AFRICAN LITERATURE TODAY

A Journal of Explanatory Criticism

NUMBERS 1 · 2 · 3 · 4 WITH INDEX
Edited by
ELDRED D. JONES

First published by Heinemann Educational Books
No. 1 1968
No 2. 1969
No. 3 1969
No. 4 1970

Combined volume no's 1-4 with Index
First published 1972
Reprinted 1978

First published in the United States of America 1972
by Africana Publishing Corporation

James Currey, Woodbridge, Suffolk

ISBN 978-0-85255-506-4

Transferred to digital printing

James Currey is an imprint of Boydell & Brewer Ltd
PO Box 9, Woodbridge, Suffolk IP12 3DF, UK
and of Boydell & Brewer Inc.
668 Mt. Hope Avenue, Rochester NY 14620, USA
website: www.boydellandbrewer.com

This publication is printed on acid-free paper

ALT 1

CONTENTS

4   *Articles*

CONTENTS

AFRICAN LITERATURE TODAY

This is the first number of *African Literature Today* which has grown out of *The Bulletin of the Association for African Literature in English*. This latter mouthfilling title was born of an attempt to provide for African Universities an information sheet 'to report on activities and developments in creative writing and the teaching of Literature'. This house magazine of African Universities soon attracted the attention of scholars all over the world and it was soon clear that if it was to fulfil their needs it had to find some more certain source of support than it had enjoyed since its inception. Heinemann offered this support, and the new venture is now born.

African Literature Today is intended to be a forum for the examination of the literature of Africa. Its language is English but it will publish criticism of literature no matter what its original language. The Editor wishes to encourage close analysis of individual works or the output of particular writers or groups of writers. Publishers publish what they decide to publish for a variety of reasons, not least among them the reason that they are in business to make money. Readers also read books with a variety of expectations, not the least being their wish to be entertained. It is the critic's business to read discerningly and demonstrate the qualities of a work and thus (a) to make it accessible to a larger readership than the absence of criticism might have opened to it, and (b) by an accumulation of such examinations to help establish literary

1

standards. The more permissive the publisher's policy is, the more necessary becomes the function of the critic.

Recognizing that even critics differ among themselves and often come quite opposite conclusions about the same work, the Editor welcomes articles, whether or not they agree with his views or the views of others of his contributors. In this issue, for example, Derek Elders' implied assessment of *The Interpreters* in his view of *A Grain of Wheat* is very different from the Editor's as expressed in "Interpreting The Interpreters" in the *Bulletin of the Association for African Literature in English* (and which he will discuss further in *African Literature Today* No 2). There is thus no party line.

Writers will be particularly encouraged to write critically of their own or other people's work. Chinua Achebe has illuminated his own work by stating in lectures and articles his aims as a writer, and by commenting on the role of the writer in Africa. John Pepper Clark's 'Personal Note' to his poems *A Reed in The Tide* only whets the appetite for more pieces by writers on themselves. Mr Wole Soyinka's article on "The Writer in An African state" *Transition*, No. 31, July 1967, is a statement of the utmost importance. (So many of our writers in Africa are in any case teachers of literature, that the business of criticism is a familiar one to them.)

Criticism of African literature has served the novel and the drama fairly well but has not done so much for poetry, which readers, particularly students, often find quite obscure and inaccessible. A certain amount of the blame for this lies in an unnecessary modish reconditeness on the part of some of the poets themselves, but quite often a good expository article could clear the way for personal appreciation. Thus we are specially delighted to publish articles the poetry of Okigbo and J. P. Clark. More critical examination of our poets are ardently desired.

This issue reflects the growing interest in African literature throughout the world. Two of our contributors for instance write from California. Literature is part of Africa's gift to the world and the world seems to have accepted this gratefully. African critics, as Mr Povey implies in his article, can however play a special role in the interpretation of their own literature. We look forward to having more contributors from Africa.

Finally we would welcome critical comments on articles and will publish them when this is possible. ●

Department of English   *Eldred Jones*
University of Sierra Leone

2

Among the Ibo the art of conversation is regarded very highly, and proverbs are the palm-oil with which words are eaten.

CHINUA ACHEBE

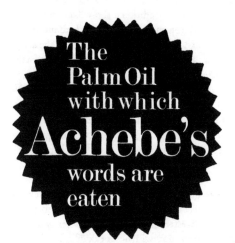

The
Palm Oil
with which
Achebe's
words are
eaten

BERNTH LINDFORS

Chinua Achebe is well known as a writer throughout Africa and even beyond. His fame rests on solid personal achievements. As a young man of twenty-eight he brought honour to his native Nigeria by writing *Things Fall Apart*, the first novel of unquestioned literary merit from English-speaking West Africa. Critics tend to agree that no African novelist writing in English has yet surpassed Achebe's achievement in *Things Fall Apart*, except perhaps Achebe himself. It was written nine years ago and since then Achebe has written three novels and won several literary prizes. During this time his reputation has grown like a bush-fire in the harmattan. Today he is regarded by many as Africa's finest novelist.

If ever a man of letters deserved his success, that man is Achebe. He is a careful and fastidious artist in full control of his art, a serious craftsman who disciplines himself not only to write regularly but to write well. He has that sense of decorum, proportion and design lacked by too many contemporary novelists, African and non-African alike. He is also a committed writer who believes that it is his duty to serve his society. He feels that the fundamental theme with which African writers should concern themselves is:

that African peoples did not hear of culture for the first time from Europeans; that their societies were not mindless but frequently had a philosophy of great

3

depth and value and beauty, that they had poetry and, above all, they had dignity. (*Nigeria Magazine*, June 1964)

Each of Achebe's novels[1] sheds light on a different era in the recent history of Nigeria. *Things Fall Apart* (1958) is set in a traditional Ibo village community at the turn of the century when the first European missionaries and administrative officials were beginning to penetrate inland. In *Arrow of God* (1964) the action takes place in a similar environment about twenty-five years later, the major difference being that the missionaries and District Officers have by this time become quite firmly entrenched. Achebe switches to an urban scene in *No Longer at Ease* (1960) in order to present a picture of the life of an educated Nigerian in the late nineteen-fifties. He brings the historical record right up to contemporary times in *A Man of the People* (1966), a devastating political satire that ends with a military coup. Achebe's novels read like chapters in a biography of his people and his nation since the coming of the white man.

What gives each of Achebe's novels an air of historical authenticity is his use of the English language. He has developed not one prose style but several, and in each novel he is careful to select the style or styles that will best suit his subject. In dialogue, for example, a westernized African character will never speak exactly like a European character nor will he speak like an illiterate village elder. Achebe, a gifted ventriloquist, is able to individualize his characters by differentiating their speech. Of course, any sensitive novelist will try to do this, but most novelists do not face the problem of having to represent in English the utterances of a character who is speaking another language. To resolve this problem, Achebe has devised an African vernacular style[2] which simulates the idiom of Ibo, his native tongue. For example in *Arrow of God* a chief Priest tells one of his sons why it is necessary to send him to a mission school:

> I want one of my sons to join these people and be my eye there. If there is something there you will bring home my share. The world is like a Mask dancing. If you want to see it well you do not stand in one place. My spirit tells me that those who do not befriend the white man today will be saying *had we known* tomorrow. (p. 55).

In an article in *Transition* (IV, 18, 1965) 'English and the African Writer,' Achebe demonstrates that he could have written this passage in a different style:

> I am sending you as my representative among those people — just to be on the safe side in case the new religion develops. One has to move with the times or else one is left behind. I have a hunch that those who fail to come to terms with the white man may well regret their lack of foresight.

Achebe comments, 'The material is the same. But the form of the one is *in character* and the other is not. It is largely of instinct, but judgement comes into it too.'

4

Achebe's use of an African vernacular style is not limited to dialogue. In *Things Fall Apart* and *Arrow of God*, novels set in tribal society, the narrative itself is studded with proverbs and similes which help to evoke the cultural milieu in which the action takes place. In *No Longer at Ease* and *A Man of the People*, on the other hand, one finds the language of the narrative more cosmopolitan, more westernized, more suited to life in the city. Here are some similes drawn from narrative portions of *Things Fall Apart* (TFA) and *Arrow of God* (AOG):

... like a bush-fire in the harmattan. (TFA, p. 1)
... like pouring grains of corn into a bag full of holes. (TFA, p. 19)
... as if water had been poured on the tightened skin of a drum. (TFA, p. 42)
... like a yam tendril in the rainy season. (TFA, p. 45)
... like the snapping of a tightened bow. (TFA, p. 53)
... as busy as an ant-hill. (TFA, p. 100)
... like the walk of an Ijele Mask lifting and lowering each foot with weighty ceremony. (AOG, p. 84)
... like a grain of maize in an empty goatskin bag. (AOG, p. 100)
... as one might pull out a snail from its shell. (AOG, p. 118)
... like a bad cowry. (AOG, p. 146)
... like a lizard fallen from an iroko tree. (AOG, p. 242)
... like the blue, quiet, razor-edge flame of burning palm nut shells. (AOG, p. 274)

Now here are some similes drawn from narrative portions of *No Longer at Ease* (NLAE) and *A Man of the People* (AMOP):

... as a collector fixes his insect with formalin. (NLAE, p. 1)
... swivelling their hips as effortlessly as oiled-ball bearings. (NLAE, p. 18)
... like a giant tarmac from which God's aeroplane might take off. (NLAE, p. 24)
... like an enchanted isle. (NLAE, p. 28)
... like the jerk in the leg of a dead frog when a current is applied to it. (NLAE, p. 137)
... like a panicky fly trapped behind the windscreen. (NLAE, p. 149)
... as a dentist extracts a stinking tooth. (AMOP, p. 4)
... like that radio jingle advertizing an intestinal worm expeller. (AMOP, p. 29)
... as I had been one day, watching for the first time the unveiling of the white dome of Kilimanjaro at sunset. (AMOP, p. 45)
... as those winged termites driven out of the earth by late rain dance furiously around street lamps and then drop panting to the ground. (AMOP, p. 51)

5

. . . like a slowed up action film (AMOP, p. 145)

. . . like a dust particle in the high atmosphere around which the water vapour of my thinking formed its globule of rain. (AMOP, p. 146)

In the urban novels one also finds similes drawn from village life, but in the novels set entirely in tribal society one finds no similes drawn from urban experience. This is altogether fitting, for Achebe's urban characters have lived in villages, but most of the characters in his village novels have had little or no exposure to cities. Here again we see Achebe using judgement and instinct to select the type of imagery that is appropriate to the time, place and people he is trying to picture. It is Achebe's sensitive use of appropriate language that lends an air of historicity to his novels.

I have taken time to comment on Achebe's artistry because the argument I intend to pursue is based on the premise that Achebe is an exceptional literary artist. I believe that he is both a conscious and an unconscious artist, that he has an instinct for knowing where things belong and a talent for putting them there, and that he possesses a shrewd sense of what is *in character* and what is not. All these qualities are displayed in his deliberate search for an appropriate language for each novel, a style that will not only suit his subject and evoke the right cultural milieu but will also help to define the moral issues with which the novel is concerned.

It is my contention that Achebe, a skilful stylist, achieves an appropriate language for each of his novels largely through the use of proverbs. Indeed, Achebe's proverbs can serve as keys to an understanding of his novels because he uses them not merely to add touches of local colour but to sound and reiterate themes, to sharpen characterization, to clarify conflict, and to focus on the values of the society he is portraying. Proverbs thus provide, as M. J. Herskovits has said, 'grammar of values' by which the deeds of a hero can be measured and evaluated. By studying Achebe's proverbs we are better able to interpret his novels.

Things Fall Apart is the story of Okonkwo, a famous warrior and expert farmer who has risen from humble origins to become a wealthy and respected leader of his clan. His entire life has been a struggle to achieve status; he has almost attained a position of pre-eminence when he accidentally kills a kinsman. For this crime he must leave his clan and live in exile for seven years. When he returns at the end of the seventh year, he finds that things have changed in his home village. White missionaries have established a church and have made a number of converts. White men have also set up a court where the District Commissioner comes to judge cases according to a foreign code of law. Okonkwo

6

tries to rouse his clan to take action against these foreigners and their institutions. In a rage he kills one of the District Commissioner's messengers. When his clan does not support his action, he commits suicide.

Okonkwo is pictured throughout the novel as a wrestler. It is an appropriate image not just because he is a powerful brute of a man, not just because his life has been a ceaseless struggle for status, but because in the eyes of his people he brings about his own downfall by challenging too powerful an adversary. This adversary is not the white man, but rather Okonkwo's *chi*, his personal god or guardian spirit.[3] Okonkwo is crushed because he tries to wrestle with his *chi*. The Ibo have a folktale about just such a wrestler; indeed it is also used by Cyprian Ekwensi and F. Chidozie Ogbalu:

> Once there was a great wrestler whose back had never known the ground. He wrestled from village to village until he had thrown every man in the world. Then he decided that he must go and wrestle in the land of spirits, and become champion there as well. He went, and beat every spirit that came forward. Some had seven heads, some ten; but he beat them all. His companion who sang his praise on the flute begged him to come away, but he would not. He pleaded with him but his ear was nailed up. Rather than go home he gave a challenge to the spirits to bring out their best and strongest wrestler. So they sent him his personal god, a little, wiry spirit who seized him with one hand and smashed him on the stony earth. (*Arrow of God*, pp. 31–2)

Although this tale does not appear in *Things Fall Apart*, there is sufficient evidence in the novel to suggest that Okonkwo is being likened to one who dares to wrestle with a spirit. A hint is contained in the first paragraph of the opening chapter which tells how Okonkwo gained fame as a young man of eighteen by throwing an unbeaten wrestler 'in a fight which the old men agreed was one of the fiercest since the founder of their town engaged a spirit of the wild for seven days and seven nights'. (p. 1) And later, when Okonkwo commits the sin of beating one of his wives during the sacred Week of Peace, '. . . people said he had no respect for the gods of his clan. His enemies said his good fortune had gone to his head. They called him the little bird *nza* who so far forgot himself after a heavy meal that he challenged his *chi*.' (p. 26)

Achebe uses proverbs to reinforce the image of Okonkwo as a man who struggles with his *chi*. Notice in the following passage how skilfully this is done:

> Everybody at the kindred meeting took sides with Osugo when Okonkwo called him a woman. The oldest man present said sternly that those whose palm-kernels were cracked for them by a benevolent spirit should not forget to be humble. Okonkwo said he was sorry for what he had said, and the meeting continued.
> But it was really not true that Okonkwo's palm-kernels had been cracked

7

for him by a benevolent spirit. He had cracked them himself. Anyone who knew his grim struggle against poverty and misfortune could not say he had been lucky. If ever a man deserved his success, that man was Okonkwo. At an early age he had achieved fame as the greatest wrestler in all the land. That was not luck. At the most one could say that his *chi* or personal god was good. But the Ibo people have a proverb that when a man says yes his *chi* also says yes. Okonkwo said yes very strongly; so his *chi* agreed. And not only his *chi* but his clan too, because it judged a man by the work of his hands. (pp. 22–3)

When Okonkwo returns from exile, he makes the mistake of believing that if he says yes strongly enough, his *chi* and his clan will agree. No doubt he should have known better. He should have accepted his years in exile as a warning from his *chi*. In his first months of exile he had come close to understanding the truth:

Clearly his personal god or *chi* was not made for great things. A man could not rise beyond the destiny of his *chi*. The saying of the elders was not true – that if a man said yea his *chi* also affirmed. Here was a man whose *chi* said nay despite his own affirmation. (p. 117)

However, as the years of exile pass, Okonkwo's fortunes improve and he begins to feel 'that his *chi* might now be making amends for the past disaster'. (p. 154) He returns to his clan rich, confident, and eager to resume his former position of leadership. When he finds his village changed, he tries to transform it into the village it had once been. But although he says yes very strongly, his *chi* and his clan say nay. Okonkwo the wrestler is at last defeated.

Quite a few of the proverbs that Achebe uses in *Things Fall Apart* are concerned with status and achievement:

... the sun will shine on those who stand before it shines on those who kneel under them. (p. 5)

... if a child washed his hands he could eat with kings. (p. 6)

... a man who pays respect to the great paves the way for his own greatness. (p. 16)

... the lizard that jumped from the high iroko tree to the ground said he would praise himself if no one else did. (p. 18)

... you can tell a ripe corn by its look. (p. 18)

... I cannot live on the bank of a river and wash my hands with spittle. (p. 148)

... as a man danced so the drums were beaten for him. (p. 165)

Such proverbs tell us much about the values of Ibo society, values by which Okonkwo lives and dies. Such proverbs also serve as thematic statements reminding us of some of the major motifs in the novel such as the importance of status, the value of achievement, or the idea of man as shaper of his own destiny.

Sometimes in Achebe's novel one finds proverbs expressing different views on the same subject. Examined closely, these proverbs can provide clues to significant differences in outlook or opinion which set one man apart from others. For example, there are a number of proverbs in *Things Fall Apart* comparing parents and their children. Most Ibos believe that a child will take after his parents or, as one character puts it, 'When mother cow is chewing grass its young ones watch its mouth.' (p. 62) However, Okonkwo's father had been a failure, and Okonkwo, not wanting to be likened to him, had striven to make his own life a success. So impressive were his achievements and so rapid his rise that an old man was prompted to remark, 'Looking at a king's mouth, one would think he had never sucked at his mother's breast.' (p. 22) Okonkwo believed that one's ancestry was not as important as one's initiative and will power, qualities which could be discerned in a child at a very early age. 'A chicken that will grow into a cock', he said, 'can be spotted the very day it hatches.' (p. 58) He had good reason for thinking so. He himself had achieved much as a young man, but his own son Nwoye had achieved nothing at all:

How could he have begotten a woman for a son? At Nwoye's age, Okonkwo had already become famous throughout Umuofia for his wrestling and fearlessness.

He sighed heavily, and as if in sympathy the smouldering log also sighed. And immediately Okonkwo's eyes were opened and he saw the whole matter clearly. Living fire begets cold, impotent ash. He sighed again, deeply. (p. 138)

It is worth noting that in complaining about Nwoye's unmanliness, Okonkwo says, 'A bowl of pounded yams can throw him in a wrestling match.' (p. 57) All the proverbs cited here are working to characterize Okonkwo and to set him apart from other men, especially from his father and his son. The proverbs reveal that no one, least of all Okonkwo himself, considers him an ordinary mortal; rather, he is the sort of man who would dare to wrestle with his *chi*.

Obi Okonkwo, who is Okonkwo's grandson and the hero of Achebe's second novel *No Longer at Ease*, is a very different kind of person. When he returns from studies in England, he is an honest and idealistic young man. He takes a high paying job in the civil service but soon finds that his salary is not sufficient to meet the financial demands made upon him. He also gets involved with a woman his parents and clan despise. In the end he is caught taking bribes and is sent to prison.

Obi is an unheroic figure, a good man who slides rather than falls into evil ways. His actions are ignoble and unworthy. When he begins taking bribes, he tries to satisfy his conscience by refusing to take them from people he knows he cannot help. Kinsmen who attend his trial cannot understand why he took such risks for so little profit; one says, 'I am against people reaping where they have not sown. But we have a saying that if you want to eat a toad you should look for a fat and juicy one.' (p. 6) But Obi lives by half-measures, by resolute decisions mollified by irresolute actions. He falls in love with Clara, a woman whose unusual ancestry Obi's parents look upon with horror, and he wants to marry her. A friend warns him not to pollute his lineage: 'What you are going to do concerns not only yourself but your whole family and future generations. If one finger brings oil it soils the others.' (p. 75) Obi, feeling he must free himself from the shackles of tradition, becomes engaged to Clara but later yields to parental pressure and breaks off with her. When she reveals she is pregnant, he arranges for her to get an abortion. More shameful, at least in the eyes of his clan, is Obi's refusal to return home for his mother's funeral, an action that leads one dismayed clansman to suggest that Obi is rotten at the core: 'A man may go to England, become a lawyer or doctor, but it does not change his blood. It is like a bird that flies off the earth and lands on an ant-hill. It is still on the ground.' (p. 160) Obi never gets off the ground, never reaches heroic heights, never stops swallowing undernourished toads.

Helping to set the tone of the story are a great number of proverbs which comment on or warn against foolish and unworthy actions. Besides those already mentioned, one finds:

He that fights for a neer-do-well has nothing to show for it except a head covered in earth and grime. (p. 5)

The fox must be chased away first; after that the hen might be warned against wandering into the bush. (p. 5)

. . . he replied that a man who lived on the banks of the Niger should not wash his hands in spittle. (pp. 10, 135)

. . . like the young antelope who danced herself lame when the main dance was yet to come. (p. 11)

When a new saying gets to the land of empty men they lose their heads over it. (p. 48)

A person who has not secured a place on the floor should not begin to look for a mat. (p. 60)

Shall we kill a snake and carry it in our hand when we have a bag for putting long things in? (p. 80)

. . . digging a new pit to fill up an old one. (p. 108)

. . . a man should not, out of pride and etiquette, swallow his phlegm. (p. 156)

. . . The little bird *nza* who after a big meal so far forgot himself as to challenge his *chi* to single combat. (p. 163)

A man does not challenge his *chi* to a wrestling match. (p. 40)

10

The last two proverbs cited here may remind us of Okonkwo, but no one could mistake Obi for his grandfather. Okonkwo erred by daring to attempt something he did not have the power to achieve; this makes him a tragic hero. Obi erred by stooping to take bribes; this makes him a crook. To put it in proverbial terms: Okonkwo wrestles his *chi*, Obi swallows a toad. It is not only the stupidity but the contemptibility of Obi's ways that many of the proverbs in the novel help to underscore.

An important theme in *No Longer at Ease* is the conflict between old and new values. Obi's people tax themselves mercilessly to raise funds to send him to England for university training. The 'scholarship' they award him is to be repaid both in cash and in services when he finishes his studies. They want him to read law so that when he returns he will be able to handle all their land cases against their neighbours. They expect a good return on their investment because Obi is their kinsman; they have a saying that '... he who has people is richer than he who has money'. (p. 79) Obi, however, immediately asserts his self-will by choosing to read English instead of law. When he returns, he starts to pay back the loan but refuses to allow his kinsmen to interfere in his personal life. He especially resents their efforts to dissuade him from marrying Clara. Having adopted western values, Obi believes that an individual has the right to choose his own wife. It is this that brings him into conflict with his parents and kinsmen. Obi's western education has made him an individualist, but his people still adhere to communal values.[4]

Obi's people attach great importance to kinship ties, and their beliefs regarding the obligations and rewards of kinship are often revealed in their proverbs. Even when a prodigal son like Obi gets into trouble they feel it is necessary to try to help him: '... a kinsman in trouble had to be saved, not blamed; anger against a brother was felt in the flesh, not in the bone'. (p. 5) They also have a song which cautions:

He that has a brother must hold him to his heart,

For a kinsman cannot be bought in the market,

Neither is a brother bought with money. (p. 129)

Certainly it would be very wrong to harm an in-law for '... a man's in-law was his *chi*'. (p. 46) And conflict within the clan should be avoided for in unity lies strength: 'If all snakes lived together in one place, who would approach them?' (p. 81) Those who prosper are expected to help those who are less fortunate: '... when there is a big tree small ones climb on its back to reach the sun'. (p. 96) But all the burdens should not fall on one man: '... it is not right to ask a man with elephantiasis of the scrotum to take on small pox as well, when thousands of other people have not had even their share of small diseases'. (p. 99) Obi accepts some of the values expressed in these proverbs,

11

but his own individualistic attitude is probably best summed up in the saying, 'Ours is ours but mine is mine'. (p. 32) Obi's problem lies in having to make choices between the old values and the new, between 'ours' and 'mine'.

Ezeulu, hero of Achebe's third novel, *Arrow of God*, is faced with a similar problem. As Chief Priest of a snake cult Ezeulu is committed to traditional ways, but just to be on the safe side he sends one of his sons to a mission school to 'be [his] eye there' and to learn the white man's ways. This action draws criticism from some of the leaders of the clan, criticism which rapidly mounts into angry protest when the Christianized son is caught trying to kill a sacred python. Ezeulu also falls foul of the District Commissioner by declining to accept an official appointment as Paramount Chief of his village. For this he is thrown into prison for two months. When he returns to his village he sees himself as an avenging arrow in the bow of his god, an instrument by which his god intends to punish his people. Ezeulu therefore refuses to perform certain rituals which must be performed before new yams can be harvested. This precipitates a crisis which results in the destruction of Ezeulu, his priesthood and his religion.

To understand Ezeulu one must comprehend his deep concern over the way his world is changing. This concern is expressed both in his decision to send one of his sons to a mission school and in the proverbs he uses to justify his decision. He tells his son that a man must move with the times: '. . . I am like the bird Eneka-nti-oba. When his friends asked him why he was always on the wing he replied: "Men of today have learnt to shoot without missing and so I have learnt to fly without perching." . . . The world is like a Mask dancing. If you want to see it well you do not stand in one place.' (p. 55) Months later Ezeulu reminds his son that he must learn the white man's magic because 'a man must dance the dance prevalent in his time'. (p. 234) Ezeulu explains his decision to the village elders by comparing the white man to a new disease: 'A disease that has never been seen before cannot be cured with everyday herbs. When we want to make a charm we look for the animal whose blood can match its power; if a chicken cannot do it we look for a goat or a ram; if that is not sufficient we send for a bull. But sometimes even a bull does not suffice, then we must look for a human.' (p. 165) Ezeulu's son is to be the human sacrifice which will enable the clan to make medicine of sufficient strength to hold the new disease in check. In other words, Ezeulu decides to sacrifice his son in order to gain power to cope with the changing times.

The question is whether Ezeulu's action is an appropriate response to the problem. Some elders think it is not and blame Ezeulu for bringing new trouble to the village by taking so improper a step. The importance that Ezeulu's people attach to appropriate action is reflected in many of the proverbs in the novel.

12

For example:

> If the lizard of the homestead neglects to do the things for which its kind is known, it will be mistaken for the lizard of the farmland. (pp. 20–1)
>
> ... let us first chase away the wild cat, afterwards we blame the hen. (p. 122)
>
> We do not by-pass a man and enter his compound. (p. 138)
>
> We do not apply an ear-pick to the eye. (p. 138)
>
> ... bale that water before it rises above the ankle. (pp. 156, 197)
>
> If a masked spirit visits you you have to appease its footprints with presents. (p. 190)
>
> ... a traveller to distant places should make no enemies. (p. 208)
>
> ... a man of sense does not go on hunting little bush rodents when his age mates are after big game. (p. 209)
>
> He who sees an old hag squatting should leave her alone; who knows how she breathes? (p. 282)

Sending a son to a mission school is regarded by some elders as a highly inappropriate action for a Chief Priest to take, no matter what his motivation. Ezeulu's enemies interpret his deed as a gesture of friendship toward the white man. Thus, when the District Commissioner rather curtly commands Ezeulu to appear in his office within twenty-four hours and Ezeulu calls, the elder replies in no uncertain proverbs that Ezeulu must either suffer the consequences of friendship with the white man or do something to end the friendship:

> ... does Ezeulu think that their friendship should stop short of entering each other's houses? Does he want the white man to be his friend only by word of mouth? Did not our elders tell us that as soon as we shake hands with a leper he will want an embrace? ... What I say is this ... a man who brings ant-ridden faggots into his hut should expect the visit of lizards. But if Ezeulu is now telling us that he is tired of the white man's friendship our advice to him should be: You tied the knot, you should also know how to undo it. You passed the shit that is smelling; you should carry it away. Fortunately the evil charm brought in at the end of the pole is not too difficult to take outside again. (pp. 177–78)

It is worth noting that the proverb about bringing ant-ridden faggots home is quoted twice by Ezeulu himself. He uses it to reproach himself when his mission-educated son is found trying to kill a sacred python. (p. 72) Here, momentarily at least, Ezeulu seems willing to accept responsibility for the abomination. Ezeulu uses the proverb a second time when a friend accuses him of betraying his people by sending his son to the white man's school. Ezeulu counters by pointing out that he did not bring the white man to his people; rather, his people brought the white man upon themselves by failing to oppose him when he first arrived. If they wish to blame someone, they should blame themselves for meekly submitting

13

to the white man's presence and power. 'The man who brings ant-ridden faggots into his hut should not grumble when lizards begin to pay him a visit.' (p. 163) This is a key proverb in *Arrow of God* for it enunciates a major theme: that a man is responsible for his actions and must bear their consequences.

But in addition to being responsible for his actions, a man is also expected to act responsibly. This idea is conveyed in another key proverb which is used four times in the novel: 'an adult does not sit and watch while the she-goat suffers the pain of childbirth tied to a post'. (p. 258, cf. pp. 21, 31, 189) Ezeulu uses this proverb twice to reprimand elders for encouraging the village to fight a 'war of blame' against a neighbouring village. He reminds them that elders must not neglect their duty to their people by acting irresponsibly. It is quite significant that this same proverb is used later by the elders to rebuke Ezeulu for failing to perform the ritual that will permit new yams to be harvested. (p. 258) The elders suggest that Ezeulu is doing nothing to prevent or relieve the suffering of his people. They urge him to do his duty by performing the necessary ritual. They urge him, in other words, to act responsibly.

Ezeulu answers that he has a higher responsibility for his god, Ulu, has forbidden him to perform the ritual. The elders then say that if Ezeulu will perform the ritual, they themselves will take the blame for it: '... if Ulu says we have committed an abomination let it be on the heads of the ten of us here. You will be free because we have set you to it, and the person who sets a child to catch a shrew should also find him water to wash the odour from his hand. We shall find you the water'. (p. 260) Ezeulu answers, '... you cannot say: do what is not done and we shall take the blame. I am the Chief Priest of Ulu and what I have told you is his will not mine'. (pp. 260–61) Ezeulu sincerely believes that he is the instrument of a divine power, 'an arrow in the bow of his god'. (p. 241) When his actions bring disaster upon himself and his people, he does not feel responsible but rather feels betrayed by his god:

> Why, he asked himself again and again, why had Ulu chosen to deal thus with him, to strike him down and cover him with mud? What was his offence? Had he not divined the god's will and obeyed it? When was it ever heard that a child was scalded by the piece of yam its own mother put in its palm? What man would send his son with a potsherd to bring fire from a neighbour's hut and then unleash rain on him? Who ever sent his son up the palm to gather nuts and then took an axe and felled the tree? (p. 286)

Tortured by these questions, Ezeulu finally goes mad.

The elders come to regard Ezeulu as a man who brought tragedy upon himself by failing to recognize his own limitations. In order to act appropriately and responsibly, a man must know what he is capable of doing. This idea finds expression in many of the proverbs in the novel:

14

... like the little bird, *nza*, who ate and drank and challenged his personal
god to a single combat. (p. 17)
... no matter how strong or great a man was he should never challenge his
chi. (p. 32)
The man who carries a deity is not a king. (p. 33)
A man who knows that his anus is small does not swallow an udala seed.
(pp. 87, 282)
... only a foolish man can go after a leopard with his bare hands. (p. 105)
The fly that struts around on a mound of excrement wastes his time; the mound
will always be greater than the fly. (p. 282)

To sum up, Ezeulu, in trying to adjust to the changing times, takes certain
inappropriate actions which later lead him to neglect his duties and respon-
sibilities. Not knowing his limitations, he goes too far and plunges himself and
his people into disaster.

Achebe's most recent novel, *A Man of the People*, is set in contemporary Nigeria
and takes as its hero a young school teacher, Odili Samalu. Odili, who tells his
own story, is moved to enter politics when his mistress is seduced by Chief the
Honourable M. A. Nanga, M.P. and Minister of Culture. Odili joins a newly-
formed political party and prepares to contest Nanga's seat in the next election.
He also tries to win the affections of Nanga's fiancée, a young girl Nanga is
grooming as his 'parlour wife'. In the end Odili loses the political battle but
manages to win the girl. Nanga loses everything because the election is so rough
and dirty and creates such chaos in the country that the Army stages a coup and
imprisons every member of the Government.

In Nanga, Achebe has created one of the finest rogues in Nigerian fiction.
Claiming to be a 'man of the people', Nanga is actually a self-seeking, grossly
corrupt politician who lives in flamboyant opulence on his ill-gotten gains. He is
fond of pious platitudes: 'Not what I have but what I do is my kingdom,' (p. 3)
'Do the right and shame the Devil'. (p. 12) But his ruthless drive for money
and power is far from pious. When criticized, he accuses his critics of 'character
assassination' and answers that '... no one is perfect except God'. (p. 75) He
frequently complains of the troubles and burdens that Government Ministers
have to bear and readily agrees when someone remarks, 'Uneasy lies the head
that wears the crown'. (p. 68) Nanga has enormous power which he is willing to
use to help others provided that they in turn help him. In a country in which
'it didn't matter *what* you knew but *who* you knew' (p. 19), Nanga was obviously
a man to know.

The maxims quoted here help to characterize Nanga and his world. They are sayings borrowed from a foreign culture and are as often misapplied and abused as are the manners and institutions which have also been borrowed from Europe and transplanted in contemporary Africa. Nanga quotes these maxims but does not live by them; similarly, he gives lip service to democratic elections but does everything in his power to subvert and manipulate them. Detribalized but imperfectly westernized, adhering to no systematic code of values, Nanga battles to stay on top in a confused world. He is one of the most monstrous offspring produced by the tawdry union of Europe and Africa, and his misuse of non-African mottoes and maxims exposes not only his own insincerity and irresponsibility but the moral chaos in the world in which he lives.

Odili, a more thoroughly westernized African, is a man of far greater virtue and integrity. His narrative is sprinkled with imported metaphors and proverbial expressions as, for example 'kicked the bucket' (p. 28), 'pass through the eye of a needle' (p. 63), 'one stone to kill two birds with' (p. 152), 'attack . . . is the best defence' (p. 162), 'a bird in the hand'. (p. 165) But he always uses them appropriately. Whatever he says can be trusted to be accurate and honest. Somehow Odili has managed to remain untainted amidst all the surrounding corruption and his clear vision provides an undistorted view of a warped society.

Contemporary Nigeria is, after all, the real subject of the novel. What sort of society is it that allows men like Nanga to thrive while men like Odili suffer? Some important clues are provided in the proverbs in the novel. In contemporary Nigeria one must, for example, be circumspect:

> . . . the proverbial traveller-to-distant-places who must not cultivate enmity on his route. (p. 1)
> . . . when one slave sees another cast unto a shallow grave he should know that when the time comes he will go the same way. (p. 40)
> . . . if you respect today's king, others will respect you when your turn comes. (p. 70)
> . . . if you look only in one direction your neck will become stiff. (p. 90)
> But one must not be unduly inquisitive:
> . . . naked curiosity – the kind that they say earned Monkey a bullet in the forehead. (p. 153)
> The inquisitive eye will only blind its own sight. (p. 164)
> A man who insists on peeping into his neighbour's bedroom knowing a woman to be there is only punishing himself. (p. 164)

One should take advantage of opportunities ('. . . if you fail to take away a strong man's sword when he is on the ground, will you do it when he gets up . . .?' p. 103); capitalize on good fortune ('[would] a sensible man . . . spit out the juicy morsel that good fortune placed in his mouth?' p. 2); and avoid wasting time on trivialities ('. . . like the man in the proverb who was carrying the carcass of an elephant on his head and searching with his toes for a grass-hopper.' p. 80). Most important of all, one must be sure to get one's share. Like the world of Obi Okonkwo in *No Longer at Ease*, this is a world in which 'Ours is ours, but mine is mine'. (p. 140)

One must not only get one's share, one must also consume it. Eating is an important image in the novel. Politicians like Nanga tell their tribesmen, 'our people must press for their fair share of the national cake'. (p. 13) Those who stand in the way of such hungry politicians are branded as 'the hybrid class of Western-educated and snobbish intellectuals who will not hesitate to sell their mothers for a mess of pottage'. (p. 6) These intellectuals, Nanga says, 'have bitten the finger with which their mother fed them.' (p. 6) Although some people believe that God will provide for everyone according to His will ('He holds the knife and He holds the yam', p. 102), the politicians know that the fattest slices of the national cake together with the richest icing will go to the politicians who hold the most power. This is the reason elections are so hotly contested. In these elections people are quite willing to support a corrupt politician like Nanga in the belief that if he remains well-fed, he may let a few crumbs fall to his constituents. When someone like Odili protests that such politicians are using their positions to enrich themselves, the people answer cynically, 'Let them eat, . . . after all when white men used to do all the eating did we commit suicide?' (p. 161) Besides, who can tell what the future may bring? '. . . who knows? it may be your turn to eat tomorrow. Your son may bring home your share.' (p. 162) It is not surprising that Odili sums up this era as a 'fat-dripping, gummy, eat-and-let-eat regime . . . a regime which inspired the common saying that a man could only be sure of what he had put away safely in his gut or, in language even more suited to the times: "you chop, me self I chop, palaver finish".' (p. 167)

The reason such an era comes to an end is that the politicians make the mistake of overeating, of taking more than their share. In proverbial terms, they take more than the owner can ignore. This key proverb is used four times in the novel. Twice it is applied to a miserly trader who steals a blind man's stick: 'Josiah has taken away enough for the owner to notice', people say in disgust. 'Josiah has now removed enough for the owner to see him.' (p. 97) Odili later reflects on the situation and the proverb:

I thought much afterwards about that proverb, about the man taking things away until the owner at last notices. In the mouth of our people there was no greater condemnation. It was not just a simple question of a man's cup being full. A man's cup might be full and none the wiser. But here the owner knew, and the owner, I discovered, is the will of the whole people. (p. 97)

In the middle of his campaign against Nanga, Odili wishes that 'someone would

17

get up and say: "No, Nanga has taken more than the owner could ignore!"' (p. 122) But it is only after much post-election violence and an Army takeover that Odili's wish comes true. Only after such upheavals result in the establishment of a new order do people openly admit that Nanga and his cohorts 'had taken enough for the owner to see'. (p. 166)

Thus, in *A Man of the People*, as in Achebe's other novels, proverbs are used to sound and reiterate major themes, to sharpen characterization, to clarify conflict, and to focus on the values of the society Achebe is portraying. By studying the proverbs in a novel, we gain insight into the moral issues with which that novel deals. Because they provide a *grammar of values* by which the actions of characters can be measured and evaluated, proverbs help us to understand and interpret Achebe's novels.

Achebe's literary talents are clearly revealed in his use of proverbs. One can observe his mastery of the English language, his skill in choosing the right words to convey his ideas, his keen sense of what is *in character* and what is not, his instinct for appropriate metaphor and symbol, and his ability to present a thoroughly African world in thoroughly African terms. It is this last talent that enables him to convince his readers 'that African peoples did not hear of culture for the first time from Europeans; that their societies were not mindless but frequently had a philosophy of great depth and value and beauty, that they had poetry and, above all, they had dignity'. (*Nigeria Magazine*, June 1964) ∎

NOTES

1. *Things Fall Apart*, London, 1958; *No Longer at Ease*, London, 1960; *Arrow of God*, London, 1964; *A Man of the People*, London, 1966. All quotations are from these editions.

2. I discuss this at more length in 'African Vernacular Styles in Nigerian Fiction', *CLA Journal*, IX, 3 (1966), 265–73. See also Gerald Moore, 'English Words, African Lives', *Présence Africaine*, 26, 54 (2nd Quarterly 1964), 90–101; Ezekiel Mphahlele, 'The language of African Literature', *Harvard Educational Review*, 34, 2 (Spring 1964), 298–305; and Eldred Jones, 'Language and Theme in *Things Fall Apart*', *Review of English Literature*, V. 4 (October 1964), 39–43.

3. There has been some controversy about the meaning of 'chi'. (See Austin J. Shelton, 'The Offended *chi* in Achebe's Novels', *Transition*, III, 13 [1964], 36–7, and Donatus Nwoga, 'The *chi* Offended', *Transition*, IV, 15 [1964], 5.) Shelton prefers to translate it as 'God within', but Nwoga, an Ibo, supports Achebe's translation of it as 'personal god'. Victor Uchendu, an Ibo anthropologist, describes *chi* as 'the Igbo form of guardian spirit' (*The Igbo of Southeast Nigeria*, New York, 1966, p. 16). I have followed Achebe and Uchendu here.

4. This theme is discussed by Obiajunwa Wali in 'The Individual and the Novel in Africa', *Transition*, IV, 18 (1965), 31–3.

18

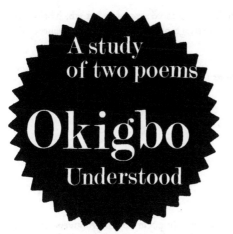

A study of two poems

Okigbo

Understood

Born August 1932
Killed in action 1967

O.R.DATHORNE

When you have finished
& done up my stitches
Wake me near the altar,
& this poem will be finished.

In isolating two poems of Christopher Okigbo for close examination, one must be aware that they belong to, and are indicative of, a larger overall meaning. All his poems concern themselves with archetypal experience, except that in all cases the protagonist's view of the world is essentially a religious one. There is no single accepted ethic that dominates it; it sums up the variety of human experience and distils it in enigmatic form. Because of this all words contribute to the religious density of meaning that the poet intends. Because of this also every word has an almost telegraphic precision about it as well as associations that belong to the encyclopedia of the poetic experience.

The two poems in this article have been intentionally chosen from *Modern Poetry from Africa*, ed. Gerald Moore and Ulli Beier (London, Penguin, 1963) as this is the most accessible source of Christopher Okigbo's poetry. Other poems by the same poet will be examined in another article.

19

An examination firstly of a poem that was printed separately but which belongs to a larger cycle will demonstrate the telegraphic nature of the statement. This is the poem:

The moon has ascended between us
Between two pines
That bow to each other

Love with the moon has ascended
Has fed on our solitary stems

And we are now shadows
That cling to each other
But kiss the air only.

At first sight this is seemingly a simple love poem about two lovers who have achieved physical proximity, even though emotional nearness is denied them. The moon which has ascended represents this spiritual divorce and the lovers remain merely as 'shadows', robbed of the true substance of love which has departed with the moon. The poem can certainly be enjoyed at this level of meaning.

On closer inspection, however, the cumulative nature of its meaning becomes apparent. In the first stanza the most important word is 'between'. This word appears twice and on both occasions is so placed syntactically that it appears to be superfluous. But the importance of the word is emphasized by the repetition and by the placing of a single 'us' in the middle. 'Between' therefore serves the visual purpose of emphasizing the separation of the two protagonists. It is almost as if the word 'us' is cut in half. Because of this, 'us' takes on a new and different meaning. The word suggests that some former cohesion had previously been shattered and the moon comes to represent the separation. Such a separation is not one between two people but is the ritual re-enactment of a folk-belief which details the manner in which sky and earth became separated.

That this is a tragedy of colossal importance is brought home by 'pines' which suggest both the tree and the archaic meaning of the sufferings of hell. This latter meaning adds force to the more apparent meaning by implying that the tree probably has an allusion intended in it to the fall, and man's consequent separation from God. The prevalence of darkness in the first stanza helps with the understanding of the 'pines / That bow to each other'. Man is lost in the darkness of his own making – the bowing is not ritualistic; it suggests the worship of false gods that have taken the place of the truth in which he lived before.

20

Until the second stanza, 'ascended' has no religious significance. It is merely indicative of the position of the moon, paradoxically light and yet the barrier between earth and sky. Also until the second stanza there is little hope of a possible reunion. However the adroit way in which 'The moon has ascended between us' is balanced rhythmically and meaningfully with 'Love with the moon has ascended' brings in the idea of 'God is love' and the Ascension. It is through this ascension of love, acting as it were as a modifying influence on the moon, that the word 'bow' alters in a subtle manner to 'cling' in the last stanza.

In the second stanza the image of sacrifice is equated with the crude ritualism of sacrifice. The 'solitary stems' on which love has fed refer to the insubstantiality of the pines and therefore man. Sacrifice, the image suggests, can only partially placate the evil of a primordial crime. Intentionally 'Love' is placed at the beginning of a line to give it the ambiguous benefit of a capital letter, which all the more insists on the cruelty of the expiatory sacrifice. There is something almost cannibalistic about 'fed', made all the more harsh since 'has fed' comes immediately after 'has ascended'.

With the third stanza there is an abrupt shift in time which is meant to shock. The primordial crime and sacrifice have both occurred. 'We' is more personal than 'us', 'now' more definite than 'has ascended'; the third stanza is a religious stocktaking — where does man stand today in relation to the universe? The agent of separation, paradoxically, helps the anonymous 'us' to become 'shadows', for it is due to the moon that this occurs. 'Cling' suggests a desperate desire to hope, but this word also confirms the implications of 'between us / Between', that is the link has not really been completely broken.

In the first stanza 'bow' had referred to the meaningless gestures that had taken the place of proper ritual. In the last line of the final stanza, 'kiss' is substituted. 'Only' of course modifies the meaning or rather sets up the limitations for the reassociation with sky. However, because of love 'we are now shadows' and because of love man is capable of the partial link with sky which he acknowledges when he makes an oath, or as Okigbo puts it, when he is able to 'kiss the air only'. The reacquaintanceship with sky involves man in the continuous gestures that seek to placate the universe.

Not only is the poem just considered indicative of Okigbo's technique of meaning-accumulation but it also shows something of his interests. There is an assumption in all of the poetry that the primordial rift between matter and essence, earth and sky, man and his gods has to be atoned for. There is as well the assumption that the rift is not a complete break but a severance that can be bridged by expiation.

21

The opening poem in the *Heavensgate* sequence indicates how this can be done and states the dilemma:

Before you, mother Idoto,
naked I stand,
before your watery presence,
a prodigal,

leaning on an oilbean,
lost in your legend. . . .

Under your power wait I
on barefoot,

watchman for the watchword
at heavensgate;

out of the depths my cry
give ear and hearken.

The posture is one of abject humility; indeed 'naked' and 'barefoot' suggest humiliation. These are the two key-words of this section and they introduce a sexual element in the quest. Like the cannibalistic love which fed on its own stems, in the poem considered before, this nudity is a pointer towards the ritualistic abnormalities the devoted must undergo – here incest. The 'mother' – Eve, Mary, a minor river goddess, the mother of the protagonist – is the sexual means through which the heavenly connection can be made. But the separation has already taken place – hence the seeker is 'a prodigal', conjuring up, of course, its strong biblical allusion. The 'watery presence' of Mother Idoto, contrasts with the harsh sound of the name which ought to suggest more substance. Because of the initial crime, her presence is however 'watery'.

Okigbo's words, as we have noticed, are heavily loaded. In this instance the water (like the moon in the previous poem, the cause of separation and the means of reunion) is the means of cleansing. Out of the trivia of his disinherit-ance man hopes to construct the spider's web to the godhead. The opening stanza with the way in which 'before' is finely balanced, suggests that 'mother Idoto' is an easy means. This is shattered in the third stanza when the sexual conquest does not take place, for the male protagonist is 'under your power'.

There is the obvious humility in the first stanza, if the meaning of 'before' is taken as suggesting the position of the seeker. However, Okigbo intends another meaning here as well – 'before' is also meant in the sense of time. Therefore the opening lines of the *Heavensgate* sequence begin not with humility but with a certain braggadocio; the protagonist only comes in feigned humility for his nakedness vaunts his powers of procreation and his boast suggests that the male in him preceded the female in her. The paradox of his situation is further dramatized in the next two lines. The familiar image of the tree appears, the tree that cannot hope to support him. Its relevance is that it suggests strong phallic associations which are meant to contrast with the suggestion of 'lost in your legend' or the goddess as whore. The

22

rhythmical contrast is also striking with regard to these two lines – the 'I' alliteration links them and forces the comparison between the harshness of the first line and the mystic wonder of 'lost in your legend' with the open sounds that suggest awe.

Next comes the disillusionment, but the protagonist pretends that he had craved for the omnipotence of the goddess, that his bareness was not a way of flaunting sexual power but of admitting the lack of it. Therefore the lines can be read 'wait I on' with the obvious meaning of endurance (still of course hinting at the sexual theme). However, because 'I stand' of the first stanza has now become 'Under your power wait I', there is a suggestion not only that the goddess has overcome the protagonist in the ritual of sex, but that he is flat out in all humility like a sleeping watchman.

In this way these two apparently dissimilar meanings continue to merge – the protagonist as victim and as agent. The two aspects to the personality of the protagonist are present in each line, even the ones that suggest his apparent humility. The two aspects to the meaning are present in 'watchman for the watchword' (recalling the sleeping disciples) but at the same time with its flaunting balance of sound, suggesting flaunting self-praise.

Not until the final two lines of the 'overture' does the poem and the lover/worshipper shed all desire for sexual mastery. In biblical language the almost hysterical plea is made that:

out of the depths my cry
give ear and hearken.

'Depths' is a reference to the 'watery presence' of the first stanza and is a truly contrite cry of the anguished. The next line recalls the fact that though the desire for sexual mastery has been lost, the wish to conquer and through conquering to unite, is still there. 'Give ear and hearken' is both a plea and a command, balanced so delicately from the point of view of sound that one cannot be detached from the other.

These two poems can stand alone only because they introduce one to the vocabulary of the poet's world and because they both seek redemption for the protagonist. Their essential difference in form is that the first poem sought to *narrate* the process whereas the second *dramatized* it. The first poem is lyrical, the second has a basic theatricality about it so that the complacent 'us' and 'we' of the first poem become the assertive 'I' and the apparently passive 'you' of the second. The poems belong to two periods in Okigbo's poetry – the one representing a narrative desire to chronicle archetypes of experience, the other, assuming the experience, inquires into the conflicting loyalties of the present. ∎

23

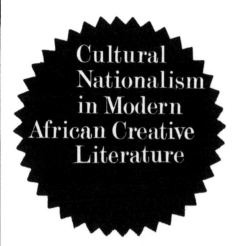

Cultural Nationalism in Modern African Creative Literature

E.N.OBIECHINA

The growth of modern creative writing in West Africa by indigenous West African writers is a post-war phenomenon which developed side by side with the nationalist movement for freedom from colonial rule. This literary upsurge has been dominated in French West Africa by the literary vogue known as 'Négritude'. Whereas in the English-speaking West Africa there has been a definite emphasis on the reconstruction and re-evaluation of the autochthonous West African cultures, especially in so far as they still form an essential part of the composite post-colonial culture of West Africa. The close correspondence between political nationalism and literary nationalism is not just an accident; it is a natural result of the nature of colonial relationship.

The direct result of European colonization of Africa was the depreciation of the African image in popular European imagination, for the imposition of political control also involved conscious or unconscious devaluation of the African culture. Loss of political freedom was also inevitably attended by loss of cultural confidence by Africans, induced by the dynamics of domination. Furthermore, African primitivism, essentially a by-product of political domination, received in the second part of the nineteenth century an almost authoritative stamp from evolutionary anthropology which on the evolutionary scheme of cultural hierarchy placed the African culture at the bottom and Western culture at the top.

It is not difficult to see that the standards of cultural assessment were based on the factors of Western civilization. Any people who did not invent writing or who had not had an industrial revolution were regarded as

24

primitive and so of course Africa not having had both was regarded as primitive. In the nineteenth century then, the popular image of Africa in the European mind was of a primitive place with primitive institutions, inhabited by primitive irrational people on whom should be imposed the civilizing will of Europe. Christian missionary pressures and the opinion of philanthropists began to influence the general attitudes towards the colonies. The idea of 'the white man's burden' grew with the pride of colonial possession and westernization of Africans through education received increased attention. Colonization was no longer regarded as barefaced political domination and economic exploitation but as a humane and philanthropic mission for civilizing and Christianizing the 'primitive' and 'benighted' natives. This is what the Madagascan poet, Jacques Rabemananjara means when he said in *Présence Africaine* (June–Nov. 1956): 'The Negro only became a barbarian the day the white man realized the advantage of this barbarism; the development of capitalism in the XIX century, and its expansion overseas had to have an excuse; the myth was born of the desire for moral elegance, and the fable of the civilizing mission continues to haunt the conscience of noble souls. For the barbarism of the Negro is an irreplaceable gold mine for certain modern midases.'

Le mission civilisatrice is not altogether the fraud Rabemananjara implies, but its basic assumption of the qualitative inferiority of African culture vis-à-vis European culture is not in doubt. It is an assumption which was so widespread and pressed so strongly on the consciousness that even the Africans came to believe in it. The result was an uncritical imitation of Western cultural behaviour and a feeling of uneasiness for the African culture.

It could be said that the colonial relationship involved the assertion of cultural superiority by the colonizing people and a devaluation of the culture of the colonized people, leading to their loss of cultural confidence and the death of the creative impulse within their indigenous cultural milieu as well as a lack of creative confidence within the introduced culture of the colonizers. Nationalist movements geared towards the ending of colonial domination were therefore attended by cultural nationalism aimed at rehabilitating the autochthonous culture (or such aspects of it that could still be rescued), and restoring the creative impulse of the peoples emerging from colonialism. This cultural phenomenon which sociologists call 'nativism' is of such immense significance in national resurgence that the Irish, just to give one example, in the assertion of their cultural independence of Britain have not only resurrected the ancient and moribund Erse language but have painstakingly revived their antiquarian literature and mythology.

Cultural nativism, or that aspect of it called literary nationalism, is so fundamentally universal a phenomenon in unequal social situations such as that engendered by colonialism that its inevitability hardly deserves an argument. In the West African scene, then, it is not surprising that the artistic creative impulse which had been smothered under the impact of colonialism began to bud once more with the awakening of national consciousness after the Second World War and that it has actually been flowering since the attainment of national independence. Cultural nativism and its expression in literature in English-speaking West Africa cannot be altogether isolated, as is very often imagined, from the main body of cultural revivalism which is sweeping over Africa and in an even larger context, over all those places inhabited by people of African descent – in the Americas as well as in the Caribbean. Whether this nativism or cultural affirmation finds expression in psycho-political terms such as the African Personality or in the literary ideology of Negritude its cultural implications are obvious. There is a fundamental assumption that the African has had a civilization which is distinct from all other civilizations and which distinguishes him from all other human beings. Historical disasters overtook this civilization in the nature of the slave trade and European colonialism; they resulted not only in its partial disintegration but in the distribution of African peoples to new geographical areas. It is the belief that this African civilization and its outpost in the Americas and the Caribbean, even though temporarily submerged under the impact of the technological civilization of Europe, is not completely lost. This has stimulated in varying forms the attempts at reconstruction and the evolution of a new synthesis.

The Negritude movement is the most coherent, because most ideological, of these attempts at African or rather Negro-African cultural rehabilitation. The movement took root among Negro-African intellectuals of French expression perhaps because their French intellectual background with its 'ideological orientation, neat intellectual habits and quality of elegance' equipped them to construct an ideological framework to meet a situation which Negro-African intellectuals and writers of English expression, who are less doctrinaire, are content to treat in a more or less pragmatic manner. The word 'Négritude' was invented by Aimé Césaire, the coloured poet-politician from Martinique, in 1932 in his well-known poem 'Cahier d'un retour au pays natal', but its ideology has been defined mainly by the Senegalese poet-politician, Léopold Sédar Senghor. This article, being essentially a brief survey, cannot go into a detailed discussion of Negritude (which is a vast promising field of investigation by itself) or into its merits and demerits as a literary slogan. One of the most excellent essays on Negritude is Jean-Paul Sartre's *L'Orphée Noir*, a prefatory essay to Senghor's *Anthologie de la nouvelle poésie négre et Malagache de langue française.* Brilliant as are its insights into Negritude, one must imagine that Sartre's Marxist expectations of the movement are bound to meet with disappointment since, even though many of its exponents are ardent Marxists, the ethnocentricity of its ideology definitely precludes the militant cosmopolitanism of the Marxist line. That is perhaps why some non-Negritudinous African Marxists tend to regard Negritude with suspicion and profound horror. For instance, the Senegalese Marxist author-critic, Sembene Ousmane, author of *Le Docker Noir* and other novels, takes a strong stand against Negritude and the kind of African culture its theoreticians advocate. In his view, Negritude is racist, deviationist, fake and retrogressive. It is, he said, a kind of intoxication being used by the rising bourgeoisie in Africa to fool the masses and the progressive intellectuals. That is why, he asserted, the advocates of Negritude lean to a cultural past that favoured the caste system, feudalism and the spiritual oppression of the masses, the aim being to justify the rising bourgeoisie's own acquired rights and privileges after its take-over on independence. Already Aimé Césaire has resigned from the Communist party (though still a professed Marxist) and President Léopold Senghor has begun to preach in earnest a brand of socialism which he regards as distinctly African. (*West Africa*, 11 November 1961).

The cultural significance of Négritude can best be seen from the background of the usual pattern of cultural nativism which characterizes the struggles of every colonized or oppressed people to re-establish and raise the status of their devalued culture. In accordance with this pattern, cultural assertion may take the form of their extolling of the virtues of specific aspects of their indigenous culture, their debunking of some specific aspects of the culture of the colonizing or dominant group or both forms. Thus Negritude as a typical nativistic movement repudiates certain intrinsic values of European civilization such as its machine technology, its extreme materialism, its contractual determination of social relationships, and its slavish adherence to scientific planning of every detail of life. While on the other hand it extols the African's close attachment to the soil and to nature, the warmth of his humanity expressed in relationships which are purely personal and his immense vitality and zest for a life which is not circumscribed by much planning. As a reaction to European racism Negritude poets extol the Negro physique and physical beauty, especially the beauty of African womanhood. The anti-Westernism of the Negritude ideology is important only in so far as by devaluing the Western culture the African culture will once more find its pristine dignity. Just as European colonialism by postulating the superiority of its attendant culture undermined the African culture, so, by a natural process of reversal, the African culture will regain his lost dignity by the destruction of colonialism

27

and through an undermining of the superiority complex of the European culture.

Rejection of Western civilization in its entirety is not part of the ideology of Negritude – criticism is not rejection; nor should the Negritude ideology be regarded as advocating a total return to pre-colonial cultural life. Negritude is really concerned with finding a synthesis of old and new, a synthesis within which the old will form the dominant element in composition with the new. What is resisted so vehemently is the idea that the traditional culture is primitive and inadequate for rational human existence and that the African, as implied by the French colonial policy, can only reach a full and civilized life by espousing the Western culture. The chief premise of Negritude is that Africans are Africans and not Europeans and can only feel confident and give rein to their creative impulse within their African culture. It is only within their own cultural climate that they can contribute something substantial to the corpus of world civilization.

In *Liberté I*, Senghor defines Negritude thus: 'La Negritude, c'est l'ensemble des valeurs culturelles du monde noir, telles qu'elles s'expriment dans la vie, les institutions et les œuvres des noirs.'

Aimé Césaire stated the case for Negritude when he said at the First International Conference of Negro Writers and Artists (*Présence Africaine*, June–Nov. 1956): 'I believe that the civilization that has given negro sculpture to the world of art; that the civilization that has given to the political and social world the original communal institution such as village democracy, or fraternal age-groups, or family property, which is a negation of capitalism, or so many institutions bearing the imprint of the spirit of solidarity; that this civilization that, on another plane, has given to the moral world an original philosophy based on respect for life and integration within the cosmos; I refuse to believe that this civilization, imperfect though it may be, must be annihilated or denied as a pre-condition of the renaissance of the native peoples.

'I believe that, once the external obstacles have been overcome, our particular cultures contain within them enough strength, enough vitality, enough regenerative power to adapt themselves to the conditions of the modern world and that they will prove able to provide for all political, social, economic or cultural problems, valid and original solutions, that will be valid because they are original.'

Negritude is therefore not so much a rejection of Europe as an affirmation of Africa.

In English-speaking West Africa, unlike in its French-speaking counterpart, the impact of the Negritude movement was insignificant. Apart from a few poets like Francis Parkes, Gabriel Okara, Efua Morgue, Dei Anang and Adebayo Bablola, whose Negritudinous poems are slight compared with such French-speaking poets as Senghor and David Diop, there is hardly any recognizable trace of the Negritude ideology in English-speaking West African writing. In fact, the Negritude ideology tends to be treated with scepticism, derision or blatant hostility in this part of West Africa. Wole Soyinka's statement that the tiger does not go around proclaiming 'its tigritude' any more than the Negro should go around proclaiming his Negritude sums up the general attitude of English-speaking West Africans towards Negritude.

An objection to this facile dismissal is that it does not seem to recognize the immense significance of the ideology to the assimilated French African intellectuals in their effort to regain cultural initiative. Dr Davidson Nicol, the versatile West African intellectual and, until recently, Vice-Chancellor of the University of Sierra Leone has made a more balanced review of Negritude than any other English-speaking West African before him. He put these ideas to the Seminar on African Literature and the University Curriculum at Fourah in April 1963. The display of unsympathetic and impatient attitude to Negritude by some West Africans who have never been completely cut off from their cultural roots and made to acclimatize themselves within a foreign culture, as had the French African intellectuals, smacks of complacency.

Ardent exponents of the African Personality in English-speaking West Africa, like former President of Ghana, Kwame Nkrumah, also tend to treat Negritude with considerable suspicion no doubt because its pan-Negroism tends to distract efforts from the building up of pan-African solidarity even though on purely cultural grounds, the African personality, which includes the Arab peoples of North Africa as well as the sub-saharan Africans, does not seem to have a more convincing validity than Negritude. It may be supposed, however, that as a result of spatial contiguity, the realization of pan-Africanism, the political objective of the African Personality cultists, is a much more feasible proposition than the pan-Negroid ethno-aesthetic dream of Negritude.

No clear ideological definition of the African Personality and pan-Africanism approaching that of Negritude has yet emerged but it seems that pan-Africanism is an essentially political movement aimed at continental co-operation between independent African states (its most positive achievement to date is the formation of the Organization of African Unity). Whereas the African Personality is a psycho-ethnological concept resembling Negritude but differing from it because it applies to the African continent alone.

Kwame Nkrumah originated the term at the Accra conference of African nationalists in December, 1958. For a time, it became mere slogan for rallying pan-African political solidarity until W. E. Abraham in his book, *The Mind of Africa*, attempted to explore its cultural implications. However, it soon became obvious from his paradigmatic treatment of African culture that a single cultural frame-work is inadequate for the diversity of cultural types within the continent. His use of the Akan culture as a paradigm of African culture is valid only in reference to the sub-Saharan Africa.

The pragmatism which characterizes the thinking of most English-speaking West Africans on the cultural question clearly contrasts with the Cartesianism of the Negritude school. It has its root in the nineteenth century when some intellectuals of English expression began to be seriously concerned that the impact of Western culture might lead to the destruction of indigenous African culture. Scholars like Dr Africanus Horton, Dr Edward Blyden and J. E. Casely Hayford, began to canvass the idea of a West African university within which West Africans would be able to imbibe higher education; it would maintain international standards, while at the same time it would encourage the utilization and development of the indigenous culture. Dr Blyden proposed a university system which would not promote the 'despotic Europeanizing influences which had warped and crushed the negro mind.' Such a university would, in addition to inculcating classical scholarship, make provision for the teaching of African languages, songs and oral tradition. Hayford would have university education given in the vernacular with provision made for the translation of books into Fanti and a working correspondence forged with the best teaching institutions not only in England but also in Japan, Germany and America. In 1920 the First Conference of Africans of British West Africa inspired by the views of these intellectuals, especially as spearheaded by Hayford, addressed a memorial to King George V asking that a British West African university be established 'on such lines as would preserve in the students a sense of African Nationality'. The significant thing about these early efforts to have a local university installed in West Africa is the relationship the proponents see between the existence of a university in West Africa and the preservation of the indigenous West African culture.

There was a definite continuity between the early cultural nationalists like Blyden, Hayford and the local historians and amateur anthropologists and the contemporary creative writers of West African whose writings in the early part of this century' are in a way a practicalization of the dreams and cultural aspiration of the former.

There was of course always a sense of uneasiness during the early efforts to record the African cultures and assert them creatively. The professional elite of the coastal towns, who were very conscious of their status and, often imitative European culture, controlled the press and determined aesthetic standards, and as long as they did it was difficult for the traditional culture to find outlet through artistic expression except on the lower level where teachers and some missionaries encouraged experiments in vernacular drama and music. The democratization of outlook in the press which followed the establishment of such newspapers as the Pilot group in Nigeria and the appearance of university men with their roots in the provinces, however, gave a great impetus to creative effort which derived its inspiration and material largely from the traditional culture. Anglophone West African writers of the fifties and sixties are therefore translating into reality what earlier West Africans had dealt with in abstraction. In so far as they are conscious in their writings of the cultural question and allow it to determine the texture of their works, they are as *engagé* as the Negritudinous poets.

National independence, when it came, liberated the energies of young West Africans with creative talent from preoccupation with nationalist politics and increased their awareness of the individuality of being. But this awareness brings with it cultural frustration. Political independence is meaningless without cultural independence for only the cultural values of a people can inspire them with a national pride, give them a separate identity and something to live and die for. This challenge of culture cannot be met through the cosmopolitan culture of the departed colonial powers; it can only be met through the neo-African culture which is a composite of African and European cultural elements.

The upsurge of creative writing, which is a phenomenon of the fifties and sixties, reveals that the writers are aware of the challenge and are meeting it in their individual ways. The pattern which seems to be emerging is this: in the treatment of the neo-African culture, the traditional aspect (which by and large outweighs the foreign aspects) is restated to emphasize its logic, its dignity and intrinsic beauty; whereas the foreign aspect appears as disintegrative, corruptive and often antithetical. The musico-ethnologist Kwabena Nketia of Ghana records and interprets the funeral dirges of the Akan. The Sierra Leone novelist William Conton invoked the beauty of the country life in Sierra Leone. Achebe reconstructed the Ibo traditional culture in its full dignity and autonomy before the colonial impact undermined it. Tutuola assembled and embellished Yoruba folk-tales. And many other young poets and playwrights draw elaborately not only from traditional themes and motifs but also from the mythology and symbolisms of West African traditional cultures. In the work of all these traditional elements stand out and give the literature a characteristically West African flavour.

We can now speak of the West African literature which has grown and drawn its inspiration from the West African culture. It has no recognizable and overtly formulated ideology as is the case with the literature of Negritude. Rather, it arises out of certain cultural compulsions which are both natural and induced by a recent colonial past. These compulsions are implicit in the contemporary cultural situation of West Africa and the writers instinctively stumble towards them because they synchronise with the national literary expectations of the West African reading public. As Middleton Murry observes in his book *The Problem of Style*, 'At a certain level of general culture, with certain combinations of economic and social conditions . . . certain artistic and literary forms impose themselves. These forms the writer is almost compelled to accept, either because he relies on his writing for his living, or because he feels instinctively that he must embrace the means necessary to reaching the largest possible audience.'

The West African writer is not only writing in the way he does in order to reach the largest reading audience (though this surely has something to do with it) but he is also aiming at satisfying the literary expectation of this generation of West Africans. His book will possibly be more widely read by overseas readers but he cannot afford to disappoint the new spirit of national independence. He is expected, as a creative member of his country's literate class, to participate actively in the business of national reconstruction. His contribution is cultural and he is expected to play the important role of rehabilitating the African culture; he is to give the people a new vision of life, to rescue them from the trauma of cultural confusion in which they have been left as a result of European acculturation, to provide them with new values, new outlooks and new spiritual bearings with their base in the African culture and psychology.

Chinua Achebe knows the seriousness of the duty which the West African audience imposes on its writers. At a lecture on 'The Role of the Writer in a New Nation' (reproduced in *Nigeria Magazine*, June 1964), after he had cited several examples to show that many European writers on Africa portray the African as a man without culture, he went on: 'In a world bedevilled by these and much worse beliefs is it any wonder that black nations should attempt to demonstrate (sometimes with exaggerated aggressiveness) that they are as good as – and better than – their detractors?

'This presents the African writer with a challenge. It is inconceivable to me that a serious writer could stand aside from this debate, or be indifferent to this argument which calls his full humanity in question. For me, at any rate, there is a clear duty to make a statement. This is my answer to those who say that a writer should be writing about contemporary issues – about politics in 1964, about city life, about the last coup d'état. Of course these are all legitimate themes for the writer but as far as I am concerned the fundamental theme must first be disposed of. This theme – put quite simply – is that African peoples did not hear of culture for the first time from Europeans; that their societies were not mindless but frequently had a philosophy of great depth

32

and value and beauty, that they had poetry and, above all, they had dignity. It is this dignity that many African peoples all but lost in the colonial period, and it is this that they must now regain. The worst thing that can happen to any people is the loss of their dignity and self-respect. The writer's duty is to help them regain it by showing them in human terms what happened to them, what they lost. There is a saying in Ibo that a man who can't tell where the rain began to beat him cannot know where he dried his body. The writer can tell the people where the rain began to beat them . . . In Africa he cannot perform this task unless he has a proper sense of history'.

The above is the testimony of one who feels the pulse of contemporary West Africa and discovers with striking accuracy its innermost yearnings and cultural aspirations – the urgent need to rehabilitate the cultural past especially as it still forms a part of the present. The responsibility on the modern West African writer is immense. He is not only called upon to draw from his imaginative resourcefulness, he is also expected to fulfil other functions which in firmly established cultural communities are fulfilled by sociologists, anthropologists, archaeologists, cultural historians, psychologists or philosophers. Above all, he is expected to be a dedicated nationalist and patriot. There is no room in this particular point in time and place for the artistic philosophy of 'art for art's sake'. All art is committed and directed towards the expression of the integrity and autonomy of the West African culture. There is therefore a didactic streak in contemporary West African writing, a purpose implicit or explicit, to correct the distortions of the West African culture, to recreate the past in the present in order to educate the West African reader and give him confidence in his cultural heritage and also, in order to enlighten the foreign reader and help him get rid of the false impressions about the West African culture acquired from centuries of cultural misrepresentation.

This strong didacticism of the modern West African writing sometimes intrigues and often irritates the English reader who, because literary didacticism has ceased to be a strong element in his literary tradition since Dr Johnson and the neo-classicists, does not take kindly to its recurrence in contemporary literature. (Although one can point to 'the angry young men' as an exception.)

Typical of the way in which some English readers react to the new West African writing is Professor Martin Tucker's article in *West Africa* (28 July, 1962) titled 'The Headline Novels of Africa'. His main criticism seems to be that the new African novels are sacrificing art to propaganda, that because these novels are expected (by West Africans) to spring from the native African roots and to preoccupy themselves with contemporary issues they are increasingly becoming political and sociological pamphlets. He makes a plea for African writers to get above their material and to worry less about the immediacy of

33

their fictional milieu. What this type of criticism shows is a lack of proper awareness of the real compulsions which are determining and conditioning creative
writing in West Africa. It is obvious that the West African writer, for the
time being at any rate, cannot write without strong cultural commitment and
propaganda motive if he is to contribute to the rehabilitation of the traditional
culture and correct its previous misrepresentations. Judging from the impassioned
polemical tone of the replies to Professor Tucker's article, especially from the
West African novelists themselves, it is obvious that this kind of criticism is
resented as an attempt 'to impose a false pattern on the West African novel'.
These words are quoted from the rejoinder from the Society of Nigerian Authors
of which Achebe, Ekwensi, Nzekwu and others are members.

From Achebe's manifesto quoted above and the statements of other writers
(*Nigeria Magazine*, September 1963), it is clear that the West African
writers' rejection of the philosophy of art for art's sake and the preoccupation with artistic purism for a definitely utilitarian and didactic literary
outlook at this particular point in time and place is to a large extent a
necessity imposed by a historical antecedent and the pressures of cultural
nationalism. Social change in West Africa is proceeding at a rapid rate.
Old values are quickly crumbling and solid new values are not evolving as
rapidly with the result that there is confusion in the minds of many. The
individual lacking cultural direction tends to constitute himself into a
culture-maker. He evolves personal values which would often be determined
by self-interest-altruism as a generating principle of individual action is
replaced by egocentricism. The committed writer, as well as the other intellectuals of society, has the duty of explaining his cultural predicament to
the individual and, what is more, of helping him to evolve new values which
will accommodate the shock of change. The West African writer is therefore
not out only to entertain and please his West African audience but also to
instruct it. In this endeavour, the West African writer bases his authority
on the traditional culture within which art was functional and utilitarian as
well as providing aesthetic pleasure.

The phenomenon is not unique whereby the writers of a period, especially of
a period of cultural disintegration and confusion, are expected to bear the burden
of providing cultural direction and creating or suggesting new cultural values
or restating old ones. It is in fact universal in all such situations of cultural
anarchy. The writer, because of his imaginative insight into the social situation,
brings out with lucidity the real causes of conflict and spiritual unhappiness,
not necessarily overtly but implicitly, and his success or failure depends on
how subtly he is capable of doing this. He can give his readers their true cultural
bearings ('tell the people where the rain began to beat them' as Achebe proverb-

34

ializes it) and imply the obvious values which will lead to a new social integration and fulfilment. This is the kind of thing Leavis and Thompson suggest literary education could do for the English society to ensure cultural continuity and obviate the disintegrative effects of industrialism, urbanism and mass-communication media on the English culture. Literary education, their book *Culture and Environment* implies, should stress the puritan virtues which had given solidity to the English culture. The West African writer is impelled in his writing to strengthen the cultural present with a matrix of the old traditional West African culture. Under the prevailing cultural nationalism he stands or falls by how successfully he has undertaken this duty in his writing.

There is a definite danger in this nationalist pressure on the writer. It is the danger of producing a literature of a new 'Celtic Twilight'. Recreation of the past in the present can easily degenerate into a mere romantic idyllism as false as the European image of a barbaric irrational Africa. One falsehood could easily be replaced by another falsehood. The English-speaking West African writer is fully aware of this pitfall into which the French African writer of the Negritude school has plunged. The French African writer, often the product of the best French intellectual tradition, residing in Paris which has always been a centre of philosophical primitivism and under the shadow of the Rousseauist phantom called *le sauvage noble*, may not easily see the danger of glamorizing his African heritage and thereby calling its authenticity in question. The English-speaking West African with his background of British education and pragmatic outlook, side-steps the pitfall. He regards his cultural heritage as needing no idealization and no apology. All that is required of him is to recreate the traditional culture with fidelity, without flourishes and false colouring. A West African writer whose book fails to satisfy this minimal requirement of fidelity to cultural facts finds it rejected, very often in a cruel and angry manner.

West African writers are in the forefront of this mission to lead Africans from the old to the new Africa. The strong didactic streak in and the pronounced sociological nature of their writings derive from a sense of this cultural mission. Asked by the present writer what the main influence on their writing had been, William Conton replied, '. . . my growing awareness of the sharp conflicts between African and Western culture, and in particular the frequent triumphing of the materialism of the latter over the spiritualism of the former whenever they do clash.' Achebe answered simply, 'My greatest inspiration has been Ibo culture and civilization.' It could be said therefore that whether glaringly obvious or merely implicit, cultural nationalism is one of the determining factors of contemporary West African fiction by indigenous West Africans. ∎

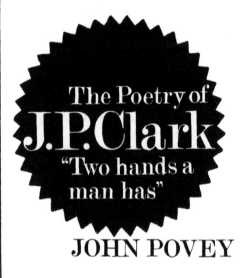

The Poetry of
J.P.Clark
"Two hands a man has"

JOHN POVEY

J. P. Clark is among the best of contemporary African poets, for his work has both a technical and emotional range, more extensive than that measured by his contemporaries. If he lacks the rigorous technical precision and intellectual structure of Christopher Okigbo, he avoids the attendant coldness and detachment of such poetry as he exposes his intimate and unexpectedly tender vision.

Clark is a poet who exists between two worlds and two cultures. I realize nowadays how carefully one must hedge about such a hackneyed truism with equivocal qualifications but the critical commonplace must still be allowed a rough general truth. As an African poet he draws his verse out of his environment, which is the traditional and contemporary life of Nigeria. As an English language poet he derives his style from the multiple influences which fashion the diction and imagery of contemporary poetry. He uses the English, which he handles with such fluent skill, to seek a necessary synthesis, an English language poetry that is localized yet not parochial simultaneously uniquely national, yet inherently universal. The titles of many of his best poems indicate his natural attachment to the African scene, its landscape and its heritage: 'Fulani Cattle', 'Abiku', 'Olumo Rock', 'Olokun', 'Ivbie'. But for the outsider, Clark's international audience, the apparent mystery of these titles can be readily resolved from a footnote and the experience which Clark conveys is invariably a human one. Clark begins with the African scene, charges it with his style forged out of the discipline of English poetry and then leads the reader to his personal, even intimate, revelation. As Clark himself has explained in his introduction to *A Reed in the Tide* (p. vii): 'As our epigraph goes, a man has two hands. In other words, he comes of a mother, and he comes of a father, each of a different family with a separate set-up. As the offshoot of such a union, a man not only fuses elements of both sides but he also constitutes a new independent whole.' It is this 'new independent whole' that we must seek in Clark's work if he is to be other than merely derivative. His achievement of this synthesis is the mark of his quality for it eludes another Nigerian poet, Gabriel Okara, when, in the last stanza of his most famous poem he records his continuing division both spiritual and artistic.

And I, lost in the morning mist
Of an age at a riverside, keep
Wandering in the mystic rhythm
Of jungle drums and the concerto.

From the English side the two most obvious influences which impinge upon Clark's style are the ubiquitous forms of T. S. Eliot and G. M. Hopkins. It is possible to find other echoes. There is the rumble of Dylan Thomas in lines of 'Night Rain' such as:

Doped out of the deep
I have bobbed up bellywise.

'Why Should I Rage?' seems to mirror Yeats' Olympian anger at the unresponsiveness of Maud Gonne. But these are passing moments. The more significant derivative elements are those which become absorbed within the truly personal style.

It would be possible to see the styles of Hopkins and Eliot as the extremes of twentieth century English poetic attitudes. Hopkins' lush, rhetorical excess, charged with sensuous force in both sound and vision, is almost the antithesis of Eliot's verse; dry, acid, with its occasional sharply flippant comedy standing amongst the powerfully repetitive logic of his spiritual diagnosis made in words as precise as cold. Hopkins as a poet celebrates his own passion; Eliot confronts his world with sardonic detachment.

The influence of Eliot is probably more common in Clark's work though it is less simply demonstrable in that its nature is less ostentatious and so more readily absorbed into inconspicuousness. It is most clearly seen in Clark's poetic plays. Eliot had demonstrated that a poetic rhythm could be devised for the stage from the effects of Anglo-Saxon verse. It served to liberate the English stage verse from the inevitable and tedious blank verse which had become the obligatory technique for poetic drama. The boredom caused by the irrelevance of this form to modern situations and characters, had done much to allow until relatively recent times that dearth of poetic drama in England. The stressed lines of *Murder in the Cathedral* and *Family Reunion* are the initial steps in forging a new language for the theatre. The same technique so successfully employed, particularly in Clark's first two dramas *Song of a Goat* and *Masquerade*, derives from Eliot's stage experiments.

In Clark's poetry the influence is also present though less obvious. 'Ivbie' owes much of its language and structure to Eliot's *Waste Land*. It is indicative of the recognition of a more individual style that when Clark reprints 'Ivbie' in *A Reed in the Tide* he eliminates the most obviously derivative sections and republishes only the latter, most African and original sections. In this poem there are the same apparently haphazard sequences which mirror the muddled and dissonant range of experience. There is the characteristic emphasis derived from the studied repetition typical of the opening lines:

> It is not late now in the day
> Late late altogether late,
> Turning our doubled backs upon fate . . .

Common in Eliot too is the arbitrary but emphatic line division that becomes almost a mannerism in Clark's dramatic speeches.

> In the irresolution
> Of one unguarded moment
> Thereby hangs a tale . . .

The hint of pop comedy in the creation of 'sweet Mrs Gamp' recalls a female Sweeney, the characterization maintained in this tone by the nursery rhyme lilting nonsense in which the Austin Hereford pun is curiously English, being derived from the marque of a British car.

> And Austin Herefords go toot
> Tooting in mad rush for loot,
>   Go hooting,
> Blazing wide trails of gold . . .

The influence of Hopkins is more obvious but perhaps this may partly be because he is less easily assimilated. His unique stressed, sprung-rhythm form is immediately recognizable. This obviousness may also derive from one's feeling that Hopkins' style is, in fact, much closer to Clark's own natural voice, for

38

what may sometimes appear like Hopkins may rather be a fresh verbalizing of Clark's own inherently sensuous poetic vision. On several occasions Clark openly admits that he is playing with a style, contriving a pastiche, and yet the results are more poetically serious than that word would generally make us expect. 'Variations On Hopkins' has as its opening couplet:

> *Ama are you gall bitter pent*
> *Have paltry pittance spent.*

In 'Of Faith' both the sonnet form and the very theme are taken from Hopkins for the first lines are:

> *Faith can move mountains, will move whole mountain,*
> *Over seas sail their main, tap-root, buttress*
> *And crest . . .*

Both of the above too obvious examples are eliminated in his collection but Clark retains 'Ibadan Dawn' adding to its title 'After "Pied Beauty"' (though it sounds closer to the poem 'The Windhover' to my ear).

> *Who, ah, looks at! walks over there wide*
> *Velvet greens dipping out of sight:*
> *Rush outdoor concession-strong . . .*

This tiresome academic exercise is not undertaken to suggest any plagiarism of course; it is to establish the significant presence of the influence of the English literary tradition upon the style of Clark, to set him – that 'one hand' of him – into the wider tradition. The language he is using has been shaped by a series of influential writers yet he must take this language, absorb and incorporate it with all its 'foreign' limitations into a style with which he seeks to describe the African experience that constitutes his 'other hand'.

It is here that an outsider such as myself has to admit limitations. The choice of English for this poetry is dangerous because it sets up the expectation of a too ready and total comprehension. How can an English critic evaluate this other African part? I can recognize that the setting and occasionally the attitudes and assumptions will seem 'foreign' to me. Clark is undoubtedly right when he poses the inevitable question, 'How can one speak of or detect vernacular rhythms, influences and sources present or imagined in works by African creative writers in English and French, unless one is versed in the vernacular of a particular author?' (*A Reed in the Tide*, p. viii) This is unchallengable, yet it is also a counsel of perfection that would lead a reader to despair, for it would imply that the only valid criticism of Clark could come from someone fluent in Ijaw. Ideally this might be true but such a study would be a hard enough task for any outside critic and even success would, by this argument, bring him no nearer toward the comprehension of the poetry of Soyinka, Awoonor-Williams or Lenrie Peters who come from other linguistic backgrounds. Even an African critic would be limited by the narrow area of his comprehension. One begins by admitting in courteous honesty the obvious limitations that make one tread cautiously avoiding the brazenly dogmatic. Yet one might observe in self-defence, that all criticism is based upon the application of gradually increasing knowledge and experience to an art work, but if criticism could only begin at the moment of total understanding it could hardly begin at all. There is, for all the limitations in one's specific, and in this case African, knowledge an area where critical observation can be delimited. The starting point for this assertion is the fact of the choice of the English language which, no matter how modified by African usages remains a language available to the tools of English literary criticism if those devices are handled with modesty and good sense. Clark himself has observed of his language choice, '... language-which for me, a Nigerian, is English, a language that no longer is the copyright of any one people or nation'. (*A Reed in the Tide*, p. viii) It is necessary to admit frankly that I am incapable of detailing, or even demonstrably perceiving, the effect of Ijaw epic oral poetry upon Clark's writing. This would be an important task and perhaps some Ijaw critic could indicate the association of this contemporary poetry with an older vernacular tradition in a manner similar to my own recognition of the English elements which I discussed above. Yet one can still point to another synthesis more obvious than the linguistic one and one much more apparent to the outside reader. This is the application of the English language style to the description of the African scene.

Clark records with joy and warmth the African landscape. Rarely is his writing simply descriptive. It is apparently so in 'Ibadan' perhaps because its almost haiku-like brevity permits minimal speculation. The economy here better exposes the sudden visual impact which is the mark of the successful poetic image.

Ibadan,
> *running splash of rust*
> *and gold ... flung and scattered*
> *among seven hills like broken*
> *china in the sun.*

Those who have flown from Lagos to Ibadan will recall that as the plane descends the corrugated iron roofs of the houses catch the sun suddenly and brightly and Pepper Clark's image precisely captures that scene. There are many points in this poem worthy of mention but enough to point out the subtle rhetoric achieved by the line division and the balanced colour antithesis of gold and rust, to see how competent a piece it is. In 'Girl Bathing' the description and the response are more openly sensual. The scene is archetypal in literature. One recalls the moment when witnessing the girl wading thigh deep into the sea Stephen Dedalus makes the supreme dedication of his aesthetic soul. It is interesting that there is only one specifically 'African' word in this lyric – 'cassava' in her basket. Yet there is in this poem such warm intensity that it appears that the dazzle of the scene becomes part of the vision of the woman and Clark's halting separation of phrases becomes a measure of his passing witness. 'And as she ducks / Under, with deft fingers plucks / Loose her hair . . .' When after the description he rhetorically celebrates her beauty 'O girl . . . so ripe with joy', he records his own equal and generous response. 'Girl Bathing' is a simple example of the way in which Clark moves from description, which is by its nature static, into intimate involvement. The effect can be seen more obviously in 'Olumo Rock' with its passionately personal concluding note. Olumo Rock is a sacred rock in Abeokuta. Clark begins by describing its awesome power:

> *Stone reared on the crest of Olumo*
> *And far-out-flung by lightning-hand*

But when he gets to the concept of the purgation through sacrificial fire the poem immediately becomes intimate self critical:

> *So blest be my loving-unloved flesh,*
> *That fanned so long in flames of passion*
> *Lapping futile for consummation,*
> *Turns this pillar of ash;*
> *But curst my heart that stubborn*
> *As Joan's yearns and wouldn't burn.*

The concluding reference to Joan, clearly Joan of Arc, takes us into another area. In seeking the analogy for his own heretic pride he has sought in the European histories. His equation of experience has here brought together both the Western and the traditional elements of knowledge to cope with the balance of world cultures. The attempt to handle this dualism, to make synthesis rather than record oppositions, to make a single focus out of such diversity is the supreme problem for the African poet and a difficulty that has been a major preoccupation in the verse of both Awoonor-Williams and Christopher Okigbo. Sometimes it seems an impossible task of reconciliation and Clark seems almost as alienated as his French contemporaries and their Negritude concerns. He recognizes the dangers that he may have been divided from the African existence by the changes wrought by education and training.

41 This sense of division is seen very clearly in 'Agbor Dancer'. He describes

appreciatively the illustration of this dancing figure:

> *See her caught in the throb of a drum*
> *Tippling from hide-brimmed stem*
> *Down lineal veins to ancestral core . . .*

This ancestral core is of course also Clark's own but although he is affected by this dance he regards it with some of the detachment that his education makes inevitable. His appreciation no longer has that instinctive quality. One notices the auxillary verb that begins the last stanza. 'Could I', he asks:

> *Could I, early sequestered from my tribe,*
> *Free a lead-tether'd scribe*
> *I should answer her communal call*
> *Lose myself in her warm caress*
> *Intervolving earth, sky and flesh.*

The verbs and their conditional mood make the tone very clear. 'Could I . . . I should . . .' not that he IS able to and DOES. He does not lose himself and that consummation which the dancer has achieved by merging earth, sky, flesh; that universality of experience that Clark in other poems seems to seek in childhood memory is specifically denied him. He is 'sequestered' because (and how ironic the word seems) he is 'a scribe'.

This mood persists even when he attempts a more flippant tone in 'Ring Round the Moon'. The neat overemphatic rhyme of the first couplet establishes the mockery of the initial mood.

> *The moon tonight wears a hat*
> *draped in crape as a bat:*

The emotion changes completely in the second stanza which includes a self recognition more agonizing than the mere anxiety that ends 'Agbor Dancer'.

> *My heart reflects at noon*
> *this shadow of the moon,*
> *   hugging desolation*
> *as bats a blasted bough . . .*

It is a reaction encountered again in another poem called 'Darkness and Light'. The scene is set in a fairly conventional way:

> *That time when the stars are out*
> *And earth in womb of night*
> *Is double-torn in doubt*
> *Hold me like a mother tight.*

42

The heavy terminal rhymes and the awkward rhythm of these lines denies them real subtlety but it is interesting to see the way that Clark takes the conventional image of the womb of night, which has become almost a dead metaphor, and invigorates it by developing it into the more precisely visualized and quite literal idea of motherhood for later he cries 'take me by the navel . . .' It makes one remember the very intimate and tender tone with which Clark responds to his mother and grandmother in 'Night Rain' and 'To Granny'. But in this poem his concern is elsewhere, for the last stanza consists of the anxious lines:

> *But take me by the navel*
> *Close and I will go in stark*
> *Out of hurtful light*
> *For I will be again the dark*
> *Child safe from lunik blight.*

The creation of the new adjectival form 'lunik' for 'lunar' may owe something to the idea which associated full moon with madness, but the spelling seems rather to show derivation from that ubiquitous Russian 'sputnik'. If this is so the 'blight' becomes a very different and technological threat. Confronting this Clark wishes to fall back into the security of childhood, to become 'dark child safe . . .'

This significance of child memory is common in Clark's work and is the basis for his most tender and sensitive poems. His poem 'For Granny, From Hospital', is a childhood memory intimate in a way that seems entirely unsentimental. It describes one of those moments when a gesture, casual in itself, becomes a supreme illumination. He recalls the time 'fifteen floods ago', when suddenly his grandmother, unaccountably 'strained me to breast'. He speculates about this sudden moment of intimacy in lines that surge with a poetic intensity, the long insistent stress of the lines matching the emotion as he concludes:

> *Or was it wonder at those footless stars*
> *Who in their long translucent fall*
> *Make shallow silten floors*
> *Beyond the pale of muddy waters*
> *Appear more plumbless than the skies?*

His vision here, both delicate and impassioned, incorporates sky, water, land, in a harmony which creates an inevitable unposing sympathy between human beings and their landscape in a natural manner that has been unobtainable in Western literature since the Romantics.

A longer poem, 'Night Rain', which has often been quoted by Gerald Moore as one of the most effective of Clark's poems shows a similar type of memory –

a memory suddenly illuminating across years, across the gulf imposed by adult experience. He begins when he is woken up from sleep by pounding rain and then, within the structure of the poem, there is a transition in time, a sudden shift from present to memory, and the poet sees himself back as a child, watching the rain dripping through the thatch of the African hut. As he describes his mother moving her bins of corn out of the way of the leaks he uses a sudden vivid and very African image. He talks of the water slopping across the floor 'like ants filing out of wood'. The image is effective in creating an exact picture of the encroaching water puddle and yet it does this through the use of an association that is only familiar to us through the illumination of this poem. The concluding lines, like several of Clark's better poems, assert the possibility of unity; of an emotional stasis. The dangerous owls and bats cannot fly so the rain brings a kind of safety:

> *And again roll to the beat*
> *Of drumming all over the land*
> *And under its ample soothing hand*
> *Joined to that of the sea*
> *We will settle to sleep of the innocent and free.*

Land, sea, the rain-filled sky are made harmonious in the poet's vision.

The last poem in the Mbari collection is 'Ivbie'. I have already mentioned the derivative nature of the early verses. The last sections are much more profound and are the sections rightly preserved in *A Reed in the Tide*. With part four the over-clever dross is eliminated and a more profound and, significantly a more African note is stressed. The section lists a series of ominous threats; a ghost, 'his wings flapping in the twigs', is manifest by unpredictable events:

> *A snake bird fell down early flat*
> *in the market place.*

'Race and riot', 'poison', 'repulsive waves' are all symptoms of the unrecognized horror for only the poet, 'saw all'. But the poet recognizes the dangers and he colloquially cries his distress, 'I can not sleep. I can not sleep'. 'Yet in my father's house I can not sleep.' There is a clear irony in the use of 'father's house' which works both ways and applies to the missionary promises of religion and more generally to the traditional heritage of Africa. It is not resolved for although, Clark cries about 'a violated past' which appears to be a taking sides, the section concludes when he accuses himself of being a 'bastard child'. Clearly the deliberately chosen term implies the unreconciled parentage of Clark's own intellectual existence. He attempts to sum up this continuous dilemma in the last shorter section. At a superficial level the resolution is a cry of 'a plague on

44

both your houses'. He dismisses the West,

> *missile-hurled*
> *In your headlong flight to fool the world.*

He insists that he is other than this missile world:

> *I, Reared here on cow-dung floor,*
> *From antedeluvian shore*
> *Heard all, and what good it did!*

He reserves the poet's implicit right to stand aside ordering the mad technology to 'pass on in mad headlong flight . . .' All he asks of it is that it

> *leave behind unhaunted*
> *An innocent in sleep of the ages.*

The irony is less in the words of this line than in the contradiction of concept. Clark knows that he can never be 'unhaunted'. His lack of sleep, in the symbolic sense is permanent. But it is the accuracy of the contemplation of this fact, not the attempt, or our desire, to find a simplistic resolution of this irreconcilable paradox which makes these stanzas approach a new assertion.

The publication of *A Reed in the Tide* in 1965 was a significant event because it was the first international publication of a volume of verse by an individual poet from Africa. Before this, although the work of the better known poets had quite often been published in anthologies, their individual volumes had all been published in Ibadan under the auspices of the Mbari Writers Club. These attractively produced books had received rather irregular and haphazard international distribution. Clark's new volume included from his earlier Mbari collection largely those poems which were already best known through the anthologies. The greater part of the rest were taken from the poetic interludes in Clark's autobiographical record of his abortive scholarship year at Princeton, *America Their America*. This is a sharp, sometimes perceptive but generally ungenerous book. The disgruntled mood that must have very understandably possessed Clark as he came up against the patronizing restrictions of his Princeton scholarship is not restrained and invades the poetry of this period in his life. The poems are not improvements upon the sensitive involvement of, say, 'Agbor Dancer' or 'Abiku'. Yet this is not evidence of a diminution in Clark's obvious and genuine literary talent. America, even had it not been the source and occasion for so much personal irritation to Clark himself, is not kind to the visiting poet. The impact of its staggering excess invites an attitudinizing which reflects only the inevitable shock at its vehement materialism, its violent self-assertion. The temptation to capture this surface grossness in sharply satirical lines is apparently irresistible, and causes a particular, false, kind of cleverness. The tone hollowness is exposed more obviously in the facile attack of the poem's lines than in the American social fabric so scathingly displayed. After all American urbanization is a more subtle and complex thing than the lines which record the first shock of the poet-tourist's arrival can indicate. Lines like these are just as slick and superficial as the gadget culture they seek so scathingly to denounce.

> *A dime*
> > *in the slot,*
> *And anything*
> > *from coke to coffee*
> *Spews down your throat,*
> > *from crackers to candy . . .*

The rhythm of these lines takes on that same cheap syncopation as the matching sound of the juke box which would in reality accompany this scene.

This American mood is anticipated even before landing on the continent for the stereotype expectation is total. In the plane the language of 'Boeing Crossing' has a loose structure, part casually colloquial, part merely sloppy.

> *New York, however,*
> *Whether and wear permitting, is*
> *Where we are scheduled for the come down*
> *(That-mine!) with a thud and*
> *A dash or more, should certainly send*
> *Us all packing and about our several ways . . .*

In a similar way the description of the New York subways will not be forged into poetry that makes a statement. The description is adequate but a 'So what?', in the brash American idiom comes to mind as we read the details.

> *till like thunder tunnelling*
> *The earth, the centipede train*
> *Lunges full into station*
> *And pulls us all to attention.*
> *Multiple doors of their own slide*
> *Open all at once down the platform,*
> *Each the magnetic yawn*
> *Of a monster.*

Clark can show moments of concern for 'my brothers in the wild America', but it is a mood that would require involvement and that is not a noticeable reaction in this series of poems. The merciless impact of the American scene

46

enforces a kind of shocked repulsion which allows only a posturing both in deed and in poetry.

Clark comes closer to his authentic voice in three poems he wrote while living down in New Jersey: 'Three Moods of Princeton'. Here he was not merely the passing spectator he had been in New York, so perhaps time allowed a contemplation more contemplative than the tourist glimpses of 'Times Square'. Yet it is interesting to see that even here the 'three moods' are the three moods of the landscape and not the moods of Clark and the moods are those rather obvious pathetic reactions to the decline of autumn and winter's death. The picture created is, in the final analysis, only descriptive while Clark's better poetry — as all valid verse — must move beyond the visual to establish the under-lying intellectual and emotional awareness that engages the poet's awareness. Suggestively enough Clark deliberately describes the Princeton scenes in the images of Africa, linking the two continents with his careful metaphor.

The elm trees, still
Shaven bald and gaunt,
In the brief buba
They wear after snow
Are a band of alufa
Deployed down the neighbourhood.

The last poem is this collection entitled, 'The Leader' begins:

They have felled him to the ground
Who announced home from abroad,

There is an ironic way in which the lines are true of Clark as he wrestled with America in his verse. Yet the observations one was able to insist upon in relation to his earlier poems are still critically valid. The poetic conception is still sharp, the gradually forged new style becomes more flexible, there is still an intimacy and awareness in his vision. At the moment the sad distress of Nigeria's turmoil must be dampening the ready hope that celebrated the African scene in the earlier poems, yet one has a specific confidence that the later work of Clark will carry out the achievement of his earlier verse into a more profound maturity, which will not only be a technical but also a perceptual advance. With an emphasis that applies more strongly now that Clark could have imagined when he created these lines, he had declared

Okuapolokpolo!
When he's done, we shall sing.

'He' refers far more widely than any contemporary politics but Clark's song will most certainly be heard with delight and admiration. ∎

Aimé Césaire, *Une Saison au Congo*, Editions du Seuil, Paris 1966

The poet Aimé Césaire has broadened the scope of his literary endeavours in recent years by adding a series of plays to the volumes of poems for which he first became known. The most recent of these plays is an interpretation of the meteoric career of Patrice Lumumba, a subject dramatic in itself, yet one which can inspire violent reactions even today, especially among the radical young Africans to whom he remains the symbol of intransigent resistance to Western imperialism. To the Belgians, Americans and others, who were genuinely horrified by the tales of massacres, and who stood to lose their substantial investments because of Lumumba, he was a symbol of another sort: primitive barbarity, madness, and atheistic communism. Césaire's play, *Une saison au Congo*, reviews the events of the days from independence to Lumumba's death, and reveals both the source in reality and the relevance of the Lumumba myth.

In one of the opening scenes, the problem of mobilizing the popular imagination is suggested. The joyful crowd is singing and dancing in anticipation of the great day of independence, or 'Dipenda', as they call it:

A WOMAN: How will Dipenda come?

By car, by ship or by plane?
A MAN: It's coming with the little white king, bwana Kitoko, he's bringing it to us.
MNC CITIZEN: They aren't bringing us Dipenda, citizens, it's we who are taking it!
MUKONGO TRIBALIST: Makes no difference! Given or seized, all I know is that now that we have our Dipenda, all those Bengalas will have to go back to their villages . . . .

The menace from the colonial power is made explicit; the bankers plot their strategy for keeping control of Congolese wealth after Independence; and the Belgian king and his army commander make a display of granting independence as a gift rather than acknowledging any natural right to enjoy it. The mutiny of the army, the Belgian financiers' invention of Katangese autonomy, and the subsequent civil disorder bring the crisis rapidly to a head.

Lumumba has to face the multiple threats all by himself. The President, Kala-Lubu, is jealous and ineffectual, the army has proved itself unreliable, and the senate is too busy enjoying its material comforts to act. When the senators complain that he can never be found in his office Lumumba replies:

As for me I should like to be able to

48

multiply and divide myself, have innumerable selves, so that I could be everywhere at once. Matadi, Boma, Elisabethville, Luluabourg, to be able to undo the innumerable plots of the enemy! But even Lumumba's dynamism is unavailing: the problems are too great. The weapon he chooses against the Belgians, after threatening to call in Soviet aid, is the UN. The arrival of Hammarskjöld, the man of peace, brings a note of light and hope into the situation. But the first act does not end with this reassuring scene. While the crowd dances the Independence cha-cha in the background, the Great Western (US) ambassador tells the audience that Lumumba's appeal to Moscow was an incendiary act, and that his nation, whose foreign policy is to fight fires – the fireman is a stock character in French force, a bit pompous and not at all clever – will not stand idly by.

The second act begins with the confrontation between Lumumba and Hammarskjöld, and traces the intensifying crises of secession, internal dissension and unending bloodshed, as the National Army slaughters thousands of Baluba in its advance towards Katanga. Lumumba passes this off by saying: 'A military campaign isn't carried out anywhere by using confetti!' As for world opinion, Lumumba defies it to celebrate the army's victory by dancing with a girl from the Lulua tribe, blood enemies of the slain Lubas. Lumumba remains confident of the loyalty and co-operation of Kala-Lubu and Mokutu, the army commander – the names of characters still alive are given a transparent disguise in the play – even though his wife Pauline is anxious for his safety. When Kala-Lubu deposes Lumumba to install Ileo as Prime Minister, Mokutu comes to arrest the incredulous Lumumba and makes the now familiar claims that the army will restore order and put an end to politicians' rule in the Congo.

Lumumba is in prison as the Third Act opens, but easily wins over his guards and talks his way out. And once free, he refuses the entreaties of his wife Pauline to flee: Stanleyville? How can I, while I am struggling against secession, organize a secession of my own to shelter myself

from the blows of my enemies? I want neither to flee nor to desert.

Likewise he is begged by Kala-Lubu and Mokutu to join a coalition government. He insists that he is still the only legitimate government of the Congo, and protests:

Africa needs my intransigence! ...
And to answer your very precise question, I do not wish to guarantee by my presence a policy I disavow, and still less to boss a team formed from a lot of sellouts and traitors.

The Katangese refuse to co-operate with Mokutu even after the price of their co-operation has been paid: Lumumba's arrest. Tzumbi, the Katanga premier, demands that he be handed over. Lumumba is taken to Elisabethville and brutally treated by the Katangese army. Holding a knife to Lumumba's chest, his assassin M'siri shouts:

You're living your death and you don't realise it!

LUMUMBA: I'm dying my life, and that's enough for me.

M'SIRI: There! (*He shoves the blade in.*) Now then, prophet, what do you see?

LUMUMBA: I shall be of the field, of the pastures

I shall be with the fisherman Wagenia

I shall be with the Kivu herdsman

I shall be on the hill, I shall be in the gorges.

M'SIRI: Let's put an end to this. (*He bears down*).

LUMUMBA: Oh! This dew on Africa! I am looking, I see, comrades, the flame tree, pygmies, with an axe, busying themselves about the precarious trunk, but the head grows and quotes to the quavering sky the rudimentary froth of a dawn.

M'SIRI: Filthy bastard! (*Lumumba falls*).

Three figures appear to speak their final words: Hammarskjöld, tormented by his guilt in Lumumba's death; the banker, pleased at having kept his own hands clean; and Pauline, who sees him return, in the form of the African musician, the sanza player, singing a warning to death, and ending with a war cry 'Luma! Luma!', which is answered by Pauline and taken up by the drums, to mark the end of the play.

Patrice's last words are pure poetry, and

recall the symbol of fire which occurs whenever people talk about Lumumba. His identification with diverse kinds of people in the Congo repeats the recurrent theme of this conscious embodiment of the nation. The language is that which Césaire uses in the fervent poems about his own Antilles, and by making Lumumba speak in this way, he means to show that poetry and the power of the Word are powerful weapons of the revolution. While Lumumba was not a poet, he was a master of language in another way. Everyone who saw and heard him speak to a crowd testifies to his eloquence. In the opening scene he is using it to sell beer, but his speech to the crowd on Independence day, his articulate defense to Hammarskjöld of his line of action, and his persuasiveness when talking to the prison guards show that he was aware of his gift. Aware of it, and of its limitations as well. Neither a messiah nor a mahdi, he says:

My only weapon is my speech: I speak and I arouse; I am not a righter of wrongs, not a miracle-worker, I am a righter of life: I speak, and I give Africa back to herself! I speak, and I give Africa to the world! I speak, and attacking oppression and servitude at their base, I make fraternity possible for the first time.

But Patrice is a musician, too. He uses a song to encourage the Parliament to resist the Belgians, he accompanies himself on the guitar and sings a Swahili song to comfort Pauline, and later sings a slave lament to Mokutu. The action of the play is constantly interspersed by music of all kinds: the strains of the Independence cha-cha, songs of people in the crowd, girls singing in the African bars, and the chorus-like figure of the sanza-player.

Although even a white mercenary sings between violent outbursts of insults, it seems clear that music, like the Word, means life and liberty to Césaire and to his hero. Indeed Lumumba's eloquence corresponds exactly to the people's need to be educated by the Word. The Belgian financiers speak only in ridiculously parroted formulas parodying French classic alexandrine verse. Lumumba, as a lover of song, beer, and dance – he is remembered as an excellent and avid dancer – represents the vitality of the Congolese people – the Belgian king speaks significantly of the Congo as a 'machine' – and as such his own life is far less important than his symbolic role. He is aware of all this, too, not because he is a prophet, but because of his clear vision: he alone sees what *must* be done.

Among the other characters in the play, the most interesting are Hammerskjöld, Mokutu, and Kala-Lubu. When Lumumba first mentions Hammarskjöld's name to the Congolese Senate, he praises his integrity and neutrality, and claims to have complete confidence in him. Hammarskjöld himself claims to be completely impartial and just, and is presented by Césaire as genuinely attempting to be so. In the final scenes, Hammarskjöld discovers that certain of his aides were purposely restraining Lumumba's movements against Katanga, all the while knowing about the dispatch of supplies to Katanga by the Belgians. Only at this point does Hammarskjöld suddenly realize he has been the dupe of these policies, and has struck down the one man capable of saving the Congo. In the final scene he reappears to lament in almost Biblical language:

Oh! how injust the Just Becomes;
And honesty a tool to be used only
to strike down honesty
Lord! Why choose me
To preside over the satanic alchemy?

Hammarskjöld is thus innocent and well-intentioned, but cannot really understand Lumumba or Africa. In some respects, he is as much a tragic figure as Lumumba, as he engages himself in the Congolese labyrinth, armed only with his purity.

Kala-Lubu is a chief and likes to think of himself as 'King' of the Congo. His independence speech is one of moderation, praise of the tribal culture and traditional values, and of reconciliation. Surprisingly enough, he rather admires Lumumba, and is desperately jealous of the latter's popularity. The spectacle of Kala-Lubu accompanying Lumumba like a new bride on all the frantic movements to and fro in the struggle to hold the new nation, together makes Kala-Lubu ridiculous and weak. Still, he sneers at reports that Patrice is communist and, not knowing what to do, turns to bishop Malula for advice. Only thus can he be persuaded that it is his duty to depose and arrest Lumumba.

50

Accompanying him on his visit to the bishop is Mokutu. He has been a close companion of Lumumba during the struggle for Independence, and while Patrice appreciates his intelligence and finesse, he recognizes his weakness of character. This betrayal makes the Mobutu government's official cult of Lumumba's memory grimly ironic.

Césaire gives us a more accurate myth of the martyr of African independence. The Lumumba he presents is a visionary: his ideal of a free, united Congo was one that he would not compromise, not even with the stubborn realities which finally destroyed him. But the play, if revolutionary in its message, is not doctrinaire. As Mokutu says in an early scene:

All roads are good. In any case at the present moment in the Congo all roads lead to revolution, so take any of them, but take one.

The anti-clericalism of the play is not atheism, and must be seen in the light of the Church's role in the colonial power structure. Lumumba in the last act talks even of non-violence and compares himself to Gandhi, a willing martyr to the cause he has lived for.

If Césaire hopes, in *Une Saison au Congo*, to rehabilitate Patrice Lumumba from the slanderers and to rescue him from some of his dubious champions, it is not for the benefit of an invisible posterity. His historical study of Toussaint Louverture and his earlier play about King Henri Christophe, Negro heroes of Haitian independence, show that his primary preoccupation is the liberation of his own people in the Antilles. The popular tone of most of the text, including the use of songs and dance, contrast agreably with the intense poetic and philosophical passages, giving the play a broad appeal, very much in the manner of Brechtian theatre. Césaire tells the un-liberated peoples, and especially the people of his native Martinique, that 'all roads lead to revolution, so take any of them, but take *one*'. As mayor of Fort-de-France and deputy to the National Assembly in Paris, but more truly as the greatest French-speaking poet of Negro *engagement*, Césaire is taking all the roads, armed like his Lumumba, with the gift of the Word. ∎

Garry Spackey

JAMES NGUGI

JAMES NGUGI
A Grain of Wheat, Heinemann 1967.
African Writers Series 1968

James Ngugi's new novel is longer and more ambitious than his two earlier works. Both *Weep not, Child* and *The River Between* impressed by their meticulousness but disappointed somewhat by their ultimate caution, their refusal to venture beyond a simple narrative statement: here was a writer of distinct quality but whose self-imposed range seemed too narrow to permit a complete assertion of his talent. And the 'simple beautiful English' or the 'simple evocative prose' so lauded by reviewers might well have seemed to a less charitable reader more accurately described as impoverished. Indeed, European critics, uncertain of their ground before novels owing little to a definable literary tradition, tend to retreat too readily into ritual genuflections in the direction of Bunyan or the Authorized Version (though the Bible is the most clearly demonstrable literary influence on African fiction), hailing a workmanlike narrative as a skilful work of art and transmuting a scattering of Yoruba or Swahili words into a grand assertion of African dignity and nobility.

On the other hand, whilst density of verbal

texture is notably absent in many African novels, it is not, in spite of modern critical orthodoxy, a prime desideratum — as the desperate modishness of Soyinka's *The Interpreters* sadly illustrates. When compared with the tedious and finally aimless virtuosity of Soyinka's novel, one may see Ngugi's continence of language as the acceptable price of an alternative kind of development: a structural complexity serving a satisfying depth of moral awareness. An isolated page of Soyinka may seem to hold more promise than a page of Ngugi but *A Grain of Wheat* is a greater whole than *The Interpreters*.

A Grain of Wheat is set on the eve of Kenya's achievement of independence. Uhuru has become a reality but not quite the panacea that was half optimistically expected and half uneasily hoped for. The problems latent in the earlier novels now reveal themselves as living issues and their appearance is a severe test of the writer's integrity and artistic skill. The weakness of the first two novels lay in the distance of their themes from the concrete relationships figuring in the plot. The visionary dreams attached to the idealized view of education in both *Weep Not, Child* and *The River Between* simplify problems rather than solve them. Neither are matters assisted by the introduction of an adolescent love interest vaguely reminiscent of Romeo and Juliet. And both these novels end on a note of despair: *Weep not, Child* with the narrowly averted suicide of the hero, Njoroge; *The River Between* with Waiyaki and Nyambwa united in an unconvincing love but with Honia, the symbolic river of life, dividing rather than joining the antagonistic forces represented by the opposing ridges.

This third novel is remarkable for approaching the theme of Uhuru in terms of the minute conflicts that actually make up life. The central characters have a resilience and solidity hitherto lacking; their intimate relations and inner lives animate and explore the ground plan of the novel with a subtlety and insight altogether admirable. These characters are not postulates in an illustrated debate but people with a recognizable identity as individuals, living their lives and facing their problems in a vividly caught environment — consider the almost Laurentian quality of this passage

describing the newly married life of Gikonyo, the carpenter and his wife, Mumbi:

Wangari, his mother, was also happy. She had found a daughter in Mumbi with whom, even without the medium of speech, she could share a woman's joys and troubles. The two went to the shamba together, they fetched water from the river in turns, and cooked in the same pot. The soul of the mother warmed towards the young woman crossing the abyss of silence no words could reach, revelling in the tension of new recognition. Together they looked beyond the hut to the workshop, where the man held a saw or a plane. They listened to the carpenter's voice singing with the tools and their hearts were full to bursting.

The merging of the rhythms of everyday activities with the way a human relationship develops is but a minor example of how this kind of evocation in the novel is used to flesh out the skeletal statements which punctuate the political theme:

One night it happened. Jomo Kenyatta and other leaders of the land were rounded up. Governor Baring had declared a State of Emergency over Kenya.

These two extracts conveniently epitomize the linked interests of the novel: the inner lives, the personal aspirations of the chief characters are brought into conflict both with each other and with Uhuru, to whose inexorable movement they must pay willing homage or else conceal their secret antagonism. It is to Ngugi's credit that, in this novel, he fully recognizes that the compromises and disappointments of personal life are not solved by a political 'new deal'. Uhuru is not the easy solution to problems: it is their inescapable context — and one which will include not just the end of white domination but also the corruption of the new black political elite in Nairobi.

To accomodate the moral discovery of his novel, Ngugi employs a narrative structure based on flashback and reminiscence. The shifting chronology delays information and suspends judgment. All the main characters have some private guilt: Mugo, the village hero, owes his stolid suffering in the detention camps to a self-inflicted expiation of his betrayal of Kihika, the leader of the Freedom

Fighters. Gikonyo, having escaped from detention by confessing to the Mau Mau oath, returns to his wife, Mumbi, only to find her nursing the child of his old rival Karanja — himself a government chief and willing tool of the whites. The easy certainties of the struggle for Uhuru are superseded by the personal complexities of the achieved event. The ready decisions of Mau Mau no longer obtain; motives become obscured by time, and guilt difficult to assign. When Mugo, like Razumov in Conrad's *Under Western Eyes*, finds that he cannot retire from himself, he makes a public confession of guilt which at the same time exonerates the unworthy Karanja from suspicion. General R., a former Freedom Fighter, treats the situation with the confident rectitude of the unsubtle soldier:

'Your deeds alone will condemn you', General R. continued without anger or apparent bitterness. 'You — No one will ever escape from his own actions.'

Ngugi knows that the problem is not that simple; and in a short muted chapter following the above extract he presents the puzzled uncertainty of two elders of the village which admirably represents the atmosphere of this novel. Summary execution has left only a different kind of guilt which is intensified by Mumbi's revelation that she already knew of the betrayal of her brother, Kihika.

Lack of information at the right time is the novel's structural equivalent of lack of sympathy and self-knowledge in life's actual moral decisions. The exploded time-scheme constantly undermines moral complacency. When Gikonyo returns home, the reader is inclined to accept his evaluation of Mumbi's adultery; but when Mumbi gives Mugo her account of Karanja's behaviour, adultery becomes seduction and the reader's moral perspective shifts. This kind of moral ambiguity permeates the novel — with the unfortunate exception of the treatment given to the European characters. John Thompson, the English colonial officer, is allowed none of the rounded and circumspect sympathy shown to the Africans. Thompson is a paste-board character whose presentation is fairly indicated by this extract:

After the war he returned to his interrupted studies at Oxford. It was there,

whilst reading history, he found himself interested in the development of the British Empire. At first this was a historian's interest without personal involvement. But, drifting into the poems of Rudyard Kipling, he experienced a swift flicker, a flame awakened. He saw himself as a man with destiny, a man poised for great things in the future.

The tone of this is too near to the similar effusions on the glorious destiny arising from education promised to Waiyaki and Njoroge in the first two novels for one to suspect the presence of a deflating irony. Even when he introduces a prospective publication of Thompson's to be entitled *Prospero in Africa* the context has sufficient callow logic for it to stand as Ngugi's genuine view of the European colonialist. Thompson's notes for this manuscript include some of the more patronizing remarks of Schweitzer and these too are assimilated in the characterization. The only irony is Thompson's explicit reflection on the futility of his life's effort — but this is based on his view of Uhuru as British betrayal and not on any realization of the fatuity of his own premises.

One is not condemning the presentation of this level of colonialist naivety as past belief. What one objects to is the facile glibness of the character drawing in a novel which is generally praiseworthy for avoiding two-dimensional types. And when Thompson's role suddenly changes from the visionary-turned-bureaucrat to the brutal head of a detention camp, the switch lacks plausibility in terms of the novel's own system of moral evaluation. It is here perhaps that close comment on verbal texture becomes relevant; for it is unfortunately easy for an African writer to remain unaware of the resonances of the language and hence unwittingly invite the wrong kind of ironic response from a European reader.

However, it would be grossly unfair to conclude on this note without at the same time giving James Ngugi's novel the warmest commendation. *A Grain of Wheat* deserves an enthusiastic reception — it both endorses one's prior sense of its author's quality and promises greater achievement in the future.

Derek Elders

EQUIANO

Oloudah Equiano: *Equiano's Travels* (edited by Paul Edwards) African Writers Series Heinemann (also in boards)

The publication of this abridged edition of Equiano's autobiography as *Equiano's Travels* is the natural step following Paul Edwards' two anthologies of African narrative prose. It is most welcome.

The value of what Paul Edwards is attempting to do for the fast-growing readership of West African writing in English cannot be overestimated. As his two prose anthologies have shown, he is deeply interested in establishing in this readership a sense of an African 'literary history'. These books are not intended exclusively for a West African readership, it is true, but few reading his introductions can long doubt where he feels his first duties lie. This is, of course, quite proper, for though the establishment of this sense of history is desirable in a wider readership, in West Africa, so deeply involved in the evolution of a modern cultural identity, it is essential.

Paul Edwards has by careful research given substance to previous, rather vague assertions of the long-standing and dignity of West African writing in English. Few, certainly not Paul Edwards, would claim more than competence for Phyllis Wheatley, Ignatius Sancho, Cuguano (or his accomplice) and Equiano. Equally few would deny their relevance to West African literature for, although all of them wrote as members of alien cultures, they were paradoxically the beginning of their adaptation towards a new cultural identity, a process which, with the recent increase of published work from West Africa, has already proved rich and exciting. Equiano and the others were almost entirely absorbed into the societies for which they wrote. The constant dispute as to whether they could have written what they did is a measure of the extent to which this was so (pp. xv–xvi). But what is important is that they were the springboards for the leaping towards separate identities. A springboard is necessarily anchored at one end.

No one would care to pretend that the original version of Equiano's autobiography makes easy reading today in all its parts — indeed the temptation is to think that this cannot have been the case in the eighteenth century either. Mr Edwards is well aware of this and *The Interesting Narrative of the Life of Olaudah Equiano, or Gustavus Vassa the African, written by himself* becomes *Equiano's Travels* and, for its present purpose, the better for it. It makes good reading and it owes this as much to Equiano's narrative skill as to Paul Edwards' skill in stringing events into a coherent book without obscuring a view of the writer's personality. Here is an extract of Equiano's account of his part in an engagement with French ships when on board the *Namur*:

> At this station my gun-mate (a partner in bringing powder for the same gun) and I ran a very great risk for more than half an

hour of blowing up the ship. For when we had taken the cartridges out of the boxes, the bottoms of many of them proving rotten, the powder ran all about the deck near the match tub: we scarcely had water enough at the last to throw on it. We were also, from our employment, very much exposed to the enemy's shots, for we had to go through nearly the whole length of the ship to bring the powder. I expected therefore every minute to be my last, especially when I saw our men fall so thick about me, but wishing to guard as much against the dangers as possible, at first I thought it would be safest not to go for the powder till the Frenchmen had fired their broadside, and then while they were charging I could go and come with my powder: but immediately afterwards I thought this caution was fruitless, and cheering myself with the reflection that there was a time allotted for me to die as well as to be born, I instantly cast off all fear or thought whatever of death and went through the whole of my duty with alacrity, pleasing myself with the hope, if I survived the battle, of relating it and the dangers I had escaped to the dear Miss Guerins and others, when I should return to London. (pp. 48–49)

Equiano is often boastful often pompous, but he is always warmly human. He rarely makes more than stoical remarks about the cruelty he suffers personally:

The reader cannot but judge of the irksomeness of this situation to a mind like mine in being daily exposed to new hardships and impositions after having seen many better days and having been as it were in a state of freedom and plenty, added to which, every part of the world I had hitherto been in seemed to me a paradise in comparison of the West Indies. (p. 81)

Indeed, his cries from the agony of slavery are more of the general horror than of his own case.

O, ye nominal Christians! might not an African ask you, Learned you this from your God who says unto you, Do unto all men as you would men should do unto you? Is it not enough that we are torn from our country and friends to toil for your luxury and lust of gain? Must every tender feeling be likewise sacrificed to your avarice? Are the dearest friends and relations, now rendered more dear by their separation from their kindred, still to be parted from each other and thus prevented from cheering the gloom of slavery with the small comfort of being together and mingling their sufferings and sorrows? Why are parents to lose their children, brothers their sisters, or husbands their wives? Surely this is a new refinement in cruelty which, while it has no advantage to atone for it, thus aggravates distress and adds fresh horrors even to the wretchedness of slavery. (p. 32)

There are several illustrations – including a map of Phipp's route to Spitsbergen, which are a valuable inclusion in this edition. I particularly, and irrelevantly, enjoyed 'A Spanish Planter of Porto Rico luxuriating in his hammock'. There are two interesting appendixes. The first is an historical note on the appointment of Equiano as Commissary for Stores for the Black Poor going to Sierra Leone, and will be of interest to students of the slave trade and the settlement of Sierra Leone. The second contains what Paul Edwards charitably refers to as a 'fairly competent though dull piece of religious verse' by Equiano.

The English nation call'd to leave,
How did my breast with sorrows heave!
I long'd for rest — cried 'Help me, Lord'.
Some mitigation, Lord, afford! (p. 172)

In addition there is a short note on the West African pronunciation of English in the introduction (p. xvi). Comprehensive useful notes and references are given at the end of the book.

This book is, then, the natural extension of what was begun in Paul Edwards' two anthologies, *West African Narrative* (1963) and *Modern African Narrative* (1966), and is important as an attempt to foster an informed pride in the origins of an increasingly productive literature in English. As propaganda it is necessary and desirable; as a sensitive abridged edition of an historically interesting, often compelling narrative it is perhaps, for the general reader of today, closer to an 'interesting narrative'. ∎

Peter Young

ELECHI AMADI & FLORA NWAPA

Elechi Amadi *The Concubine* and Flora Nwapa *Efuru*. African Writers Series, Heinemann 1966

In the *Concubine* and *Efuru* Elechi Amadi and Flora Nwapa have produced two novels strikingly similar in theme. Both are set in Eastern Nigeria and deal with man's complex relationship with the gods and the supernatural. A comparison of the two writers is therefore inevitable, and it seems to me that Elechi Amadi's achievement is the more impressive.

The Concubine is Amadi's first novel, and by any account it is a most accomplished first performance. At the centre of the novel's events is Ihuoma, a beautiful, elegant and almost perfect woman who is admired and respected by the entire village. It is revealed, however, that Ihuoma had been the wife of the powerful sea-god and that, contrary to her husband's advice, she sought communion with human beings and was reincarnated. The sea-god was furious but, since he loved Ihuoma more than all his other wives, he decided to allow her to live her human span of life and to wait until her death, when she would rejoin him in the spirit world. However, he reserves his vengeance for any mortal who dares to fall in love with Ihuoma. Ihuoma's first husband, the popular and exemplary Emenike, accordingly dies of 'lock-chest', while Madume, the blustering village bully, who presses his unwelcome attentions on Ihuoma, is blinded by a spitting cobra and commits suicide. But Amadi reserves much of his narrative skill and psychological insight for the treatment of

Ihuoma's relationship with her last lover, Ekwueme. It is in this section also that his powers of characterization manifest themselves.

Ekwueme, for many years the only son of his ageing parents, has been pampered and spoilt by his mother and as a result develops a marked indifference to women. He makes a mess of his marriage to the childish Ahurole who, in order to make sure of his love, gives him a love potion. The result is disastrous and Ahurole has to be divorced. Ihuoma plays a major role in effecting Ekwueme's cure, and his old love for her is reborn. Marriage negotiations commence, but once more the sea-god exacts his terrible vengeance and Ekwueme is accidentally killed by an arrow.

At this point one is tempted to refer to that considerable Nigerian novelist, Chinua Achebe. In the work of both writers tradition and social pressure play major roles. But in Achebe's work man is primarily the agent of his own destiny. Achebe's tragic vision is therefore more conventional. In Amadi's novel on the other hand, man seems to be merely the plaything of the gods and the supernatural spirits. His tragic vision thus recalls that of the English novelist Thomas Hardy.

In a sense it might seem easier to portray man under the influence of the gods than as the agent of his own destiny. The second course demands great psychological insight and knowledge of human nature, whereas in the case of the first, it seems that all the novelist needs to do is to provide adequate supernatural machinery. But this is much more difficult than it sounds. The use of supernatural agents in a novel always presents grave difficulties; such as the problem of rendering them credible and realistic as many of Thomas Hardy's novels attest. Who believes in Old Father Time?

It is a measure of Amadi's achievement that we are induced to suspend our disbelief. Supernatural agents abound in this novel but they carry conviction. Anyika, the Dibia, or Medicine man, is most lifelike, and his prophecies and divinations have the ring of truth. Indeed there are times when the reader is induced to believe them even when the characters themselves do not. One of the reasons for this credibility is the amount of concretization in this novel. For instance, the god Amadioha is not just an other-worldly being; he makes his appearance in the form of a snake devouring the wing of a chicken. The sea-god himself has often been seen; he not only has numerous wives, he also shares the predilection of certain human beings for bright colours. It is by means of devices such as these that Amadi has rendered his supernatural element credible, convincing and acceptable. The reader is thus made to believe that in the world presented in this novel man is under the influence of the gods.

There is much local colour in *The Concubine*, but it is local colour which functions on a higher level than that of mere background. The many detailed descriptions of sacrifices, dances and even cooking reinforce the impression of a society which is stable and orderly because it clings to tradition, the wisdom of the ancients, and the worship of the gods. Yet Amadi does not sentimentalize this society, or gloss over the cruelties resulting from its adherence to tradition. Madume, for instance, who has committed suicide, is cast off unburied into the forest reserved for those 'whom the earth rejects'. Jealousy and conceit are also present here as well as love and friendliness.

Amadi's style is lucid, unpretentious and direct. He writes with the ease and assurance of a man who enjoys writing. It is difficult to find flaws in this small masterpiece. Perhaps Ahurole, Ekwueme's wife might have been introduced earlier; the narrative pace occasionally becomes sluggish. But this is a novel of some distinction.

Flora Nwapa's novel on the other hand leaves the reader with the impression that its author has not yet mastered her craft. It lacks the fluency, effortlessness and economy of *The Concubine*. It is too obviously a first novel.

The heroine of *Efuru* is the same type of woman as Ihuoma – the heroine of *The Concubine*. She is beautiful, generous, brave, upright – in fact, almost ideal. However, she has been chosen by the goddess of the Lake, Uhamiri, to be one of her worshippers. This means that although she will be rich, she will never be able to have a successful marriage or to have children. Her first husband, Adizua, deserts her and does not even return for the burial of their only child. Her second, Gilbert, has an illicit affair with another woman who bears him a child. He eventually goes to prison for an unspecified offence, and is finally divorced by Efuru for wrongly accusing her of adultery. Efuru ends where she began – in her father's house, except that her father is now dead. She is childless, husbandless, fatherless – quite alone.

These are the bones of the story that Flora Nwapa has stretched out to two hundred and eighty-one pages. The novel could quite conveniently have been half this length, for the bulk of it consists of unnecessary sociological information. One is not suggesting that sociology should not have a place in the African novel. Elechi Amadi's *The Concubine* contains some sociological information, but it is always relevant, necessary and functional. His novel, moreover, has the virtue of economy; nothing is there that should not be. It is as if Flora Nwapa has set herself the task of writing an East Nigerian epic and wants to ensure that, whatever the subject matter, her novel should embody the culture and spirit of her tribe. The reader is therefore treated, among other things, to an unnecessary description of a cure for convulsions, a lengthy story by the town's professional story-teller and numerous Nigerian songs. 'If we write novels so, how do we write sociology?' (If readers will pardon the adaptation.) Writers from Africa need to learn how to integrate political and sociological material with the main themes of the novel and make it functional, as Elechi Amadi has done.

This weakness in Flora Nwapa's novel might have been less important if she had demonstrated any psychological insight or powers of characterization. Unfortunately this is not her strong point either. She has created one perfect feminine character – Ajanupu, the bitchy but good-natured aunt of Efuru's first husband – and another reasonably good one in Efuru herself. Ajanupu is obviously based on Flora Nwapa's accurate observation of the idiosyncracies of certain Nigerian women. She is therefore a triumph. Efuru, for obvious reasons is a more difficult character to realize and she stops just short of becoming sentimentalized and silly.

The other characters are quite hollow. Certainly, Miss Nwapa seems to be incapable of creating credible masculine characters. Neither of Efuru's two husbands is convincing.

The process, for instance, whereby they lose interest in her and eventually desert her, is too abrupt and inadequately documented. One can easily imagine how Elechi Amadi would have done this. Let us take as an example a comparable passage in *The Concubine*. It is the scene in which Ekwueme, now desperately in love with Ihuoma, goes to her to confess his love. Every single action and reaction or non-reaction is given. His gestures, hesitations stutterings and general clumsiness and Ihuoma's dignified outward composure but inward confusion, are all minutely described. This, the reader feels, is the stuff of which life is made. It would have been good to see comparable detailing in Flora Nwapa's novel.

Flora Nwapa, moreover, does not show any awareness of plot as the sum-total of events causally related to each other. *Efuru* is made up of a string of episodes some of which could have been usefully omitted.

Finally, the reader puts down this novel with only a hazy idea of what it is all intended to mean. Is it the personal tragedy of a pure woman? As we have it, Efuru's destiny is not convincingly shown to be tragic. She herself cheerfully accepts her lot as a matter of course and goes about her business. It is in the final scene, in which she leaves Gilbert, that the point of the tragedy was intended to be rammed home, and Miss Nwapa tries hard to infuse pathos into the episode. The scene, melodramatic and unconvincing, shows all the signs of indecent haste to finish the novel.

Is *Efuru* then about man at the mercy of the gods? This would have been a plausible interpretation if the supernatural element had been rendered convincing and acceptable. But its role here is hardly comparable with that played by the supernatural in *The Concubine*. Society does not seem to be at the mercy of the gods; man is the agent of his own destiny.

In *Efuru* therefore, there seems to be a gap between intention and realization, and we must surely attribute this to Flora Nwapa's failure to think out her themes deeply, and to devise adequate techniques with which to convey them. Add to these deficiencies her pedestrian style and it will be seen that if Elechi Amadi's effort is rated beta plus, Miss Nwapa's must surely rank beta double minus. ∎

Eustace Palmer

58

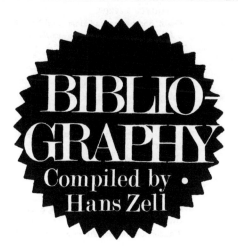

BIBLIO-GRAPHY

Compiled by • Hans Zell

This current bibliography of creative African writing is the first in a series of bibliographic listings which will appear regularly in this journal.

Its aim is to provide comprehensive and up-to-date information on new and recently published literature by African authors. It is divided into two parts: I. Periodical literature; II. Books and pamphlets. This initial list gives details of new books published since January 1967, and of forthcoming titles due to be published within the next four months or so.

The bibliography is mainly concerned with *creative* writing, but also includes critical and reference works, and anthologies. Such political, historical, religious literature, etc. is excluded, as are children's readers and similar material. Individual poems appearing in periodicals are only quoted if they are of some considerable length.

Coverage is international, although for this first list I was unable to obtain details of French and German publications in time before going to press. It is hoped to include these in the next issue.

Publishers of African literature are invited to submit to me, at Fourah Bay College, University of Sierra Leone, regular information on relevant new and forthcoming publications.

PART I: PERIODICAL LITERATURE

ANIEBO, I. N. C.
Shadows
in *Black Orpheus*, April 27, no. 21, p. 39–43
BEN AMOS, DAN
'A Young Bini Poet: Ikonmwosa Osemwegie'
in *Nigeria Mag.*, Sept. 67, no. 94, p. 250–52
BRUTUS, DENIS
'Poetic Sketches'
in *Jnl. of the New African Lit. and the Arts*
Spring 67, p. 31–2

CHIMENTI, ELISA
'Traditional Stories of the Maghreb'
in *Mid East*, Feb. 67, p. 3–6
'Culture and Criticism. African Critical
standards for African Literature and the Arts'
in *Jnl. of the New African Lit. and the Arts*,
Spring 67, p. 1–7
DAMAS, LEON G.
'Yani-des-Eaux'
in *Présence Africaine*, 67, no. 61, p. 169–76
DATHORNE, O. R.
'The Beginnings of the West African Novel'
in *Nigeria Mag.*, June 67, no. 93, p. 168–70

DATHORNE, O. R.
'Two Black Latin Poets – Juan Latino and
Francis Williams'
in *Black Orpheus*, April 67, no. 21,
p. 53–6
EGUDU, ROMANUS
'Ojebe Poetry'
in *Black Orpheus*, April 67, no. 21, p. 7–14
EGUDU, ROMANUS
'Three Poems'
in *Black Orpheus*, April 67, no. 21, p. 21–3
GBADAMOSI, BAKARE, and, BEIER, ULLI
'Two Yoruba Tales'
in *Black Orpheus*, April 67, no. 21, p. 24–7
GREEN, ROBERT
'Under the Mango Tree. Criticism of African
Literature'
in *Jnl. of the New African Lit. and the Arts*,
Spring 67, p. 25–30
HEAD, BESSIE
'Sorrow Food'
in *Transition*, v. 6, no. 30, p. 47–9
JAHN, JANHEINZ
'Bantu Literature. The Tragedy of Southern
Bantu Literature'
(Translated from the German by W. Feuser)
in *Black Orpheus*, April 67, no. 21, p. 44–52
JOHNSON, LEMUEL
'First Glimpses'
in *Jnl. of the New African Lit. and the Arts*,
Spring 67, p. 46–72
KABUSHENGA, SABITI
'Inside the Spectrum'
in *Transition*, v. 6, no. 31, p. 44–5
(Poetry)
KIBERA, LEONARD
'It's a Dog's Share in our Kinshasa'
in *Transition*, v. 6 no. 29, p. 28–9
KUNENE, D. P.
'A War Song of the Basotho'
in *Jnl. of the New African Lit. and the Arts*,
Spring 67, p. 10–20
LADIPO, DURO
'Oba Waja (The King is Dead). A Yoruba
Tragedy
in *Présence Africaine*, 67, no. 62, p. 148–167
MAUNICK, EDOUARD J.
'Avant-propos pour un dialogue en poésie:
poèmes de Guy Tirolien, Derek Walcott,
Christopher Okigbo'
in *Présence Africaine*, 67, no. 61,
p. 141–8

MPHAHLELE, EZEKIEL
'Death, Somewhere, and Homeward Bound'
in *Jnl. of the New African Lit. and the Arts*,
Spring 67, p. 36–40
(Three poems)
MOORE, GERALD
'The Arts in the New Africa'
in *Nigeria Mag.*, March 67, no. 92, p. 92–7
NICOL, DAVIDSON
'Modern African Writing'
in *Présence Africaine*, 67, no. 62, p. 13–14
OMOTOSO, KOLE
'The Honourable Member'
in *Black Orpheus*, April 67, no. 21, p. 16–20
ONYEJELI, BONA
'Two Poems'
in *Black Orpheus*, April 67, no. 21, p. 28–30
OWOMOYELA, OYEKAN
'Candles and Incense. An excerpt from a film
script'
in *Jnl. of the New African Lit. and the
Arts*, Spring 67, p. 73–80
POVEY, JOHN
'Simply to Stand'
in *Jnl. of the New African Lit. and the Arts*,
Spring 67, p. 95–100
(Profile of Dennis Brutus)
RUBADIRI, DAVID
'East African New Writing'
in *East Africa Journal*, Jan. 67
(The entire January issue of 'East Africa
Journal' is devoted to new writing from
East Africa)
RUBADIRI, DAVID
'Three Poems'
in *Black Orpheus*, April 67, no. 21, p. 37–8
RUORO, PETER
'The Return'
in *Jnl. of the new African Lit. and the Arts*,
Spring 67, p. 41–5
SCHARFE, DON; and, ALIYU, YAHAYA
'Hausa Poetry'
in *Black Orphans*, April 67, no. 21, p. 31–6
SIMON, BARNEY
'The 4th Day of Christmas'
in *Transition*, v. 6, no. 30, p. 16–19
STERLING, T.
'Africa's Black Writers'
in *Holiday*, Feb. 67, p. 131–40
THOMAS, PETER
'Poems from Nigeria'
in *Black Orpheus*, April 67, no. 21. p. 57–8

PART II: BOOKS & PAMPHLETS

Reference & Bibliography

MAGIDSON, EROLL; and, ZELL, HANS M.; eds.
Writings by West Africans, published and unpublished. Catalogue of an exhibition held in Freetown, Sierra Leone, April 20th–24th. Freetown, Sierra Leone Univ. Press, approx. Le 1.00/ 10s. od. 1967 approx. 140 p.
(Gives details of some 400 'in-print' titles by West African authors of both English and French speaking nations. Also lists unpublished manuscripts, documents, etc.)

Critical works

BEIER, ULLI; ed.
Introduction to African Literature: an anthology of critical writing from 'Black Orphans'
London, Longmans, 30s. od. 1967 272 p. illus. bibliog.
BRENCH, A. C.
The Novelists Inheritance in French Africa
London, Oxford Univ. Press, 10s. 6d. 1967 160 p.
TUCKER, M.; ed.
Africa in Contemporary Literature
New York, Ungar (in preparation)
WAUTHIER, CLAUDE
The Literature and Thought of Modern Africa: A Survey.
London, Pall Mall Press, 17s. 6d. 1967 323 p. pap. (A translation of 'L'Afrique des Africains — Inventaire de la Negritude' originally published in 1964)

Anthologies

MPHAHLELE, EZEKIEL; ed.
African Writing Today
Harmondsworth, Penguin Books, 7s. 6d. 1967 347 p. pap.
BRENCH, A. C.; ed.
Writing in French from Senegal to Cameroon
London, Oxford Univ. Press, 10s. 6d. 1967 160 p.
CAVERHILL, NICOLAS; ed.
Receuil des textes africains
London, Hutchinson, 12s. 6d. 1967 178 p.

EDWARDS, PAUL; ed.
Through African Eyes 2 vols.
London, Cambridge Univ. Press, 5s. 6d. ea. 1967 101 p. 117 p.
SERGEANT, H.; ed.
Commonwealth Poems of Today
London, Murray, 11s. 6d. 1967 288 p. pap. (Contains several contributions by African writers)

Cameroons

OYONO, FERDINAND
The Old Man and the Medal
London, Heinemann, 1968 pap. (in preparation)
(A translation of *Le vieux nègre et la médaille* originally published in 1956)

Gambia

PETERS, LENRIE
Satellites
London, Heinemann, 8s. 6d. 1967 103 p. pap.

Ghana

DE GRAFT HANSON, J. O.
The Secret of Opokuwa
Accra, Anowuo Educ. Publ, 3s. 6d. 1967 72 p. pap.
DJOLETO, A.
The Strange Man
London, Heinemann, 25s. od. 1967 296 p.
DUODO, CAMERON
The Gab Boys
London, Deutsch, 25s. od. 1967 208 p.
HIHETAH, R. KOFI
Painful Road to Kadjebi
Accra, Anowuo Educ. Publ., 4s. od. 1967 194 p. pap.
KONADU, ASARE
Come Back Dora! (A husband's confession and ritual)
Accra, Anowuo Educ. Publ., 3s. 6d. 1967 218 p. pap.
KONADU, S.
Ordained by the Oracles
London, Heinemann, 1968 (in preparation)
KONADU, S.
A Woman in her Prime
London, Heinemann, 18s. od. 1967
(Paperback edition to appear early in 1968)

SELORMEY, FRANCIS
The Narrow Path
London, Heinemann, 6s. od. 1967 184 p.
pap.

Kenya

ASALACHE, KHADAMBI
A Calabash of Life: a novel
London, Longmans, 7s. 6d. 1967 154 p. pap.
KIBERA, LEONARD; and, KAHIGA, SAMUEL
Potent Ash: Short stories
Nairobi, East African Publ. House, 1967
MPHAHLELE, EZEKIEL
In Corner B
Nairobi, East African Publ. House, 1967
NASSIR BIN JUMA BHALO, AHMAD
Poems from Kenya. Gnomic verses in Swahili.
Translated and edited by Lyndon Harries.
Madison, Univ. of Wisconsin Press, $5.00
1967 244 p.
NGUGI, JAMES
A Grain of Wheat
London, Heinemann, 25s. od. 1967 280 p.
(Paperback edition to appear early 1968)
NGUGI, JAMES
Weep not, Child; with an introduction and
notes by Ime Ikiddeh
London, Heinemann, 6s. od. 1967 162 p.
pap. (New edition with notes)
OGOT, GRACE
The Promised Land: A novel
Nairobi, East African Publ. House, 1967
P'BITEK, OKOT
Song of Lawino: A lament
Nairobi, East African Publ. House, 8/50
1967

Nigeria

ALUKO, T. M.
Kinsman and Foreman
London, Heinemann, 1968 pap. (in prepara-
tion) (Paperback edition of title originally
published, London, Heinemann, 1966)
ALUKO, TIMOTHY M.
One Man, one Wife (2nd ed.)
London, Heinemann, 6s. 6d. 1967 201 p.
pap. (Previously published, London, Nigerian
Printing & Publishing Co., 1959)
AGWUNA, CLEMENT
More than once: a novel
London, Longmans, 21s. od. 1967 211 p.

BEIER, ULLI; and, GBADOMOSI, B.; eds.
Not even God is Ripe Enough
London, Heinemann, 1968 pap. (in prepara-
tion)
CLARK, JOHN P.
America their America
London, Heinemann, 1968 pp. (in preparation)
(Paperback edition of book originally
published, London, Deutsch, 1964)
CLARK, JOHN P.
Ozidi. A Play
London, Oxford Univ. Press, 7s. 6d. 1967
121 p. pap.
HARRISON, T. W.; and, SIMMONS, JAMES
Aikin Mata
Ibadan, Oxford Univ. Press, 7s. 6d. 1967
80 p. (An adaptation of the *Lysistrata* of
Aristophanes)
MUNONYE, J.
Obi
London, Heinemann, 1968 pap. (in prepara-
tion)
NWAPA, FLORA
Idu
London, Heinemann, bsod 1968 282pp
NWANKWO, NKEM
Danda
London, Panther Books, 3s. 6d. 1967 154 p.
pap. (Paperback edition of book originally
published by Deutsch, 1964)
SOYINKA, WOLE
The Interpreters
London, Panther Books, 5s. od. 1967 254 p.
pap. (Originally published by Deutsch,
1965)
SOYINKA, WOLE
Kongi's Harvest. A Play
London, Oxford Univ. Press, 7s. 6d. 1967
90 p.
SOYINKA, WOLE
The Forest of a Thousand Daemons
London, Nelson, approx. 8s. 6d. 1967
SOYINKA, WOLE
Poems
London, Methuen, approx. 21s. od. 1967
approx. 64 p.
TUTUOLA, AMOS
Ajaiyi and his Inherited Poverty
London, Faber, 25s. od. 1967
UZODINMA, EDMUND C. C.
Our Dead Speak: a novel
London, Longmans, 6s. 6d. 1967 134 p. pap.

62

Senegal

DIOP, BIRAGO
Contes choisis. Edited with an introduction by J. Hutchinson
London, Cambridge Univ. Press, 12s. 6d.
1967 176 p.

Sierra Leone

EASMON, R. SARIF
The Burnt-Out Marriage
London, Nelson, approx. 6s. od. 1967 approx.
140 p.
FINNEGAN, RUTH; trans. & ed.
Limba Stories & Storytelling
London, Oxford Univ. Press, 60s. od. 1967
352 p.

South Africa

GORDIMER, NADINE; and, ABRAHAMS,
LIONEL; eds.
South African Writing Today
Harmondsworth, Penguin Books, 6s. od.
1967

BRINK, ANDRÉ
File on a Diplomat
London, Longmans, 25s. od. 1967 256 p.
(A translation of 'Die ambassadeur' originally published in 1963)
BUTLER, GUY
South of the Zambesi. Poems from South Africa
With an introduction by William Plomer.
London, Abelard-Schuman, 10s. 6d. 1967 31
p.
STUART, JAMES; collected by
Zulu Praise Poems
Translated by Daniel Malcolm. Edited by
Trevor Cope.
London, Oxford Univ. Press, 50s. od. 1967
180 p.

Sudan

SALIH, TAYEB
The Wedding of Zein
London, Heinemann, 1968 (in preparation)

Uganda

SERUMAGA, ROBERT
Return to the Shadows
London, Heinemann, 1968 (in preparation)

63

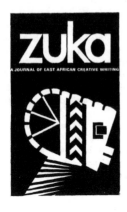
64

ALT 2
CONTENTS No 2 January 1969

1

Editorial Note

African literature presents difficulties to both African and non-African readers. The latter, if they lack an adequate knowledge of the African background, miss the significance of essential symbols and ideas. African readers on the other hand often complain that the technique of African writers which owes a lot to influences from outside Africa, makes these writers difficult to read. As a result many African teachers are reluctant to prescribe African texts because they feel insecure in tackling them. Too often they prescribe English texts in preference, not because of their literary qualities or relevance, but simply because these texts are supported by critical opinion to which both teacher and student can turn.

African Literature Today aims at providing analyses of the works of African authors, not to save readers from making their own judgements, but to provide starting points for personal appreciation and evaluation. The journal does not claim to be a dictator of taste, but hopes to be a forum for discussion through which the appreciation of works of African literature could be deepened and the readership widened.

Readers are encouraged to send in their views and comments on articles published here in the form of reasoned disagreement or further elucidation.

Eldred D. Jones

James Ngugi as Novelist

IME IKIDDEH

When *Weep Not Child* appeared in 1964 it was widely recognized as the work of a young writer of talent. No one however could have foreseen that the novel was destined to take the first prize for fiction at the Dakar Festival of Negro Arts two years later. Still less could anyone have predicted – in a continent where many a promising first novel has remained an only child – that barely three years later, James Ngugi would be publishing his third novel. *The River Between* came out a year after the first, followed by *A Grain of Wheat* in 1967. Today Ngugi is commonly counted among Africa's leading writers. Since, however, in the not too crowded Parnassus of East Africa the manuscript of his first novel alone was enough in that region to earn him the distinction of *the* novelist, doubts may well have arisen as to whether Ngugi has not been overrated as a writer – this young Kenyan (he is thirty) whose every novel and short story has been scribbled in between a university student's lecture hours and God-sent vacations. The purpose of this article is to examine Ngugi's achievement with a concentration on those areas of his writing which appear to me significant.

First, Ngugi's thematic progression. It is worth pointing out that although

The River Between was published second, it was actually the first to be written. The point is significant. It means in the first instance that Ngugi started off, like a good number of African writers, with the conflict of cultures which threw out in the wake of the fifties that hybrid of a hero who until recent years invariably passed by the simplified name of 'the man between two worlds.' Seen in that light, Waiyaki is the very epitome of such a hero, torn as he is between love for Western education and the no less passionate desire to keep tribal values intact. The historical period is the arrival of Christianity among the Kikuyu. *Weep Not Child* takes us to the Mau Mau Emergency in Kenya. The conflict is now not of cultures – though culture may be implied in it – it is more a fight for political independence. The winning of the political war leads up to present-day realities of independent Kenya. In fact a substantial part of *A Grain of Wheat* revolves around the disillusioning events on Uhuru eve.

A glance at other African writers will show several parallels to this general pattern, that is, allowing for departures in emphasis. Preoccupation with the present is fast replacing the lament over the past (not that the past ceases to matter): Achebe in *A Man of the People*, Ekwensi in *Iska*, Laye in *Dramouss*. This is as it should be. I always thought critics were being unduly worried about so many African writers exploring the theme of a clash of cultures. The subject had its relevance and its day. The emphasis was bound to shift with the passage of time, and the stage seems to have been set for a change by Lenrie Peters in *The Second Round* (1964) – the title itself is significant. For the African writer who subscribes to Achebe's belief in 'the novelist as teacher,' his present-day preoccupation can hardly be what it might have been seven years ago. Ngugi in fact felt slight embarrassment on this account, needlessly I thought, when *The River Between* was published in 1965.

The story of the rift between Kameno and Makuyu is typical of the alien ruler using Christianity as a weapon with which to disrupt a closely-knit tribal society. From that common ground of the type novel, Ngugi's individual conception takes over, and creates a social conflict substantially different from others in similar circumstances, so that Waiyaki emerges in the end as a typical hero with a difference. Waiyaki is neither an Okonkwo nor a King Lazarus. Christianity, although it is the disruptive factor in Ngugi's society, is nowhere in the hands of aliens who wield it in the battle-front. The activities of the Siriana Mission are very much in the background. The Rev. Mr. Livingstone is not a Father Le Guen or a Rev. James Smith, nor does the small government post on the ridge find it necessary to intervene in local affairs to the extent of M. Lequeux in *King Lazarus*, the District Commissioner in *Things Fall Apart* or Captain Winterbottom in *Arrow of God*. Livingstone is a second generation missionary who, in spite of obvious evangelical enthusiasm, is determined to avoid the

4

mistakes of his predecessors. He stands for moderation, and as Waiyaki sees it, the missionary has come only 'to widen the (already existing) split.' The two ridges are going to 'fight it out between themselves, the missionary encouraging his followers.'

Ngugi is content to concentrate the conflict and final disruption within the society, arising as they do largely from old feuds and present jealousies. (The situation is much the same in *Arrow of God*.) It is Joshua with his unparalleled zealotry, and Kabonyi brimful of hate and jealousy, who lead the two warring camps, with Waiyaki caught in between. And Ngugi localises the conflict for a good reason.

The underlying unity and needless split between Kameno and Mukuyu are emphasized in the novel by ironic unity-in-division symbols. The most significant of these is the Honia River, 'their common source of life', which becomes the physical gulf between the two ridges. Honia means 'cure'; it is the 'soul' of the ridges, giving life to all living things. Honia as the source of life is registered by the opening sentences of the novel: 'The two ridges lay side by side. One was Kameno, the other was Makuyu. Between them was a valley. It was called the valley of life.' (Connoisseurs of phallic symbolism may find a sample here.) But the two ridges are 'sleeping lions' which, when awake, will 'come to blows in a life and death struggle.' When the split comes, the church in Makuyu draws inspiration from Honia while the tribal rites of Kameno are celebrated on its bank. Honia all through the novel is the silent natural observer of an unnatural struggle — like the Oxus in *Sohrab and Rustom*. In the end it remains the only symbol of hope as it flows down the valley, 'its beast rising above the dark stillness, reaching into the heart of the people of Makuyu and Kameno.'

The other major ironic 'symbol' lies in the use Ngugi makes in the novel of Christian and Kikuyu myth. There is the close similarity between the myths of Gikuyu and Mumbi, and Adam and Eve (or Abraham and Sarah). Besides, the basis of hope and tribal solidarity are rooted in legends with an unmistakable scriptural ring. Murungu, the Kikuyu deity, had assured Kameno, 'This land I give to you, O man and woman. It is yours to rule and till, you and your posterity'. More recently Mugo, the Kikuyu seer, had prophesied not only the coming of white men but also a saviour for the people: 'Salvation shall come from the hills. From the blood that flows in me a son shall rise. And his duty shall be to lead and save the people.' Waiyaki is that saviour. The prophetic message as between the Christians and the tribe is so similar both in essence and language that only Joshua can fail to see the irony when he declaims to his congregation, 'Isaiah, the white man's seer, had prophesied of Jesus. He had told of the coming of a Messiah. Had Mugo, the Gikuyu seer, ever foretold of such a saviour?'

5

The Messianic motif runs through all Ngugi's novels. In *Weep Not Child*, Jomo Kenyatta is 'the black Moses' and little Njoroge sees himself as his successor. In *A Grain of Wheat*, Mugo, in flashes of righteous introspection fancies himself as perhaps a saviour by destiny. Even Kihika in his heroism — the passages underlined in his Bible tell a story — and in the people's veneration of his memory bears the Messianic image. It is not surprising that Ngugi's first title for *The River Between* was *The Black Messiah* and he has a play entitled *The Black Hermit* (this has just been published).

Waiyaki then is a Christ figure, a mediator, and therefore essentially an ideal person. Only when this is understood is it possible to see the idealization of this hero not as an artistic weakness but as an essential part of the plan of the novel. The localization of the conflict within the society and in Waiyaki himself underlines and is in line with the theme of rejection embodied in this novel.

Weep Not Child is a different creation. The missionary has taken advantage of tribal disintegration and let in his brother. The conflict now is between the aliens and their black lackeys on one side, and a deprived native population represented by the Mau Mau on the other. The issue centres around the question of who owns the land of Kenya, its indigenous people or the white settlers. The hero is a boy of tender age. The tragedy is more poignant in its effect on Njoroge and his family seen as a microcosm of the shattering of hopes and aspirations in a whole people. Ngugi's stories generally reach down to the springs of one's emotions. Waiyaki's idealism, predicament and rejection were touching enough, but it does not compare with the torture of Ngotho and Njoroge; or with the plight of Mwihaki left without a father — however much one disapproves of him — the disillusionment and frustration of Howlands and Boro, or the horror of naked violence walking the land of Kenya with all its attendant insecurity and family disasters. And the problem of *Weep Not Child* is linked up with its sentiment.

Schoolgirls have told me they wept when they read *Weep Not Child* (in spite of the author's concealed appeal in the title). This is not to imply that Ngugi is here parading any spurious tear-jerking sentiments. In fact he tries hard to balance the brutality of the homeguards with the violence of the Mau Mau including Boro, Njoroge's own brother. Nor is the tragedy over Njoroge unrelaxed — as in the comedy created around him in school, and the happy, innocent love affair with Mwihaki. But the story remains too real. For the schoolgirl who cries, the trouble is not simply that women will tend to display an overabundance of tears, but also that her age and those of Njoroge and Mwihaki make for too easy an identification.

I think the problem of *Weep Not Child* lies in a child-hero who is at the same time an innocent. For although the circumstances of Njoroge and Toundi in

6

Oyono's novel are similar, one's emotional response to *Weep Not Child* and *Houseboy* is substantially different. The torture Toundi receives from the hands of his colonial masters is far more hideous than that inflicted on Njoroge, yet what one feels at the end of *Houseboy* is more anger and revulsion than tears, largely, I think, because even in his innocence, Toundi is a more complex character than Njoroge. Besides, Oyono's tough satiric comedy does not encourage any sloppy sentiment.

The innocent child-hero affects *Weep Not Child* in some other way. The novel could hardly be built on a larger scale if Njoroge had to remain the focal point. Since he is so one-dimensional, uncomplex and passive except for his sensitive nature and make-believe, and since the incidents of the novel are unfolded more or less through his obviously limited consciousness, the writer could only have added more to the novel with the alternative risks of padding, anti-climax, or melodrama. Much of what we know of and feel for Njoroge does not arise from what he *is* in thought and action but from what affects him through external factors and what the writer tells us: 'Njoroge had always been a dreamer, a visionary who consoled himself faced with the difficulties of the moment with the hope of a better day to come.' *Weep Not Child* therefore remains a slight novel. A limitation of the author's artistic vision? Perhaps.

Yet anyone who is familiar with Ngugi's creative powers shown even in earlier short stories cannot stop at so simple a conclusion. I think that as it stands, both the plan and execution of *Weep Not Child* – with whatever limitations – are compatible with the author's artistic design. The result is not a great novel but one that is well-done and readable.

My view is that Ngugi neither intended nor needed to invest his boy-hero with any further dimensions. A pointer to this is the fact that only at the very end does Njoroge begin to grow up, and the growth has been the result of experience of the world of evil and of Mwihaki's influence. In fact Njoroge's sign of 'maturity' in recognizing the realities of the moment comes in the very last sentence: 'And he ran home and opened the door for his two mothers.' It is an act of acceptance and demonstration of a new life of responsibility. The future Njoroge could be Mugo in the next novel (or is it Kihika?) It is pointless to speculate.

Ngugi's primary interest in *Weep Not Child* is less in character study than in presenting a picture of suffering in Emergency Kenya, with the spotlight on Ngotho's family. The picture is presented in shots which often enclose groups of characters, the focus shifting swiftly from one scene to another. The excellence of the method lies in Ngugi's ability to maintain the desirable inter-relationship of scenes and therefore the interaction between characters or groups. The success of the novel is in the effective communication of the entire picture in terms of the feeling it draws, however varied the response. Feeling constitutes the compelling power of this novel within the framework of a well-told tale. Stripped of it, what is left would hardly be worth reading. Strangely, Ngugi achieves this emotional success by an economical use of the most unemotive language. I shall return to Ngugi's language later.

For a novel which is not a picture in glimpses that may partly be lost in their swiftness, and certainly one that peddles no soft emotions, one has to turn to *A Grain of Wheat*. For this novel is a panoramic drama. The actors – and they are a galaxy compared with earlier novels – make a whole world in their variety, even if that world is the village of Thabai. The fine discrimination and distinctness of outline with which they are moulded can best be appreciated by placing similar characters in the two Mau Mau novels side by side: Boro and Kihika, Jacobo and Karanja, Howlands and Thompson, Njeri and Wambui, Ngotho and Warui. There are of course the central Gikonyo, Mumbi and Mugo as well as General R. Lieutenant Koinandu, the nameless old woman – Gitogo's mother – and others. There is a greater display of animal brutality in this novel, but the sentiment here is 'tough'. The Mau Mau of the earlier novel has got more militant as the colonial government got more ruthless. Suffering is part of life in this novel for the actors in this human drama of all races are not only fighting common enemies but struggling against each other. The drama, which is psychological and emotional, is physically enacted at the end in the Uhuru Day long distance race in Thabai, and in Mugo's startling confession – they all have been running this race in other ways for so long.

When the novel opens, the Emergency is over and Uhuru is in sight. Githua can proudly show the stump that had been his left leg, and greet Mugo with, 'In the name of blackman's freedom, I salute you!' But the memory of the horrors of detention camps is still too fresh. Mugo, withdrawn and tortured by guilt, had committed treachery of which no one knows. Gitogo's old mother lives demented by grief; her only son had been shot. Thompson, the notorious detention camp D.O. of Rira fame is nervous with disillusionment. He is reading Monday's paper and getting ready to leave before Uhuru on Thursday.

From that setting the novel takes us back to events covering six or seven years of Emergency Kenya seen mainly in the life of Thabai villagers. It is not an unbroken retrospect for now and again we are back in preparations for Uhuru in a few days, so that the interlocking of then and now is maintained throughout. Even in the end when the writer takes Karanja, Mugo, Warui and Wambui, Gikonyo and Mumbi, in turns, to show how they finished this race for life, we are still looking at their past-with-the-present. The effect of the narrative method is not only to give all the major characters a parallel development, a

8

fullness of life which can draw freely from both the past and the present, one embellishing and interpreting the other, but also to ensure Ngugi's novel a solidity of plot with no easy gaps and no loose ends. This is a far cry from *The River Between*, a simple tale tracing Waiyaki's life from boyhood till he becomes the rejected 'teacher'. The real beginnings of this intricate narrative method are laid in *Weep Not Child* with its swiftly changing scenes. There no character develops to the statures we have here. The flashbacks are brief and therefore there is a lesser problem of organization.

If a finger was to be raised against *A Grain of Wheat* it would be pointed at this very facet, this artistic excellence in organization. For the problem of the writer in achieving it becomes the problem for the reader. The distinction between the past and the present is sometimes so blurred that the reader loses his way and finds himself in a tangled mesh. Ngugi is too much a believer in the social responsibility of the writer to pursue any art for art's sake. It is for this reason that one would raise a finger not of indictment but simply of caution. It is a case of clarity of story unwittingly sacrificed for the art of the novel.

Happily, Ngugi's narrative powers in part atones for this defect. As a story of betrayal, remorse and confession, I can only think of *Under Western Eyes* to parallel this. But then Conrad's novel slips out of the psychology of guilt into a spy story that runs across continents. Ngugi's story keeps up Mugo's nightmare to the end. The compelling nature of the writing makes this novel as much a triumph of language as of organization. I think it is in the art of the making, in the tremendous extension of vision and in the language that carries and overlays these that Ngugi's development in this third novel must be sought. *A Grain of Wheat* is certainly the best done of this writer's works to date. It is also one of the best made of African novels.

A sensitive handling of words runs through all Ngugi's novels. But whereas in the earlier novels one was not always sure whether his simplicity of expression did not in part arise from too limited a vocabulary, whether the vague Lawrentian echoes in portraying his characters' emotional and psychic states were not a means of covering up a certain unsureness of grasp, in *A Grain of Wheat* Ngugi dispels such doubts by showing a gift for the right word and a sureness of expression on almost every page. Here is Gikonyo at work, and this might well describe Ngugi's own performance in this novel: 'Holding a plane, smoothing a piece of wood, all this sent a thrill of fear and wonder through the young man. The smell of wood fascinated him. Soon his senses developed sharp discrimination, so that he could tell any type of wood by a mere sniff. Not that the young carpenter made it appear so easy. In fact, Gikonyo used to act out a little ritual the performance of which varied depending on who was present.'

He may sniff harder than Gikonyo for words and act out a little ritual in performance, but Ngugi has not given up that Biblical simplicity and directness in language for which he is well known. It is only that in this novel he is often dealing with more complex adult experiences than before, and the language accordingly assumes a new complexity – and this is compatible with the widening and deepening of the author's own experience. But he is careful to maintain the compatibility of language with character. When Mumbi tells Mugo the story of the destruction of Old Thabai, it is in a language that Ngugi once described in Wordsworthian fashion as 'peasant prose.' And Wordsworthian indeed it is if one compares the pathos and the lyricism of Mumbi's story with that of *The Complaint of a Forsaken Indian Woman* or similar ballads.

Again, irony in this novel has become more pungent, more subtle, and therefore more effective. As in much of Achebe and Beti, most Europeans in Ngugi are ironic characters. Livingstone, Howlands and Thompson have a lot in common; in fact in their sense of mission in Africa, Thompson is a more developed Livingstone without the Bible (the faces of both Livingstone and Howlands end in double chins). But the creation of Thompson makes him the most pathetic; even slightly tragic, he is a man who sees himself 'walking on the precipice of a great discovery' that will mean the birth of a new British Empire (nation he calls it). His proposed book on the subject, *Prospero in Africa*, draws inspiration from Schweitzer, Kipling and Lugard (excepting his 'retrograde concept of Indirect Rule'). The irony is unmistakable, ruthless without being truculent, subtle, yet carrying a certain poignancy. One of the benefits of Ngugi's English experience has been a firmer grasp of the European colonial 'type'. That experience has also meant a greater consciousness of grave social issues.

More than just a horrifying story of suffering in the fight for independence, *A Grain of Wheat* is a protest against what many of the fighters see as the lack of reward in independent Kenya. Their claim lies in their suffering. And the writer presents their feeling with considerable anger. One-legged Githua sums it up more than once: 'The government has forgotten us. We fought for freedom. And yet now!' Gikonyo and Mumbi carry between them this history of suffering, endurance, hope, frustration and near – atrophy. But Gikonyo is leaving a hospital in the end. He and his wife are reconciled and he is going to carve her a stool with a difference, with the figure of 'a woman big – big with child', the child that should mark the birth of a new Kenya.

A year before the publication of *A Grain of Wheat*, Peter Nazareth had predicted (*Transition* 24) that Ngugi's third novel would be 'committed to socialism'. I am not sure this novel shows a committment to socialism; it is a call for social justice. Yet if the two mean the same, then Nazareth was right.

10

Idealist & Mystic
Camara Laye

A.C.BRENCH

When we speak of Camara Laye, we immediately think of *L'Enfant noir*: after that, *Le Regard du roi**. They were published respectively in 1953 and 1954. Then, there was a gap of over ten years during which he published a short story, *Les Yeux de la Statue* and *L'âme de l'Afrique dans sa partie Guinéenne*, before the appearance of his third novel, *Dramouss* in 1967, which had been promised for a long time under the title: *Retour au pays natal*.

When it first appeared *L'Enfant noir* was considered by some a minor masterpiece and by others a colonialist pot-boiler. African nationalists had no time for a novel describing the happy life of a child in Central Guinea. For them, the important thing was commitment to the pressing and immediate problems of gaining African independence from European tutelage: political, cultural and economic. *L'Enfant noir* seemed to them to extol the life led by Africans under the colonial regime; though Camara, the young boy, is described as he lives

* Translations of *L'Enfant noir* or *The African Child* and *Le Regard du Roi* or *The Radiance of the King* are available in English published in Fontana paperback.

through his experiences as a child in an essentially Guinean society. The eruption of the colonial regime which decides his fate – school in Conakry and then at Argenteuil – is shown as the very factor which destroys the unity of the boy's life. His estrangement from Kouroussa, coming as it does when he is adolescent, is confused in his mind with the problems of growing-up; this double separation, physical and psychological, from the world of his childhood gives the climax of the novel its tragic undertones.

This autobiographical novel made Laye's reputation as a writer. In it, he recaptures the vivid childhood impressions of life, describing the world as if from within the child, yet at the same time showing the child's own development. He is both part of the child and outside him, sharing his experience but knowing him. There is a perpetual juxtaposition between the child's present and the adult writer's looking back. The manner in which Laye blends this dual perspective so that neither imposes on the other, so that each is reflected in the other, creates this feeling of loss and sadness which runs throughout the story. For, despite the child's happiness which he recaptures, Laye is writing in exile. Like Birago Diop, he is trying to recapture his past, to relive his past, to identify himself with a way of life from which he feels his exile is irretrievably driving him.

> . . . j'écrivais, je me souvenais, je regagnais par la pensée mes amis, mes parents, le grand fleuve Niger – et il suffisait : j'étais heureux, inexprimablement heureux; je ne me sentais plus abandonné, il me semblait que ma mère, que mon père vivaient à mes côtés; je leur parlais, ils me parlaient. Il me semblait que je vivais de nouveau dans leur chaleur, j'avais le coeur plein de leur chaleur. (p. 122)
> (. . . I used to write, to remember and in my thoughts I recaptured my friends, my parents, the great river Niger – and this was enough; I was happy, deliriously happy; I no longer felt abandoned; it was as if my mother and my father lived with me; I used to talk to them and they to me. It was as if once again I was living within their warmth, my heart was full of their warmth.)

It is these feelings which the early critics, the nationalistic, politically conscious African, ignored. For them, there was simply a story, written by an uncommitted writer, one, moreover, who seemed to be totally assimilated, who wrote about his past life with detachment, apparently unaware of the role played by the colonial power in destroying and corrupting African society. They saw in the novel a nostalgic reminiscence which ignored reality, ignored the urgent needs of the present; for them, Laye seemed to be praising a way of life which was no longer viable, which was, precisely, the way of life the colonists considered most fitting for the Africans to lead.

12

At the time there was a lot to be said for their argument. Especially as the metropolitan critics praised the work. Whether this praise was based on any racist considerations is a moot point. It could be that some critics felt that Laye was treating a subject fit for Africans, that he was acknowledging his proper station in life. That is, that their praise was patronizing and paternalistic. On the other hand, we must also recognize the fact that the novel does have merits as a creative work, that Laye is a stylist of considerable ability and that it is possible to judge his writing on criteria other than purely racist or political ones.

In retrospect, these early criticisms have little importance except to indicate clearly the kind of novel expected from the writers; novels such as Beti's, Oyono's or Malonga's, in which the conflict between coloniser and colonized, master and servant, black and white, is the central issue. From 1953 to 1959 this conflict was the central theme of nearly, if not all, the novels published by African writers in French.

L'Enfant noir has never been grouped with these 'romans de combat', has never been considered as an expression of commitment to the African nationalist cause. Yet we see quite clearly now that it is an indictment of colonial policy; that it does describe, although not as explicitly as in the later novels, the destructive influence of colonialism on traditional African cultures.

The re-creation of Laye's youth in L'Enfant noir depends for its effect on a few notable stylistic devices. His understanding of and feeling for his past are important factors, as is his understanding of the personality of characters such as his mother, father, cousins, and uncles. Yet the ultimate effect depends on his style. The most noteworthy aspect is his use of verb tenses. A friend, so Laye writes in L'âme de l'Afrique dans sa partie Guinéenne, (p. 124) advised him:

> Lisez . . . . l'Education Sentimentale: Flaubert n'a rien écrit qui passe ce roman, arraché à son propre coeur. . . . Vous regarderez la manière dont Flaubert emploie les temps, comment il passe d'un temps à l'autre – et vous ferez comme lui.
> (Read . . . . L'Education Sentimentale: Flaubert never wrote anything better than this novel which comes from his own heart. . . . You will notice the way Flaubert used tenses, how he changed from one tense to another – and you will do the same.)

In L'Enfant noir, Laye uses two crucial tenses, the past historic and the imperfect. The first of these is used when he is narrating events in his life which are unique, fixed in time and place, events such as circumcision, his departure for Conakry and so on.

The use of this historical tense which fixes events clearly in space and time

13

is contrasted with the use of the imperfect. He uses this tense when relating events which are not unique, which recur throughout his childhood and adolescence, his visits to Tindican, his years at the local school, his outings with Marie in Conakry. These episodes, instead of being fixed, lose their definite contours, appearing to be part reality, and part imagination:

> A la nuit tombante, mon oncle Lansana rentrait des champs. Il m'accueillait à sa manière, qui était timide. Il parlait peu. A travailler dans les champs à longueur de journée, on devient facilement silencieux, on remue toutes sortes de pensées, on en fait le tour et interminablement on recommence, car les pensées ne se laissant jamais tout à fait pénétrer; ... le regard de mon oncle Lansana était singulièrement perçant, lorsqu'il se posait; de fait, il se posait peu: il demeurait tout fixé sur ce rêve intérieur poursuivi sans fin dans les champs.
>
> Quand le repas nous réunissait, souvent je tournais les yeux du côté de mon oncle et généralement, au bout d'un moment, je réussissais à rencontrer son regard; ce regard me souriait, car mon oncle était la bonté même et puis il m'aimait; il m'aimait, je crois bien, autant que ma grand'mère; je répondais à son sourire discret et parfois, moi qui mangeais déjà très lentement j'en oubliais de manger.' (pp. 59–60)

(At nightfall, my Uncle Lansana would come back from the fields. He would greet me after his own quiet fashion, for he was rather timid and spoke little. Working alone in the fields all day, you get used to being silent; you think of all kinds of things, and then you start all over again, because thoughts are something you can never grasp completely; . . . . . . My Uncle Lansana's eyes were singularly piercing when he looked at you; actually, he very rarely looked at you: he would remain usually rapt in that inner dream which obsessed him endlessly in the fields.

When we were all together at meal-times I would often turn my eyes towards my uncle, and generally, after a moment or two, I would succeed in catching his eye. There was always a smile behind the gravity of his gaze, for my uncle was goodness itself and he loved me; I really believe he loved me as much as my grandmother did. I would respond to his gently smiling glance, and sometimes, as I always ate very slowly, it would make me forget to eat. (p. 43))

We see in this passage, too, how Laye links the past with the present, the transitory experience of the boy with the unchanging way of life of his uncle and those who preceded and who will follow him.

While he is describing these events concerning those people who have a fixed place in the boy's life, Laye introduces a moment of introspection in

14

which he attempts to analyse the feeling which lies at the root of the complex emotions of the boy. He takes what he feels is the key to these emotions and examines it from all sides, repeating and savouring a word or phrase until every nuance has been exhausted.

La même âme les reliait, les liait; chacun et tous goûtaient le plaisir, l'identique plaisir d'accomplir une tâche commune.

Etait-ce ce plaisir-là, ce plaisir-là bien plus que le combat contre la fatigue, contre la chaleur, qui les animait, qui les faisait se répandre en chants? C'était visiblement ce plaisir-là; et c'était le même aussi qui mettait dans leurs yeux tant de douceur, toute cette douceur dont je demeurais frappé, délicieucement et un peu douleureusement frappé, car j'étais près d'eux, j'étais dans cette grande douceur, et je n'étais pas entièrement avec eux: je n'étais qu'un écolier en visite – et comme je l'eusse volontiers oublié! (p. 72) (They were bound to one another, united by the same soul: each and every one was tasting the delight, savouring the common pleasure of accomplishing a common task.

Was it this delight, this pleasure, even more than the fight against weari-ness and against the burden of the heat, that urged them on, that filled them to overflowing with rapturous song? Such was obviously the case: and this is what filled their eyes with so much tenderness, that wonderful serenity that used to strike me with such delighted and rather regretful astonishment; for though I was among them, with them, surrounded by these waves of tender-ness, I was not one of them; I was only a schoolboy on a visit – and how I longed to forget that fact! (p. 51))

This is seen too, when Camara returns home after circumcision:

Es-tu satisfait de tes nouveaux vêtements? demanda ma mère.
Satisfait? Oui, j'étais satisfait: il allait de soi que je fusse satisfait. Enfin je crois bien que j'étais satisfait. C'étaient de beaux vêtements, c'étaient. . . Je me tournai vers ma mère: elle me souriait tristement. (p. 178) ('Are you pleased with your new clothes?' asked my mother.
Pleased? Yes, I was pleased; naturally I was pleased. At least I think I was pleased. They were fine clothes, they were. . . . . . I turned towards my mother: she was smiling sadly at me. (p. 113))

In every case, therefore, there is this attempt to recapture the essence of the past and, each time it escapes him, each time Laye, the narrator, finds himself faced with this deception. He finds, not the essential happiness of the child, but the happiness of childhood which dissipates so carelessly all the treasures of childhood. He discovers in these supreme moments of happiness the seeds of

15

their destruction. Every time, though, there is something else to carry him along, some new event or adventure which takes the place of the old. Each new phase draws him inexorably further from his childhood paradise until, finally, he leaves for France, the map of the *métro* in his pocket offering him one further hope, a last hope, one which takes us back to the beginning of the novel.

There would seem to be complete contrast between *L'Enfant noir* and *Le Regard du roi*, published only a year later. Laye prefaces *Le Regard du roi* with a quotation from Franz Kafka:

Le Seigneur passera dans le couloir, regardera le prisonnier et dira:
— Celui-ci, il ne faut pas l'enfermer à nouveau: il vient à moi.
(The Lord will walk down the corridor, will look at the prisoner and say:
'You must not imprison this one again: he is coming with me.')

The influence of Kafka is pronounced. In Kafka's novels, the central character is in search of an identity in an alien society about which he knows nothing, and in which there is no point of contact from which mutual understanding can spring. The only hope for the individual is to accept total assimilation, the dissolution of his personality and the reconstruction within himself of a totally new character imposed by the society in which he finds himself. This is, in fact, a synopsis of *Le Regard du roi*. There are other similarities: the presence in this novel and for instance, *The Castle*, of endless corridors, the tawdry inn, the village, which is a dependence of the count in one case, the king in the other, the twin-like assistants of K and Nagoa and Naoga who accompany Clarence. The King's palace and the count's castle are both strange, unknowable buildings whose architecture even escapes description. But, against Kafka's pessimism, Laye opposes an optimistic conclusion. Whereas K never manages to overcome the claustrophobic confusion which inhibits his every action, Clarence's pilgrimage is successful.

In this respect, one could say that *Le Regard du Roi* is the counterpoint to *L'Enfant noir*. Whereas Camara leaves home, his village, family, country in search of new adventures and also because the colonial system of education demands this of him, Clarence returns to the source of life. It is unimportant whether we see him as an assimilated African — Laye himself — or simply, and more probably, as a European without roots, in search of wealth or adventure. He is rejected by his own people, his own society and is therefore 'an outsider', cut off from all society.

Initially, he attempts to join the African society on his own terms as an individual, and — Laye also makes the point — as a white man. This, he soon discovers, is impossible. His encounter with the beggar is the first step in his initiation. Lost in the crowd, surrounded by unknown people, Clarence discovers that he

16

has no identity as far as they are concerned. His individuality, the one thing he thinks will preserve him, is of no avail. He is forced to depend on the beggar, a man who, in Clarence's eyes, is less likely than anyone else to be able to help him.

At the beginning of the novel Clarence is stripped of all wordly possessions. The hotel keeper confiscates his possessions, he loses his money at cards and, finally, there is the serio-comic sequence which nearly leads to the loss of his trousers and jacket. Laye therefore strips his hero of all vestiges of a western, materialized society. Clarence starts his pilgrimage divested of all the attributes which, initially, he thought would protect him, would enable him to live successfully in Africa. But these are only the superficial aspects; the novel, from Clarence's departure from the 'city' to the arrival of the King in Aziana and his welcome to Clarence, is a gradual progression, a gradual erosion of his old personality and the growth of a new.

This progression is underlined by the recurring symbol of corridors in the novel; corridors in the law courts in the city from which Clarence is unable to find the right exit until guided by a half-naked girl whose breasts he covets; corridors in the forest, endless, indistinguishable corridors which suddenly, fortuitously lead to Aziana; corridors in the Naba's palace which lead to the harem and to the small window through which Clarence sees the trial of the 'Maître des Cérémonies' and hears the proof of his suspicions about the role he has been playing as the Naba's 'stallion'. Finally, the corridor which leads to Dioki's hovel where Clarence, unconsciously, sublimates the purely physical sexuality in which he has been forced to indulge, but which now, surrounded by snakes, the symbol of sex, enables him to foresee the arrival of the king.

As in Kafka, sex is one of the central themes of *Le Regard du Roi*. Laye uses it as the symbol of man's sense of guilt as an individual. This sense of guilt is the one thing which prevents him from becoming integrated into life at Aziana. The beggar barters him for a bride and a mule, underlining from the beginning the complete absence of sexual taboos in this society. Clarence finds it impossible to accept this part of himself, this part which he looks upon as bestial, of which he tries to cleanse himself every morning with the ceremonial douche. He has done most in the village to add refinements to the act of washing, introducing a rudimentary form of shower bath and a new kind of towel.

His obsession with sexual guilt reaches its climax in his delirious dream on the river bank. Clarence dreams that he is being hemmed in by the flaccid, white breasts of the manatees; when he awakens on the shoulder of the boys he refuses to go back to Akissa, to the hut where he feels most acutely his degradation.

The role of 'Le Maître des Cérémonies' is important in maintaining and increasing Clarence's sense of guilt. 'Le Maître des Cérémonies' also has sexual inhibitions, and looks upon sexual relations as an individual, private experience. He, therefore, deplores Clarence's behaviour, innocent though it be at first, and mocks him crudely for accepting and enjoying such degradation. Clarence has, therefore, not only to overcome his own sense of guilt and degradation, but the feeling that he is guilty and degraded in the eyes of others. Only when this is finally accomplished does Clarence dare to go towards the King, naked, pure, and therefore stripped of all his prejudices and individuality.

> Mais c'est un mystère très difficile à saisir. Chaque fois que Clarence est sur le point de le voir s'éclaircir, le sommeil replonge tout dans la nuit. Pourtant Clarence n'est jamais si près de comprendre qu'au moment où il s'endort. (p. 102)
> (But the mystery is hard to solve. Each time Clarence is on the point of solving it, sleep plunges everything into darkness again. Yet Clarence is never nearer to a solution than at the moment before he falls asleep. (p. 113))

Throughout the novel, Clarence is surrounded by this air of mystification. There is a total breakdown of communication between the central character and the society in which he has to live. In many ways, this mystification is similar to the mystery which surrounds the young boy, Camara, except that, in *L'Enfant noir*, the child is able to come to terms with the new situations which occur; while Clarence is never, until the end, integrated into life in Aziana.

Laye uses essentially the same stylistic devices, the imperfect and the past historic marking those phases in his life which have a nebulous, unreal quality, and those which have a clearly defined, established place in his life. There is also the repetition of words, not now, as in *L'Enfant noir*, to savour their essence, but to try and disentangle the meaning from the many half-formed, ill-defined ideas and dreams which always crowd his mind.

> Etait-ce, cette fois, le mendiant qu'il cherchait? Peut-être. Peut-être ne cherchait-il rien, peut-être errait-il seulement, et peut-être était-ce là aussi sa seule ressource ... Il faut croire toutefois qu'aucune trace de cette désorientation n'apparaissait sur son visage. . . . (p. 121)
> (Was it the beggar he was looking for this time? Perhaps. Perhaps he was looking for nothing and no one, perhaps he was just roaming around, and perhaps after all that was the one thing he *could* do. . . . . . All the same, it must be understood that no sign of all this perturbation appeared on his face. (p. 134))

Or again:

> Il se laissa glisser le long de la paroi et se trouva assis dans le soleil levant. Maintenant ses jambes ne tremblaient plus; elles frémissaient très légèrement,

18

et elles tremblaient pour un tout autre motif: elles accueillaient le soleil. Ce rien de soleil sur le corps, tout au matin, dans l'air frais du matin, c'était extraordinairement apaisant; cela chassait la nuit, cela chassait le sud. C'était une promesse; et à l'instant où on la recevait, il importait peu que ce fût une promesse sans suite. Clarence ne s'apercevait même pas qu'il était nu . . . Clarence se laissait vivre. (p. 152)

(He slid down to the ground beside the wall and found the sun was rising. His legs were no longer trembling now; they were just shivering slightly, and for quite another reason: they were welcoming the sun's first rays. This faint touch of sunlight in the cool air of morning was extraordinarily soothing; it drove away the night and the horrors of the night, the odours of the night: it drove the South far away. It was a promise, and for the moment it did not matter that it was a baseless promise. Clarence did not even realise that he was stark naked. . . . .Clarence was at that moment enjoying life too. (p. 167))

But one cannot say that because of these similarities, *Le Regard du Roi* and *L'Enfant noir* depend on the same techniques and are, therefore, merely repetitious. The style of *Le Regard du Roi* has little of the limpidity of that of *L'Enfant noir*. In the first place, there is a much greater use of imagery, of introspection:

Oui, le sud! reprend Clarence à part lui. Ah! C'est fameux le sud, quand on habite les pays du Nord! On se berce, on se chauffe, on s'échauffe: on est comme devant un grand feu de bûches, au coeur de l'hiver. Et ce qu'on voit? Un hamac accroché à deux cocotiers, en bordure du lagon! Et puis il y a ce souffle vanillé et presque imperceptible qui fait frémir un peu les cils et les ailes du nez, et qu'on appelle l'alizé. Et ensuite des plantes plus vertes et des fleurs plus bariolées, des fleurs comme des oiseaux et des plantes comme des jets d'eau; et une mer plus bleue, plus transparente et plus bleue . . . Que ne voit-on pas? Mais on le voit parce qu'il bruine, ou parce qu'il y a du givre sur les vitres, parce qu'on n'y va pas voir. (p. 96)

('Yes, the South!' Clarence mutters to himself. 'Oh, the South, it's marvellous, the South, when you live in the North! You sway gently, you are warm, at times you even get over-heated: it's like being in front of a great log fire in the dead of winter. And what do you see? A hammock hanging between a pair of coconut palms at the edge of a lagoon! And then there's that vanilla fragrance, almost imperceptible, which makes the eyelids quiver and the nostrils faintly flare, and which is called the trade winds. And the foliage greener than anywhere else, and the flowers more brilliant − flowers like birds, and plants like fountains; and a sea that was of a profounder blue −

19

more transparent, more intensely blue. . . . . . What could you not see? But you see it only because it is drizzling, or because there is frost on the window-panes, because you think you will never see such things!' (p. 106–7))

There is in this passage, too, apart from the extensive imagery, an element of irony which does not appear in *L'Enfant noir*. Clarence's attitude towards everyone and everything is tinged with this irony throughout the novel until the arrival of the king. Clarence is mystified but also contemptuous, humorously contemptuous, of what he sees around him. The humour, though, is not limited to Clarence alone. Laye treats the majority of his characters humorously. Obviously, as this is a work of creative fiction rather than fictional recreation, as is *L'Enfant noir*, he is less restrained when developing character and situation in *Le Regard du Roi*. In the former novel, all the characters exist through their contact with the boy. In the second, although our appreciation is coloured by Clarence's perception of the other characters, they exist independently of him. This is due to some considerable extent to the use of dialogue in the novel. In *L'Enfant noir*, the dialogue is an integral part of the very formalized con-struction. Now, however, the dialogue breaks out of this pattern where it appears only in key positions when Laye needed to emphasize the effect of certain events on certain characters. It must be noted that the only dialogue in *L'Enfant noir*, indeed the only dialogue possible, is that between the boy and the other characters. In *Le Regard du Roi* there is much greater flexibility and, therefore, a greater freedom in the development of the individual characters.

This does not mean that *Le Regard du Roi* is formless; indeed it has a very complex and close-knit structure based on the progression of Clarence's quest for assimilation. Each stage of his pilgrimage from his encounter with the beggar to the King's embrace has its exact place in this progression. The whole sequence is a gradual stripping away of Clarence's individualistic personality, from the exterior, the superficial attributes such as his suit, to the innermost, sexual compulsions. Laye treats Clarence almost as if he were a psycho-analyst's patient, one step leading logically to the next, each phase having to be completed before the next can be undertaken.

To reduce *Le Regard du Roi* to a simple study in psychology is obviously to ignore the major qualities of the novel. In the first place, there is the inter-play of the various personalities. Clarence is not the narrator's 'alter ego' as in *L'Enfant noir*. Here, he is portrayed uniquely from the observer's standpoint. The effects which the other characters' words and actions have on him are brought out much more acutely than those of Camara's family and friends. This is, in part, due to the fact that while Camara is being slowly moulded, Clarence is being brutally stripped of his personality. But it is also due to the fact that

Laye is not expecting the reader to participate intuitively in his characters' life, and that he himself does not feel that Clarence is as much a part of his personality as Camara. Equally, as was said earlier, the character of Camara dominates *L'Enfant noir* and we are much more aware of his influence on others than the reverse. In *Le Regard du Roi*, Clarence is one character among many and it is his personality which is dominated by the others. This change in perspective obviously brings these other characters into sharper focus. Of them all, the 'Mendiant' has the greatest effect on Clarence. His undisguised, shameless cunning and gluttony inspire both awe and disgust in Clarence as does his unshakable self-confidence. But through his cunning and self-confidence he dominates Clarence, forces him to do his will and to follow his example. The 'Mendiant' has enormous influence over many people – over everyone except the King. This influence devolves from the fact that he has nothing, but is an integral and indispensable element in the society; he is the peoples' conscience and also, in part, the repository of their traditions. They, therefore, owe him everything. He can be compared in some respects to the Muslim marabout and to the griot – although obviously he does not sing, does not work at all, except at begging. When, however, he barters Clarence for a donkey and a wife and disappears from the novel, there is a feeling that, somehow, he has lost more than he gained. He has lost his complete independence through these new possessions. Whereas Clarence and the two boys Nagoa and Noaga were temporary companions whom he knew he could dispose of at Aziana, 'dans le sud', now, however, he has acquired something which is not so readily bartered.

The journey through the forest is an initiation. Clarence loses the sense of urgency which had dominated his initial dealings with 'Le Mendiant'. The monotony of the journey through the forest effectively deadens this urgency. On his arrival at Aziana he is ready, in this one respect, to wait for the King. Now, however, he has to learn to live in the society which has adopted him. In Aziana, he is surrounded by people in contrast with his previous loneliness in the forest. In the village he is under the authority of the Naba, who, although only visible intermittently, wields absolute authority over the inhabitants. Clarence, unwittingly at first, is his servant, carrying out the function which the Naba commands. Even when Clarence discovers his function in this society, he does not rebel against the Naba's authority, but against what he considers to be his own bestiality.

It is, however, Samba Baloum and 'Le Maître des Cérémonies' with whom Clarence comes into direct contact and who, therefore, exercise the most obvious influence on him. The former, eunuch and hedonist, good humoured and talkative, is Clarence's constant drinking companion. He tries to keep Clarence happy and in ignorance of his position. But his apparent frankness

21

and open-mindedness makes Clarence trust him and accept his words unquestioningly.

Together with Akissa, Samba Baloum helps Clarence to enjoy life in Aziana. He is fretful at being, as he thinks, so useless. He introduces some innovations such as soft towels for drying himself but can achieve nothing. Only in their presence is he at peace with himself. But their influence on him is off-set by that of 'Le Maître des Cérémonies'. He is officious and spiteful. He ridicules Clarence, discloses to him what the others want to keep hidden. For this he is punished and Clarence's intervention on his behalf only increases his spite. The role of 'Le Maître des Cérémonies' is essential. Although he may appear despicable, he is concerned with the formalities of living in Aziana. For him, Clarence's continued ignorance of his position, the manner in which he accepts the illusions with which Samba Baloum surrounds him is offensive. It offends what 'Le Maître des Cérémonies' stands for; for Clarence to continue in his ignorance means that he will continue to see no reason to respect him nor the institutions which he upholds.

But there is another obvious reason for the role which 'Le Maître des Cérémonies' plays in the novel. While Clarence can be made to accept his position in the village as long as he is still ignorant of his function, it is only after he is fully aware of his position vis-à-vis the rest of the society and can accept it without question, that he will belong to this society. His eyes have to be opened brutally on the reality of his situation. This is what 'Le Maître des Cérémonies' does. Uncompromisingly, he shows Clarence what he is in terms he understands. This awareness of himself in a situation from which he cannot escape, from which in fact he does not want to escape, drives him in on himself, forces him to face the problem of total acceptance or total rejection. If he rejects everything he loses all chance of gaining the King's favour. On the other hand, by accepting his position in society, he has to rid himself of his sense of guilt, his sense of shame in the eyes of the world. The struggle is not resolved until the last moment, when Clarence, as if in a trance, walks towards the King. Before this, however, he has suffered degradation, in his own eyes, because of his impatient desire to know when the King is to come. At the same time as he suffers this degradation, he is initiated into the mysterious, supernatural world of the manatees, of Diallo the Smith and finally, of the moment when his shame is greatest and his desire fulfilled simultaneously, that of Dioki. It is only after such experiences, when his shame is undermined but not destroyed, when his faith is vindicated, that he has the courage to present himself, naked, to the King.

While Diallo is presented as a devoted and reasonable servant of the King, attempting always to produce the perfect tool for the King, Dioki is a frightening creature surrounded by snakes in her hovel. But she is a law unto herself, exercising supernatural powers both over people and as a visionary. When Clarence, bound by a snake, sees the King's coming, Dioki is both exorcising Clarence's shame and satisfying his desire. But she does it in such a way that the mystery of what he sees and does is hidden from Clarence.

From the comparative simplicity of the autobiographical narrative of *L'Enfant noir*, *Le Regard du Roi*, introduces a new complexity and the mystical, present but not dominant in the earlier novel, becomes even more marked, and towards the end, predominates in the narrative. This move towards the mystical is even more marked in his short story, *Les Yeux de la Statue*. Here, there is again the quest for a mystical experience which offers access to complete self-knowledge. There are only two characters involved, the old caretaker and the young girl, both nameless. The action takes place in a ruined city which is in deep forest. There is no indication where the city is located. It is completely isolated and uninhabited except for the old man.

The narrative is dominated by the statue, a stone statue of the last prince, lying in the nettles which have invaded the whole of the city. It is this statue which will eventually kill the young girl. It is not just the statue, however, but more particularly its eyes, which dominate, which lead the girl inexorably to her doom. The atmosphere of *Les Yeux de la Statue* is even more obsessive than that of *Le Regard du Roi*. The young girl's obsession with the silent appeal in the eyes of the statue, which seems to echo and become vocal the more she looks at them, is even greater than Clarence's obsession for the King. The impulse which drives her to the ruined city, which forces her to explore the ruined palace, is much less equivocal than that which forces Clarence to accept his place in Aziana.

While there is great similarity between the two titles, *Le Regard du Roi* and *Les Yeux de la Statue*, implying an emphasis on the need for compassionate understanding expressed through the eyes which penetrate and see, intuitively as it were, the depths of a man's soul, there is a very different approach to the theme in the two narratives.

Clarence is initially purposeless and it is only towards the end of the novel that he is driven by an inner compulsion similar to that which motivates the girl from the beginning of her quest. 'Je suis cet Elan! dit-elle' ('I am this compulsion,' she said).

The quest could, therefore, be taken as an elaboration in different key, of the final episode of *Le Regard du Roi*. This impression is reinforced by a phrase which follows almost immediately on the exclamation just quoted: '. . . cet élan lui échappait, sa personne même lui échappait.' (This compulsion escaped her, her own self escaped her.)

But *Les Yeux de la Statue* should not be considered uniquely as a version of the final scene of *Le Regard du Roi*. As was said earlier, it possesses certain elements which make it distinct from the novel. However, one major similiarity should be noted before discussing it independently. In both there is an emphasis on a circuitous journey through the forest, labyrinthine corridors and rooms piled with rubble which are physical symbols of the mind's restless and impossible quest for fulfillment. These aspects link the two narratives to Kafka's novels, and, as J. A. Ramsaran suggests tentatively (*Black Orpheus* 3 May 1958 pp 55—7), to Sufism. The influence of Sufism, however, should be looked at in relation to Laye's last novel, *Dramouss*. It is, however, worthwhile bearing in mind the mystical aspect of Laye's work which seems progressively to dominate his writing.

Les Yeux de la Statue should be seen in this light. The ruined city represents an ideal; perfection which has been destroyed by time and by indifference. This is what the girl is looking for; perfection is also what the prince wanted to create. There remain only vestiges which the old caretaker conserves and cherishes to the best of his ability.

The girl is overwhelmed by the tragedy of this destruction. She becomes aware of the inevitability of the advance of the nettles and the erosion of the buildings by rain and wind. Yet, at the same time, she feels that she ought in some way to try and preserve something of the ideal, to perpetuate the memory of the Prince. Her effort is symbolized by the desire which both she and the old man have to replace the Prince's statue in the niche where now 'l'herbe se dressait, tourmentée comme la flamme d'une torche,' (the grass rose up, tormented like the flame of a torch) as if proclaiming its victory over the Prince.

At the end of the story, in which it seems that the surreality of the girl's sleeping nightmare replaces reality, the tide of nettles rises to engulf the palace, drowning all the last vestiges of the Prince's efforts. Only the statue remains with its plaintive, piercing eyes, floating still on top of the flood, dominating it even in its degradation until it washes over the girl, crushing her. The ideal she sought has destroyed her.

The style of *Les Yeux de la Statue* differs very little from that of *Le Regard du Roi*. Laye uses the same devices. In the short story, however, he does increase the mystification by a deliberate omission of any feature which might localize the situation of the action. Nothing, not even the statue, the old man or the palace has any distinguishing features. The architecture of the palace, its furnishings, are idealized but formless. It is as though, as with the description of the King's palace at Adramé, Laye wishes to portray the universal and unattainable. Here, though, there is something more; the formlessness is due to decay, the ideal is unattainable because it has been destroyed.

24

It is fairly obvious that the ideal the girl is seeking is within herself. It could, therefore, be argued that the girl is to some extent Clarence's African counterpart. She is seeking her true originality, which is bound up with a past now destroyed by the indifference of the invaders, and of which only remnants remain, guarded by an old man who alone has remained faithful to the old ideals. His bitterness at the visitors:

vous n'avez pas compris que tous ces visiteurs me marchaient sur la tête et s'essuyaient les pieds sur mes cheveux. J'avais beaucoup de cheveux alors. (You do not see that all these visitors used to walk over my head and wipe their feet on my hair. I had a lot of hair in those days.)

would seem to suggest that he hated these tourists who came to see but not to understand, as if the city were simply a curiosity.

Finally, of course, it could be considered that the girl, destroyed by her ideal, symbolizes the impossibility of ever returning to the ideals of the past, only vestiges of which ever survive the passage of time.

In his contribution to the *Colloque sur la littéraire africaine d'expression française*, Laye returned to many of the themes and episodes contained in *L'Enfant noir*. He entitled his paper, *L'âme de L'Afrique dans sa partie Guinéenne* and began:

je ne saurais mieux aborder ce sujet, et le mieux traiter qu'en parlant de moi-même, je veux dire, en revenant à mes souvenirs d'enfance. (I could not broach this subject nor treat it better than by speaking of myself, in other words, by returning to my childhood memories.)

While he gives some useful biographical detail, the importance of this contribution is in its statement of the main themes which Laye considers essential both to his art and to traditional African culture.

In the first place:

'Quelle était, hier, le caractéristique dominante de cette civilisation (samorienne)? Elle me paraissait être le MYSTERE même. Et pourquoi le mystère? Parce que, regardant de L'Europe vers l'Afrique, c'était d'abord le mystère de mon pays qui me frappait. Ce n'était pas que je ne reconnusse aucun mystère à l'Europe, mais je sentais mieux sa présence en Afrique.

(What was the dominant characteristic of this civilization (Samorian) yesterday? I thought it was MYSTERY itself. And why mystery? Because, looking at Africa from Europe, it was above all the mystery that struck me. This is not to say that I do not accord any mystery to Europe, but that I felt its presence more strongly in Africa.)

But there is a second, even more important element:

'Non! la vie en Afrique ne débouchait pas constamment sur le mystère bien qu'elle fût tout impregnée de mystère; et je dirais même au notre vie d'Africains de Guinée, qui ne doit pas être différente de la vie des autres Africains, débouchait plus fréquemment sur L'AMOUR...
Je parle de cet Amour qui nous unit si étroitement les uns aux autres, ... qui, a la campagne, faisait nos villages si accordés, si paisibles, si solidaires.'
(No! Life in Africa did not always stem from mystery, although it was altogether steeped in it; and speaking as a Guinean African of our own life, which cannot be different from the life of other Africans, I would say even that is stemmed from LOVE.
I mean the Love which binds us so strongly to one another......the love, which made our villages in the country so harmonious, so peaceful and so united.)

It is this love which is at the basis of the mystery of life, of man's relationship with all which surrounds him and with God. For him the greatest attribute of Europe is not its rationalism and mechanisation but 'c'est un pur MESSAGE DE L'AME'. His conclusion, therefore, is this:

'Eh bien, au mystère toujours! Au mystère qui ne va pas sans l'âme, à l'invisible, qui sans l'âme n'aurait pas d'existence en nous. A cette UNION ENTRE LE CIEL ET LA TERRE que nous partageons avec toutes les civilisations, à tout cela qui est le moteur même des civilisations'.
(And so it always comes back to mystery. To the mystery which cannot exist without the soul, to the invisible presence which would have no being in us without the soul. To this UNION OF EARTH AND SKY which we share with all civilizations, to all this which is the motivating force of all civilizations.)

Laye goes on to elaborate on this mysticism, trying to analyse its basic attributes:

'Je vois le monde visible brusquement céder, je le vois réduit à ce qu'il est: pas exactement un songe peut-être. Mais le signe, le simple signe de ce qui se trouve au delà, *et qui est plus haut, infiniment plus haut que ce signe, qui en fait, n'est qu'apparence*, n'est rien, rien qui puisse satisfaire. Je vois l'invisible surgir et je le vois remettre notre pauvre petite raison raisonnante à sa place, *qui est petite*; je vois l'inexplicable reprendre sa place, *qui est souveraine*.
— *Je vois l'âme enfin!*
(I see the visible world retract abruptly, I see it reduced to it's own size: not exactly a dream perhaps. But the sign, the simple sign indicating what is beyond,

and *what is higher, infinitely higher than that sign, what is in fact nothing but a figment of the imagination,* is nothing, nothing that can satisfy. I see the invisible rising up and putting our poor little rational reason in its place, a place which is small; I see the inexplicable take its place, a place which is supreme. — I see the soul, at last!)

Laye considers that African sculpture is the aspect of African civilization which has been most effective in revealing this civilization to the rest of the world. In sculpture, the essential elements of this mysticism are manifest. This is obviously the reason for the presence of his father in all his novels; in *L'Enfant noir* and *Dramouss* he is present as himself, in *Le Regard du Roi* he appears as Dialo the Smith. One could equally say that it is Laye's father who has most profoundly influenced his son and stimulated this mystical approach to life.

The two important elements in sculpture are 'rythme' and 'pouvoir'.

Mon père, accroupi devant le bois . . . , ne montrait point de calcul dans sa transposition de la réalité, il laissait parler son coeur avec plus de naturel, et ainsi, sa transposition le conduisait à une déformation qui d'abord, accusait et accentuait l'expression, la spiritualité, et qui ensuite, par voie de conséquence, commandait d'autres déformations, purement plastiques celle-ci, destinées à faire équilibre à la première et à l'accomplir. . . .
    Pourquoi ces plans et ces volumes font-ils penser à des variations sur un thème donné pourquoi — lâchons le mot — le RYTHME est-il ici plus frappant, infiniment plus frappant que dans n'importe quelle autre sculpture?
    Nous touchons là un des aspects fondamentaux de l'âme Africaine.
    Eh bien! hier . . . était un temps où le visage, la figurine, l'animal qui surgissait sous l'herminette de mon père, et où tout travail qu'accomplissaient nos forgerons dans plusieurs domaines était inséparable du mystère, servait directement au culte, à la magie . . . Où l'arme que sortait de ses mains était une arme qui blesse non pas seulement parce qu'elle était tranchante et bien maniée, mais parce que le POUVOIR lui avait été accordé de blesser et de trancher; où la houe du paysan n'était pas uniquement l'outil qui remue la terre, mais l'outil qui commande à la terre et à la moisson.
    (My father, crouched over the wood . . . . showed no calculation during the transposition from reality; he let his heart speak quite naturally and thus the transposition led him to a deformation which at first attacked and exaggerated the artistic expression, the spirituality, and which then, as a natural consequence, led to new deformations, this time purely plastic, designed to balance the first and to make it whole.
    Why do these planes and dimensions remind us of variations on a theme —

why is – let us keep the same word – the RYTHM more striking, infinitely most striking here than in any other sculpture?

We are touching here on one of the most fundamental aspects of the African Soul.

And so! Yesterday . . . was a time when the face, the figure, the animal which was created under my father's adze, and when all the work which our blacksmiths accomplished in their various fields, was inseparable from the mystery, and directly served the cult, the magic . . . When the tool which his hands wielded was a tool which wounded not only because it was sharp and skilfully manipulated, but because MIGHT had been granted him to wound and cut; a time when the peasant's hoe was not just the implement which turns the soil, but the implement which governs the soil and the harvest!)

These two elements serve to create perfection, an ideal reality, a reality in which are fused both the physical reality around us and the spiritual sur-reality with which everything is imbued:

La réalité. Mon père cherchait à être vrai, aussi vrai *qu'il est possible de l'être*. Son souci de *la vérité, de la réalité*, n'était tempéré que par la recherche de la *beauté idéale*, et, en corollaire, par l'établissement d'un type de *beauté universelle*.

(Reality. My father sought the truth, the truth *as far as it is possible to find it*. His care for truth, reality was modified only by the search for *ideal beauty*, and, in addition, by the desire to establish a *universal beauty*.)

These, then, seem to be the foundations on which the novels are based, which dictate their form and, to some extent, their content. In this *exposé* of his thought, Laye summarises all the main themes which run through *L'Enfant noir* and *Le Regard du Roi*. These are, equally, predominant themes in *Dramouss*, Laye's latest novel. It was not published until he had fled Guinea for Senegal. In it, he returns to the autobiographical form of *L'Enfant noir*, re-introducing the same characters. This time, however, he is a stranger looking at a world he knows imperfectly. His memories are blurred and idealized while the country has changed considerably during his absence. He looks at his country critically and seems to deplore what he sees.

Dramouss lacks many of the qualities of his earlier novels. In the first section, entitled 'Conakry', his efforts to bring alive and to interest the reader in the development of housing estates and heavy industry read like a tourist brochure. His treatment of the reunion with Mimie is more successful, but his natural reticence and desire to shield his emotions and her modesty tend to make the treatment superficial. Laye does not seem to be able to bring out the underlying emotions through the description of an action in an adult as he can with a child's.

The use of a 'flashback' to narrate his life in Paris breaks into the chronology of the novel so forcefully that the reader is transposed into an entirely different world, and any unity the novel might have possessed is destroyed. But it seems as if Laye is determined to create not a coherent fictional world but a work essentially of social criticism.

This view is substantiated in the rest of the novel. On his return to Kouroussa, Fatoman, the narrator, describes the failure of the educational programme and the disappearance of traditional crafts and beliefs which are replaced by cheap, imported products and new, basically immoral, attitudes. Especially, he attacks the nascent political parties; the epilogue, 'Retour', describing a later visit to Guinea when independence has been achieved, briefly sketches the facts which confirm his pessimism.

Against this description of the disintegration of traditional culture, Laye sets those aspects which remain: his father carving (a description which is practically identical with the one in his article 'L'Ame de l'Afrique dans sa partie Guinéenne'), the griot's story of the jealous Iman, which is related to the first part of the 'Enchanted King' in The Thousand and One Nights and shows the influence of Arab culture on the Guineans, and particularly Laye's dream 'Dramouss'. These are the aspects of life which Laye wishes to preserve and resuscitate. As he writes in the 'dédicace':

Que cet ouvrage contribue à galvaniser les énergies de cette jeunesse; et surtout celles des jeunes poètes et romanciers africains, qui se cherchent, ou qui, déjà se connaissent, pour faire mieux, beaucoup mieux, dans la voie de la restauration totale de notre pensée, de cette pensée qui, pour résister aux épreuves du temps, devra nécessairement puiser sa force dans les vérités historiques de nos civilisations particulières, et dans les réalités africaines.

... Pour que la pensée africaine ainsi réintégrée et totalement restaurée soit une force, non aggressive, mais féconde. (p. 8)

(May this work contribute towards galvanizing the energies of this youth; and above all the energies of the young African poets and novelists who are searching for their identity, or of those who have found it, in order to go further, much further along the road towards the restoration of our intellectual thought, the thought which, in order to resist the trials of time, must of necessity draw its strength from the historical truths of our individual civilizations, and from African reality.

... So that, thus reintegrated and completely restored, African thought may become a force, not aggressive, but fertile.)

Here it can be clearly seen that Laye considers that traditional values have much more relevance to contemporary Africa than the importation of alien concepts which can only destroy these established values. This is brought out most forcefully in the section entitled 'Dramouss'. Fatoman sleeps with his father's 'boule blanche' beneath his pillow and in his dream sees the future of his country. In the allegorical treatment of this future development, the influence of Kafka, which was noted in *Le Regard du Roi*, is also once again pronounced. But, more particularly, the major elements – the snake, 'Dramouss' the djinné, the black lion – are all symbols taken from the strongly islamized traditional culture. Yet the prison is a product of European culture; the guns and whips, the mind-twisting interrogations are familiar to Kafka's world. The resolution of the allegory – the whole world recreated after the flood through the intervention of the black lion, guardian of men and their skills – symbolizes the return to this traditional culture. The 'stylo mine', symbol of education, is also put into the lion's care together with the hoe, sagaie and rifle.

It is obvious that the prison and the giant warders represent the colonial régime in African countries, and that the 'revolution' which Dramouss shows to Fatoman is the post-colonial régime. But it could also be argued on the evidence of his description in the last chapter, 'Retour', that the prison is also representative of the post-colonial régime. It is in this last chapter that there is the most striking example of Laye's belief in the strength and validity of traditional culture. His father, by repeating an incantation, calls back the hawk which had pounced on a chick.

His father's words at this moment:

Oui. Ces mots ont beaucoup de force. Quand on a parlé pour Dieu, agi pour Dieu, et vécu seul dans la brousse pour Dieu, comme moi, dans la contemplation, tout cela pour Dieu. Dieu alors vous écoute quand vous lui parlez.

(Yes. These words carry much weight. When one has spoken for God, acted for God and lived alone in the bush for God, as I have done, in contemplation – all this for God. Then God listens when you speak to him.)

recall those in the *Kitáb al-Sidq* of Kharráz, the Sufi mystic:

God, said, In no way does My servant so draw nigh Me as when performing those duties which I have imposed upon him; and My servant continues to draw near to Me through works of superogation, until I love him. And when I love him, I am his ear, so he hears by Me, and his eye, so he sees by Me, and his hand, so he takes by Me.

We also see that Laye emphasizes the unity existing between his father and the universe and also his own concern for love as a unifying and transcendental

30

force which he expresses in *L'Ame de l'Afrique dans sa partie Guinéenne* which also coincides with Sufi doctrine: 'Love is indeed the gateway leading from the ascetic and contemplative to the unitive life.' Against the materialistic and corrupt society which is developing, which Laye feels is developing, he sets his mysticism which seems to owe much to Sufism combined with certain supernatural elements of residual animism.

Dramouss is a logical continuation of Laye's previous novels in so far as the mysticism which, in retrospect, can be seen in *L'Enfant noir*, becomes more overt and pronounced. However, the emphasis changes from fictional narration to direct social comment. His commitment to such mysticism and direct social comment justifies, in some respects, the criticism of 'A.B.' in *Présence Africaine* in 1954 that *L'Enfant noir* is nothing more than an exotic novel pleasing to metropolitan taste because it upholds obsolete, traditional, values. On the other hand, it could also be said that Laye's attitude is valid when the disintegration of present political systems is taken into account.

Stylistically, Laye seems to have tried in *Dramouss* to achieve the same simplicity as in *L'Enfant noir* without using the devices which give that novel its particular clarity. *Dramouss* is more direct, and in many ways more journalistic. It lacks the subtleties of his earlier works both in presentation and characterization. Fatoman seems almost to be shut off from the people he meets and even Mimie never becomes a substantial, living character. The novel, as was said earlier, also lacks coherence. It is episodic, even anecdotal in form. The effect of this is to emphasize the journalistic and autobiographical aspects and the social commitment. It is not a novel in the same sense as *L'Enfant noir* and *Le Regard du Roi*, where the narrative has a continuous thread and an inner dynamic. The narrative of *Dramouss* depends on events external to the novel; the episodes have no independent internal links which weld them together and give them continuity. In this respect, Laye seems to have broken with his earlier works; the episodic form, the absence of inner dynamic is due to his efforts to bring together two basically incompatible elements: his mysticism and social criticism. Whereas in *L'Enfant noir* the mysticism is only implicit and whereas in *Le Regard du Roi* and in *Les Yeux de la Statue* it is an organic part of the narrative, in *L'âme de l'Afrique dans sa partie Guinéenne* and *Dramouss*, Laye is making it the subject of a 'jihád'.

By committing himself overtly to reform in his creative work, Laye has destroyed much that was valuable in his writing. His latest novel, while it is a work of courage, lacks what *L'Enfant noir*, also a work of courage, possesses — coherence and poetic insight. In its place there is Laye's mysticism and a criticism of Africa's development. Like many poets before him, Laye seems to be turning into a man of action.

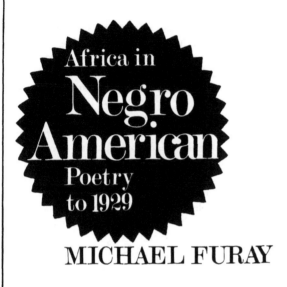

Africa in Negro American Poetry to 1929

MICHAEL FURAY

In 1961, during a visit to Israel as guest of the government James Baldwin was reminded of his own 'homelessness' and of the Negro American's relationship with Africa. On 5 October, 1961 in a letter to his literary agent which was later published as part of 'Letters from a Journey' in *Soon, One Morning* he wrote: My bones know, somehow, something of what waits for me in Africa. That is one of the reasons I have dawdled so long – I'm afraid. And, of course, I am playing it my own way, edging myself into it: it would be nice to be able to dream about Africa, but once I have been there, I will not be able to dream anymore. (p.39)

Perhaps Baldwin was afraid of finding in Africa what Richard Wright had found only a few years earlier when he told Peter Abrahams: 'I was black and they were black but it did not help me . . . I found the African an oblique, a hard-to-know man.' Wright was bitterly disillusioned by his African experience, as his book on the Gold Coast reveals. In any case, Baldwin knew he had to confront finally the reality of Africa; he was too honest to continue believing in the old dreams which he felt had assuaged but blinded Negro Americans.

The Negro writer's relationship with Africa, as Baldwin's remark illustrates, is problematical. Indeed it has been the subject of a continuing and often lively controversy among writers, a recent example of which is to be found in the

32

selected papers of The First Conference of Negro Writers, held in March of 1959 (published as *The Negro Writer and his Roots*.) Since the 1920's, when Alain Locke compiled his important anthology, *The New Negro*, black writers have turned to Africa sometimes utterly confused in order to define their cultural past and its relevance for Negroes in American society. The Harlem writers whose works appeared in Locke's collection understood that in order to interpret Negro life with any measure of honesty or force they had to reject the traditions of the past. The need to reconsider the Negro heritage and hence the meaning of Africa became obvious. They began to ask as Countee Cullen phrased it simply and beautifully in his long poem 'Heritage':

What is Africa to me:
Copper sun or scarlet sea,
Jungle star or jungle track,
Strong bronzed men, or regal black
Women from whose loins I sprang
When the birds of Eden sang?
One three centuries removed
From the scenes his fathers loved,
Spicy grove, cinnamon tree,
What is Africa to me?

Cullen's response was laden with romantic images of 'wild barbaric birds,' 'Great drums throbbing through the air,' and 'outlandish heathen gods.' It was the imaginary Africa which told him, 'My conversion came high-priced,' now I must 'Quench my pride and cool my blood.' His poem underlined the cultural dilemma of the 'New Negro' writer: '... although I speak With my mouth thus, in my heart Do I play a double part.'

A few years earlier Claude McKay had reached a similar conclusion. He wrote in 'Outcast':

For the dim regions whence my fathers came
My spirit, bondaged by the body, longs...
I would go back to darkness and to peace,
And I may never hope for full release
While to its alien gods I bend my knee.

As Langston Hughes recalled in 'The Twenties: Harlem and Its Negritude,' which appeared in *African Forum* in Spring 1966 a year before Hughes died, Claude McKay was 'the first of the New Negroes, of whom Dr. W. E. B. Du

Bois, Alain Locke, and James Weldon Johnson were the deans.' He has also been called the *enfant terrible* of the Negro Renaissance.

The Negro Renaissance, probably the most important event in the history of the American Negro since emancipation from slavery, marked the end of the old order which leaders like Du Bois had begun to challenge in the early 1900's. Alain Locke described it in retrospect as a 'mass movement of the urban immigration of Negroes, projected on the plane of an increasingly articulate elite.' The urban centre of the great migration of Negroes to the North which began soon after the outbreak of World War I became of course Harlem, the largest Negro community in the world, where young intellectuals gathered to express in their works and lives the rebellious mood of the Renaissance. According to the little magazine *Fire*, its founders intended to 'burn up a lot of the old dead, conventional Negro ideas of the past.' Looking back, the most colourful founder of *Fire's* one and only issue wrote, '. . . we set out to publish *Fire*, a Negro quarterly of the arts to *épater le bourgeois*, to burn up a lot of the old stereotyped Uncle Tom ideas of the past, and to provide us with an outlet for publishing not existing in the hospitable but limited pages of *The Crisis* or *Opportunity*.' In 'The Negro Artist and the Racial Mountain' Langston Hughes urged his fellow artists to interpret the beauty of black people, especially the 'lowdown folks' as he called the black majority. Hughes wrote a bold manifesto for his generation:

> We younger Negro artists who create now intend to express our individual dark-skinned selves without fear or shame. If white people are pleased we are glad. If they are not, it doesn't matter. We know we are beautiful. And ugly too. If colored people are pleased we are glad. If they are not, their displeasure doesn't matter either. (*Matian* CXXII 1926 p.94)

Writers before the twenties had of course written about Negro life and experience in the United States; they had also protested against slavery and other forms of racial injustice. But they were inhibited essentially by conventional ideas of the black man, or worse by their own 'stereotyped Uncle Tom ideas of the past'; furthermore they were intimidated by their predominantly white audience. They could hardly have identified with the 'primitivism' of Africa and the black man which the Harlem writers of the twenties exalted. In the earliest known Negro poetry in America there is in fact evidence of the extent to which even former slaves accepted the half-truths about pagan Africa along with their absurd implications for Negroes in the New World. Phillis Wheatley, for example (whose first published poem, 'A Poem by Phillis, a Negro Girl in Boston, on the Death of the Reverend George Whitefield,' appeared when she was seventeen) referred to her passage from Senegal as a child slave in 1761 as though she had actually been freed from bondage: 'Twas mercy brought me from my pagan land.' In 'Lines to the Students of Cambridge University,' which she wrote during her visit to England in 1773 where she became a literary success, as she had been in the U.S., she described Africa in a manner which Puritan New England could have appreciated:

Twas not long since I left my native shore —
The land of errors and Egyptian gloom.

Unfortunately, the concept of Africa as a 'land of errors and Egyptian gloom' did not die with Phillis Wheatley's generation. It persisted in one form or another throughout the nineteenth century, notwithstanding the Abolitionist Movement or the Civil War. Moreover, as an assumption about Negro heritage it was largely responsible for the ideologies behind the Negro missionary movement whose educational institutions were dedicated to 'the redemption of Africa' and the general 'elevation of the Negro race in America.' Such beliefs were even reflected in the verse of Paul Lawrence Dunbar, the first major Negro poet in American literature to appear after Wheatley. In 'Ode to Ethiopia' he wrote:

Go on and up! Our souls and eyes
Shall follow thy continuous rise;
*   Our ears shall list thy story*
From bards who from thy roots shall spring,
And proudly tune their tyres to sing
*   Of Ethiopia's glory.*

Dunbar was celebrating a new race of Negroes, whom he described in his ode as 'Proud Ethiope's swarthy children' standing alongside 'their fairer neighbor' – epithets which partly explain why the Harlem writers of a later generation did not consider themselves in the tradition of Dunbar or older Negro poets.

The writers of the New Negro Movement became contemptuous of middle-class whites and Negroes alike who talked about progress in terms of saving heathens and 'improving' the black race. Rather than worry about the redemption of Africa or suggest an even greater assimilation of Negroes into the majority culture of the United States, they were busy describing the evils of white America and defining the Negro's cultural autonomy. They identified with the Negro masses – not with bourgeois 'white' Negroes – whose frustration and disenchantment with white society formed the emotional base for such phenomena as Marcus Garvey's 'Back to Africa' movement. Garvey's Universal Negro Improvement Association with its affiliated organizations was the largest emigrationist movement in American history. No doubt Garvey was an

35

embarrassment to Negro intellectuals (certainly to the dominant leaders of organizations like the National Association for the Advancement of Coloured People and the National Urban League) who were critical of his Utopian scheme to leave America and build a new civilisation in Africa. Nonetheless, the mass appeal of the Garvey Movement indicates that emigrationist sentiment was not only alive but decidedly more widespread among the Negro masses than was generally acknowledged. If the New Negro writers were not bodily among the estimated one to four million supporters of the Garvey Movement they surely were in spirit, as their poetry affirms. 'I want to see the slim palm trees,' Gwendolyn Bennett wrote in her poem entitled 'Heritage,'

Pulling at the clouds
With little pointed fingers. . . .

I want to see lithe Negro girls,
Etched dark against the sky
While sunset lingers.

I want to hear the silent sands
Singing to the moon
Before the Sphinx-still face. . . .

I want to hear the chanting
Around a heathen fire
Of a strange black race.

The New Negroes' estrangement from American society made their symbolic journey to Africa inevitable, for they lived and worked in the United States unlike the many white writers of the *avant-garde* who opted to become exiles in the capital cities of Europe. When their repudiation of white America failed to close measurably the gap between the promise and practice of democracy, their longing for distant Africa and neo-Pagan ways became more pronounced. The lesser Harlem poets, like Gwendolyn Bennett, were frequently sentimental about Africa, which came to represent a solution to the problems of an alien society: to them Africa was a romantic homeland, a curious mixture of 'palm trees' and 'silent sands,' a 'Sphinx-still face' and heathen chanting. It was truly an imaginary continent, beyond reach. *Afrika Singt*, the first German anthology of Negro American verse, published in 1929, included among other well-known Renaissance poems Waring Cuney's 'No Images,' a simple and forced though very popular poem about the primitive loveliness hidden from a Harlem girl:

36

If she could dance
Naked,
Under palm trees
And see her image in the river
She would know.

But there are no palm trees
On the street,
And dishwater gives back no images.

To Claude McKay, whose *Harlem Shadows* established his reputation as a major writer of the Renaissance soon after the volume appeared in 1922, Africa was a land of vivid colour and plentitude like his native Jamaica which he left in 1912 to study and take up residence in the United States.

Bananas ripe and green, and gingerroot,
Cocoa in pods and alligator pears . . .

Such things made him 'hungry for the old, familiar ways,' he said in 'The Tropics in New York.' McKay longed for the fecundity of the tropics and its primeaval strength; the tragedy of the black man, he believed, was his removal from their source, Africa. In the title poem of *Harlem Shadows* he described the Negro prostitutes as 'dusky, half-clad girls' of 'my fallen race.' Similarly, the Harlem dancer in his poem of that title, who 'seemed a proudly-swaying palm Grown lovelier for passing through a storm,' did not belong in a tawdry dance hall: '. . . looking at her falsely-smiling face, I knew her self was not in that strange place.'

McKay's poetry, especially that written in America before he went to Europe or settled for a time in North Africa, is a record of his own spiritual journey; its central theme was a consequence of his preoccupation with exile and the oppressed of the world with whom he identified himself. He said with sincerity in 'Outcast':

. . . I was born far from my native clime
Under the white man's menace, out of time.

He was outraged more than any of his contemporaries by the 'white fiends' of America who were responsible for Negro suffering, and which such poems as 'Tiger,' 'The Lynching,' 'Rest in Peace,' 'White Houses' illustrate; in fact, some of his verse breaks down artistically under the strain of his emotion. Yet he hated more the causes of universal human suffering, and his best poetry displays his ability to sublimate his feelings without losing their intensity or candour. The most famous example is 'If We Must Die,' a sonnet written after

the Washington race riot in 1919 and, not surprisingly, popularised by Sir
Winston Churchill as a call to arms during World War II:

If we must die, let it not be like hogs
Hunted and penned in an inglorious spot,
While round us bark the mad and hungry dogs,
Making their mock at our accursed lot.
If we must die, O let us nobly die . . .

Unquestionably, the verse published posthumously which McKay wrote
shortly before and after his conversion to Catholicism lacks the urgency of his
earlier poems. It does, however, reveal a part of McKay's temperament which
was generally ignored during his lifetime and which today is still misunderstood
by some critics and readers, for instance his passion for human understanding
and tolerance. McKay did not consider himself a 'Negro' poet, as he emphasized
in a preface to a recording he made of his poetry, and it troubled him that
people identified him as a poet of 'racial' protest. Lewis Nkosi, for example,
missed the mark when he wrote in *Home and Exile* 'Poets like Claude McKay
would have readily identified with the Black Muslims today.' If he desired anything for himself as a poet he wanted his verse to stand as evidence of a single
man's search for truth and reconcilliation with his past, which, as he revealed
in 'Africa', could never be a simple matter for him:

When all the world was young in pregnant night
Thy slaves toiled at their monumental best.
Thou ancient treasure land, thou modern prize,
New peoples marvel at thy pyramids!
The years roll on, thy sphinx of riddle-eyes
Watches the mad world with immobile lids . . .
Thou art the harlot, now thy time is done,
Of all the mighty nations of the sun.

Among the younger Harlem writers who shared McKay's sense of kinship
with primitive Africa the two most outstanding poets were Countee Cullen
and Langston Hughes. Sterling Brown described Cullen as 'the most precious'
of the Negro poets of the twenties. He was definitely more sophisticated in
technique and range of subject than his fellow poets. Like other Negro poets
of the period, as well as white poets such as Carl Sandburg or Maxwell
Bodenheim, he used poetry as a means of social protest, as in 'The Black Christ', a
poem about lynching; in fact, he reproved Negro poets for failing to write about
racial atrocities. He also expressed a profound loyalty to his race, as 'Shroud
of Color' illustrates:

Lord, I will live persuaded by mine own,
I cannot play the recreant to these:
My spirit has come home, that sailed the doubtful seas.

Yet Cullen wrote a good many poems devoid of racial sentiment as well, which reveal the keen awareness he had of social history and his literary past; 'Karenge ya Marenge', 'Medusa', 'To John Keats', 'Not Sacco and Vanzetti', and 'For Helen Keller' are examples. Indeed most of his poetry is about all men's misery and triumph, written in an idiom largely influenced by the Bible and the English poets he admired most. A poem like 'Heritage', for example, which is in a literal sense about personal struggle emphasizes finally the moral paradox of life:

Lord, forgive me if my need
Sometimes shapes a human creed . . .
Not yet has my heart or head
In the least way realized
They and I are civilized.

To Cullen, the meaning of Africa was nothing less than the meaning of selfhood.

Langston Hughes, who was more interested as a poet in the rhythm of jazz than the cadences of Romantic verse which inspired Cullen, looked upon Africa as part of the historical past which resonates within the poet and allows him, perhaps more than others, to discover the meaning of existence. In the prize-winning poem which launched his career as a young writer of promise, 'The Negro Speaks of Rivers', he wrote:

I've known rivers:
I've known rivers ancient as the world
and older than the flow
of human blood in human veins

My soul has grown deep like the rivers.

I bathed in the Euphrates
when dawns were young.
I built my hut near the Congo
and it lulled me to sleep.
I looked upon the Nile
and raised the Pyramids above it.
I heard the singing of the Mississippi
when Abe Lincoln went down to New Orleans
and I've seen its muddy bosom
turn all golden in the sunset.

I've known rivers:
ancient dusky rivers.

My soul has grown deep like the rivers.

For Hughes Africa was a song, not completely understood and thus a trifle
bewildering. In 'Afro-American Fragment', which was orignally published in
the July 1930 issue of *The Crisis*, he spoke of Africa in a brooding and nostalgic
tone:

So long,
So far away
Is Africa . . .
Subdued and time-lost
Are the drums — and yet
Through some vast mist of race
There comes this song
I do not understand . . .

The Harlem poets of the twenties described Africa in terms which reflected
their own understanding of Negro heritage: it was a song, an unremittent beat,
a homeland viewed from exile, a harlot, it was savage power, palm trees, or
tom-toms, it was pristine innocence and fecundity. In a word, Africa was not a
country; it was:

a concept,
Fashioned in our minds, each to each,
To hide our separate fears,
To dream our separate dreams.

This was as Abioseh Nicol defined it in his widely quoted 'The Meaning of
Africa'. The New Negro poets' fascination and identification with Africa
separated them fundamentally from earlier Negro poets who thought of Africa
as a 'land of errors and Egyptian gloom' or who otherwise made apologies for
Negro heritage, just as their absorption with everything Negro distinguished
them from preceding generations. They denied the stereotyped ideas of the
past which had become fixed in the traditions of both white and black America
and which prevented writers from interpreting Negro experience with honesty
and dignity.

The impact of World War I on American life and the social problems which
followed in its wake, the unemployment and racial violence, the emigrationist
solutions such as Garveyism, the poverty in a decade of wild prosperity,
Prohibition, in short the Roaring Twenties — all in one way or other influenced

40

the Harlem Renaissance. By the end of the twenties the Renaissance had already begun to influence world literature, but by then it was over, like the decade itself which ended abruptly after the Stock Market crash of 1929. In the words of Langston Hughes, 'By the time the thirties came, the voltage of the Negro Renaissance of the twenties had nearly run its course. Ellison and Wright were about the last of the young pilgrims to come to Harlem seeking its sustenance. The chain of influences that had begun in Renaissance days ended in the thirties when the Great Depression drastically cut down on migrations, literary or otherwise (*African Forum* Spring 1966). Negro writers of the thirties began to look inward, at the problems of an economically sick nation, as indeed the N.A.A.C.P. and similar organizations did, an organization which had been preoccupied during the twenties with world problems such as pan-Africanism. Inevitably, their new concerns altered the nature and direction of their literature: the dominant spirit of the Harlem Renaissance, which has been termed negritude without much risk of oversimplification, would have to wait out the Depression before its revival in the writings of Negro Americans.

41

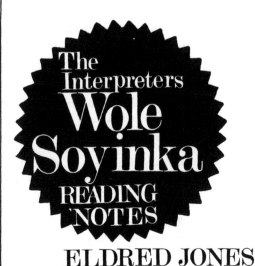

The Interpreters Wole Soyinka READING NOTES

ELDRED JONES

The Interpreters is Wole Soyinka's first novel although by 1965* when this novel was first published, Soyinka had become established as one of Africa's foremost playwrights. He had written a small but distinguished corpus of poems, and several literary and critical essays. He brings to *The Interpreters* from his poetry a cryptic, image-laden style, from his drama a sense of setting and character, and from his essays a fluency of exposition and critical observation.

All these qualities combined with the style of narration give the work a complexity which has earned it the reputation of being difficult. Once Soyinka's technique is grasped, however, the book reveals itself as a well-conceived whole even though at first sight the parts may not seem to fit easily together. In fact there is little that is wasted. It is tightly written, giving the impression of having been totally conceived before the first word was set down.

The Technique of Narration. Soyinka does not narrate the events of the story chronologically; that is he does not start from the beginning, leading us through consecutive episodes to the end. The novel starts in the middle of the affairs of the main characters, and gradually builds up a picture of their histories, their

* Wole Soyinka, *The Interpreters* André Deutsch. All page references in these reading notes are to this edition.

characters, their frustrations and their successes by stepping back in time and filling in pictures of their past, and sometimes darting from the present into the future to complete a particular picture of an individual or a situation.

Thus the novel opens with a strange sentence by Sagoe: 'Metal on concrete jars my drink lobes', and moves straight into a scene of confusion as various characters dash for shelter from a cloudburst. Gradually the scene builds up – the tables, chairs, dancers, and the band – and we know the scene is a night-club. From this present we are soon ushered into a scene from the past when one of the characters who has just been introduced, Egbo, retreats in his thoughts, taking us with him to an earlier episode of an inconclusive boat trip, and the choice which had faced him then: whether to make the break with his way of life and go on to take over his gradfather's small kingdom, or continue in his job at the foreign office. As the choice is put later, it is one between 'the war-lord of the creeks against the dull grey filing cabinet faces of the foreign office' (p. 12). Egbo makes his choice to 'go with the tide' and we return once more to the night-club. The cliché implies a comment on Egbo's choice.

The reader must be prepared for these changes in time, or he will make nothing of the novel. Sometimes the leap is into the future instead of the past. Thus Soyinka gives us a vivid picture of Sekoni the newly qualified engineer, as he leans on the deck of the ship that is bringing him home dreaming of how he is going to transform his country with his engineering skill (pp. 26–7). Then with-out a break he is swept from the height of his imagination to his office desk and shown performing humdrum tasks like signing bicycle permits and vouchers. His frustration and its consequences are then vividly portrayed without reference to the time it all takes to happen, and all this, while Sekoni is sitting with his friends in the night-club.

This style of narration gives the novel compactness of structure and a feeling of wholeness of conception. This feature is clearly one of the excellencies of the novel, but it is vain to deny that some of the difficulties complained of spring from this switch backwards and forwards in time.

The Characters. Several dozen characters appear in the course of the novel, but interest is centred on the five friends, Sagoe, journalist, Bandele and Kola, university lecturers, Egbo, foreign office, Sekoni, engineer and sculptor, Lasunwon, lawyer. These are all young professional men trying to make careers, enjoy themselves, produce art, and generally influence affairs in their own country. By no means a band of saints, their great virtue is their vigour and their determination to think for themselves. They soon find themselves barking their enthusiasm and ideals against hidebound corruption, vested interests, and a hollow hypocritical conventional morality. The characters who exemplify

43

these evils are often important people in society. Sir Derinola is a respected judge and a member of a newspaper board who is not, however, averse to demanding small bribes before doing his duty. In this regard he is no better than the loud and more obviously empty Chief Winsala. Professor Oguazor, a stuffy university professor with a superficial concern for 'merals' (this absurdly affected pronunciation is itself a comment) is an older version of the younger Faseyi (radiologist) and Dr Lumoye, who both seem destined to go the same way, offering a superficial brand of morality; in the symbolism of the play, plastic fruit for the real thing.

The author distinguishes between individuals in these two main groups of characters. For example each of the friends has quite clearly defined characteristics. Egbo's tendency towards a glib atheism is balanced by the intense religious concern of Sekoni. The difference in the outlook of these two friends is well illustrated when during the night club storm a building crashes. Egbo is glad that one unit of the slum has been demolished:

'The sky-line has lost a tooth from its long-rotted gums'.
Sekoni is concerned for those rendered homeless:

'Th-th-they will b-b-be homeless to . . . n-night. P-p-perhaps we should stop there and see if w-w-we can h-h-h-help.' (p. 16).

Similarly among the other characters, Chief Winsala walks brazenly into Sagoe's hotel, and while drinking his gin, asks him for a bribe in exchange for a job. Sir Derin, the respected judge sits in the car outside waiting for the spoils, until tired of waiting, he gingerly steps in to observe the progress of the negotiations – from behind a pillar.

Soyinka has a great gift for quick and economical character portrayal. The nameless Managing Director is a very effective portrait of an empty, corrupt leader, sailing aimlessly all over the world at his country's expense, collecting junk. Soyinka invents an idiom which suits him perfectly – a mixture of pomposity and just sub-standard English: 'How can an interview be conductable with someone who is not taking the matter serious?' (pp. 78–9) Professor Oguazor's stuffiness, the superficiality of his 'meral' pose is transparent in his affected 'We mesn't keep the ledies wetting'.

Among the women, characters like Dehinwa, Sagoe's emancipated girl-friend, and the unnamed self-possessed girl student who gets pregnant for Egbo, are feminine versions of the new interpreters. They face life with no illusions, and without an affectation of coyness. The older Mrs Faseyi on the other hand illustrates the fact that enlightenment is no monopoly of the young. She and her expatriate daughter-in-law make common cause against her stuffy, phoney son. Simi, the seductress is also memorable. Soyinka's ambivalent portrayal shows at once her charm and its dangerous consequences. When her

44

eyes met Egbo's for the first time, he 'reeled with the wanton strike of a snake and welcomed the poison through his veins'. (p. 53) She is persistently the the 'queen bee'. The imagery of sting and poison makes the point without excessive description.

Joe Golder, the American, and Peter, the visiting journalist, are two of the expatriates treated. These two characters are vivid enough, for Soyinka hardly mentions a character who does not take on a haunting reality. Nevertheless they, and to a lesser extent Lazarus and Noah, seem to have been stuck in to fill the canvass. Indeed, in an otherwise tightly textured novel, the only sign of slack writing is in the sections where these two appear. Joe Golder suffers in particular. As individual portraits the two are as successful as any other portraits in the book, but they do not have the same inevitability as most of the other characters.

Lazarus is a deeper study of the beach prophet than Soyinka's hero in *The Trials of Brother Jero*. Even so, his full potential as a serious study is not realized; Kola's Pantheon seems a rather tame destiny for one who rose from the dead.

Language. The Interpreters was written by a poet. This is clear from the sensitive use of imagery throughout. The novel itself is an extended metaphor. The technique frequently reminds us of the author's poetry. A few parallel passages will illustrate this point:

'Bandele filled himself *wall-gecko*, into a corner' (p. 16)

'Where darkness crouches *egret wings* Your love is gossamer. 'Requiem'

Sekoni's death in a car crash is from the same imagination which produced 'Death at Dawn':

'A futile heap of metal, and Sekoni's body lay surprised across the open door, showers of laminated glass around him, his beard one fastness of blood and wet earth.' (p. 155)

                                    Brother
Silenced in the startled hug of
Your invention – is this mocked grimace
This closed contortion – I? ('Death at Dawn')

(The instant transformation of life to death which a car accident often effects is a frequent theme in Soyinka's work. It is almost the basis of *The Road*.)

The same sacrifice image is the basis of these two passages though their effects are different:

45

'Joe Golder had assumed an after-sacrifice fierceness, bits of slaughtered feather sticking to his face.' (p. 102)

Cascades
Of white feather – flakes . . . but is proved
A futile rite. ('Death at Dawn')

To take up the question of metaphor again, Soyinka continually uses this device to fuse two images together and give us a double picture in one action. Egbo's fat guardian's figure is fused with that of the *amala* which made him fat: 'his flabby paunch overflowing downwards, huge rolls of soft *amala* over a leather rim.' Similarly Usaye the albino girl is a moth: 'A warm yellow moth brushed him on the cheek and wedged itself between him and the low table. It peered short-sightedly into the glass in his hand, drank from it, screwed its face at the bitter taste. Then it pressed its face almost against Kola's relaxed fingers from which the nuts had nearly begun to drop. With her back against him, nuzzling his face with short plaited yellow hair stood an Albino girl' (p. 48).

Soyinka avoids either obviousness or prurience in his description of Egbo's first sexual encounter with Simi by portraying the episode through poetic imagery:

And a lone pod strode the baobab on the tapering thigh,
leaf shorn, and high mists swirl him, haze-splitting
storms, but the stalk stayed him . . . .

parting low mists in a dark cave . . .
in darkness let me lie, in
darkness cry . . . (p. 60).

(Typical of the structural style of the novel is the fact that this episode is broken off at this point to be resumed as late as page 123.)

The fat dancer in the night-club is 'Owolebi of the squelching oranges' (p. 122); the policeman on point duty averting his eyes from Noah's predicament is 'Pontius Pilate . . . washing his hands in the stream of traffic' (p. 114). Professor Oguazor's daughter is 'the plastic apple of his eye' (p. 149). Thus Soyinka by the short cut of metaphor imprisons features, ideas, and personalities in a brief phrase.

The syntax is often highly condensed, as some of these examples have shown, and what runs between two full stops may not be a conventional prose sentence, although it conveys meaning and suggestion. For example, the Managing Director and his radiogram reflect each other: 'Like two halves of a broad bean, the pachydermous radio-gram and the Managing Director.' Not a 'sentence', but a highly compact meaningful and suggestive statement nevertheless.

Throughout, the author's feeling for words is obvious; not only existing ones but those he creates himself, like 'matterdom' (p. 76). And 'tightwad' could seldom have been more suggestively used than on page 107. Soyinka can make poetry out of the most unlikely material. The picture of the night soil men is a good example: 'faceless janitors, pail surmounted silences, short-broomed swathings flitting dusk to dawn, the cherished emblems of the vintage air' (p. 102).

Indeed Soyinka's gift for making something out of anything could have its disadvantages. The danger is well signposted by Boyd M. Berry in a review of Soyinka's play *Kongi's Harvest* when he writes, 'Mr Soyinka must reckon with the fact that he can arouse our interest, and in non-essential matters, handle that talent carefully.' (*Ibadan* 23 p. 55)

In this novel the playful essayist in Mr Soyinka occasionally prevails over the novelist, making for example, the philosophy of voidancy (a good joke to start with) loom too large, and assume a disproportionate importance in relation to the rest of the work. Perhaps Sagoe's 'drink lobes' also play too large a part for an organ that is literary rather than physiological.

The Interpreters as a whole takes a critical look at the human situation in modern Nigeria. Because of Soyinka's allusive style of writing there is a great deal of incidental satire. The main satirical butt is phoniness; the phoniness which makes a judge pronounce oracular sentences from the bench, but wait behind pillars for a bribe; the callousness with which people talk about moral issues while totally ignoring the human predicament of those involved. Nowhere is this better illustrated than in the final scene of the novel where the outwardly respectable old guard (and they are by no means all old in years) and the new interpreters (not all young either; the old Mrs. Faseyi would qualify) as it were confronting each other. The Oguazors mouth their unpitying formulas about 'meral terpitude'; Lumoye, the doctor, covers up his failure to seduce the young student with malicious gossip about her. But her dignity and courage, along with the frank, sometimes even crude honesty of the interpreters shows up the thinness of the veneer of the old guard.

NOTES

p. 7 drink lobes: A poetic rather than a physiological organ. It seems to be the seat of all Sagoe's sensibilities. Sagoe's own explanation of this elusive organ is given on p. 35.

p. 8 'Two puddles . . . .' – A flashback to an earlier episode when Egbo tried to decide whether to take his grandfather's chieftaincy or to continue to work in the foreign office.

p. 8 'Your Chinese sages . . .' – A favourite thought of poets not only Chinese. See for example John Donne:

Nor are (although the river keeps the name)
Yesterdaies waters and todaies the same.
    ('Of the Progresse of the Soule – Second Anniversary')

p. 8 Oshun – One of the principal Yoruba river deities from whom the river takes its name. There is a famous Oshun Shrine at Oshogbo.

p. 9 Sekoni the stutterer is a deep thinker. His deep religious attitude contrasts with Egbo's flippant atheism. Soyinka distinguishes his 'interpreters' very well by their personal characteristics.

p. 10 A good incidental glimpse at the futility of war – 'fishes over whom the hunting rights were fought fed on the disputants'. Osa, the name of Egbo's grandfather's Kingdom.

p. 12 Egbo's choice well expressed – 'the warlord of the creeks against the dull grey filing cabinets of the foreign office.' His descision on this occasion is expressed in words which imply a mild condemnation; he decides to go 'with the tide'.

p. 17 Egbo's adventures with his guardian – an example of Soyinka's neat economical narrative and descriptive technique.

pp. 20–21 The *apala* band another good economical description in depth.

p. 22 Sekoni has been making a sketch of the dancing woman and distorting her features in the process, giving her a goitre among other things. This arouses Sekoni's 'cobbles'.

p. 27 The sudden translation from the excitement of Sekoni's imagination to his boring desk job makes his frustration plain without need for excessive comment.

p. 27 A good example of Soyinka's satirical portraiture is the Chairman of Sekoni's board.

p. 36 The contrast between Dehinwa, now a sophisticated city girl, and her mother and aunt is very marked. Their painful and unnecessary solicitude for her is described in p. 139 as 'blood cruelty'. In spite of their fears, however, Dehin is no cheap slut.

pp. 37–40 Monica is contrasted with her husband Ayo. Monica is natural in her reactions while Ayo is pretentious and over-conscious of protocol. Their incompatibility is hinted at here. She and Kola have a lot more in common. Usaye is something of a bond between them. By p. 50 Kola is beginning to feel 'an insidious beginning of a great yearning'.

p. 50 Simi: The language with which she is described suggests not only at her great attractiveness but also the fatal nature of this attraction. We are reminded of cannibals (p. 50), snakes and bees (pp. 53, 54) 'the beast that lay in wait to swallow him' (p. 54), and the thornbush (p. 56).

pp. 59–60 The interrupted portrayal of this encounter has been commented on in the Introduction.

p. 63 Sagoe's nightmare or prolonged day-dream is the means of satirising the corrupt judge. The wardrobe, a symbol of cheapness and lack of good taste – 'cheap wood overlaid with varnish' – makes a good symbolic home for Sir Derin. It is interesting too that Sir Derin is naked (p. 68) as it were bared of the facade which he had kept up in life. Now, in death 'the truth has lately begun to matter'. The nightmare leads back to Sagoe's first encounter with the newspaper world (p. 68). A highly satirical passage.

p. 70 The voidante philosophy: This is Soyinka the lighthearted essayist – in the mood of 'Salutations to the Gut' (*Reflections*, ed. Ademola, F., A.U.P., Lagos, 1962). The 'philosophy' is defined on p. 72.

p. 71 'She farted like a beast'. Here and elsewhere Soyinka adopts a Chaucerian directness in matters flatulent.

p. 73 Winsala's entry – a dramatic near-fantasy. From now on the satirical touches come thick and fast. Sir Derin, the chief, the Managing Director, are all vehicles for the satire on falseness and corruption.

p. 91 Note how the real image of the waiter dressed in green – 'greenbottle' – fades into that of flies ('greenbottle' is formed by analogy from 'bluebottle') '... swarm of greenbottles on fruit ... buzz ...'

p. 91 Winsala's thoughts given in a series of proverbs to suggest his glibness.

p. 96 Sekoni's dreams had ended in frustration. Sagoe's attempt to publicise the story meets the same fate; obstructed by the corrupt establishment. On p. 98 the situation is neatly summarised: 'Because the good Knight must be saved, they roast the sheik'.

p. 98 Sekoni's quarrel with his father for marrying a Christian girl (they were Moslems), his illness, his father's remorse, his pilgrimage are all portrayed in the compact oblique way of the novel. All Sekoni's frustrated energy at last finds expression in sculpture.

p. 99 'Their run of forty times' – One of the activities of the Mecca pilgrimage is the circling of the Kaaba, which contains the Black Stone, seven times. Forty here is an exaggeration.

p. 102 Kola was painting a Pantheon of Yoruba deities, using his friends as his models. Egbo was Ogun, the explorer, warrior, creative god. Golder was Erinle, an animal spirit, Lazarus was Esumare, the rainbow, Usaye was Obaluwaiye's hand-maid. See the glossary for complete list of figures in the Pantheon.

p. 102 Esau and Jacob – Obvious reference to the biblical story of the usurpation of Esau's birthright. A number of Soyinka's allusions are to the Bible. Dehin is referred to appropriately as Jael (p. 67) for sending a pain through Sagoe's head. The Biblical Jael had driven a tent nail through Sisera's head. See *Judges* chapter 4, verse 21.

p. 106 Sagoe's remark about Dehin's grandmother leads back to his first encounter with her ... 'The grandmother *had* taken a long look etc.' This old lady is a grand matriarchal figure uninhibited by prudish attitudes to sex and marriage.

p. 111 Ikoyi: the old colonial residential area of Lagos now occupied by the African successors of the old administrators. Soyinka tilts at what is pictured here as the deadness of their lives.

p. 113 This section (Section 8) is primarily concerned with the chase and rescue of the young thief, Noah, but it is also a vehicle for satire. In it is portrayed the more general chase of the petty thieves by the bigger thieves in authority; it is the story of the mass, strong only in numbers bearing down on the individual. There is much implied social criticism here.

pp. 119–20 'Perfunctory doles ....' – This is the sort of passage that could be called difficult. Soyinka portrays Egbo's thoughts with the same headlong tumble with which the mind can run through its business, recalling images formed in childhood: the Osun grove, the bridge etc.

p. 123 'Egbo stirred in his sleep....' – Without notice we are taken back to the episode with Simi, p. 60. This kind of sudden switchback occurs frequently in the novel.

p. 126 Egbo's strange whim to pass the night under the bridge is no doubt connected with the associations of a bridge in his childhood at Oshogbo.

p. 128 Egbo growing out of Simi? It is interesting that the thought first occurs to him after his meeting with the self-assured undergraduate girl.

p. 128 This encounter develops rapidly; and although we are supposed to see in it the independence of the two people and the fact that they instantly find themselves totally in tune, it is one episode in the novel which seems forced and rather stagey.

p. 136 'And then it's ....' A typical side swipe at the rapid touchy assertions of nationalism which sometimes pass for the real thing.

p. 139 'A buzz of wit....' – With the Professor's party Soyinka's satirical genius comes into its own. Into this deadly sedate house 'the house of death', devoid of any real initiative, and enslaved to what other people say is right, enters the iconoclast Sagoe. His outrageous thoughts are fortunately not uttered ('humming inside him' p. 141) but soon the oppressive atmosphere of artificiality (the plastic fruit and foliage are symbolic) get him down, and he starts throwing things. By the time Sagoe bends and kisses the plastic rose decorating Mrs. Oguazor's navel the scene has become a hilarious farce, reminiscent of the adventures of another young hero, similarly placed – lucky Jim in Kingsley Amis' novel of that name.

p. 155 The parallel between Sekoni's death and Soyinka's poem 'Death at Dawn' has been mentioned in the Introduction.

pp. 155–6 A reflection of the differences between the interpreters is their differing reactions to Sekoni's death.

p. 160 Lasunwon reappears – the least developed of the group. He is more of a foil to the others.

p. 162 'Its good business . . . religion'. Soyinka has a more extended study of a businessman-prophet in Brother Jero, the leading character in his play *The Trials of Brother Jero*. Lazarus' portrait is not of an obvious charlatan. There are suggestions of complexity which are not fully explored.

p. 164 A good example of Soyinka's disregard for conventional prose structure is the description of Kola's grief – 'Kola risen . . . in his hands.'

p. 164 Lazarus and his church steal the centre, and almost edge the interpreters out.

p. 177 Kola's facile blasphemy is countered by Lazarus' quiet assertion of faith.

p. 188 Golder is something of a bonus in this novel. Interesting though his character is, it seems to be superarogatory to the structure. He is linked at the end with Noah's death.

p. 202 Faseyi is almost overdone. His type does exist but his portraiture lacks the characteristic subtlety of the rest of the novel.

p. 203 'So the pollen is blowing. . . .' – Kola's deepening feelings for Monica referred to here.

pp. 203–4 A quick glimpse at the tussles of exuberant students with authority.

p. 209 To describe Mrs. Faseyi as a stallion sounds odd, but it suggests her magnificent figure and personality. There is something male about her.

p. 212 Mrs. Faseyi is almost more emancipated than the young interpreters.

p. 213 To expose Ayo's pretentiousness he is isolated in feeling not only from his wife but also from his mother.

p. 215 The trials of a homosexual in an alien society.

p. 216 'Cockroach gut . . .' as a description of the literal-minded swot this is a good image.

p. 217 *Giovanni's Room* – a novel by James Baldwin which has been described as one of the most sensitive portrayals of a homosexual relationship in fiction.

p. 220 The novel has resumed its tense narrative texture; the almost simultaneous depiction of the past and the present. Sekoni's sculpture goes back years for its inspiration. All this suddenly merges with the adventure of Kola and Egbo's search for the church.

pp. 223–4 Noah seems to be subjected to a kind of ordeal by fire which he fails. The details are not very clear.

p. 235 Egbo's affinity with the mysterious undergraduate girl has been noted. Here he says of her, 'this is the new woman of my generation'. Gradually her image seems to eclipse even the reality of Simi.

p. 236 Noah reacts in fear where the thugs would have reacted with violence at Golder's homosexual advances, and falls to his death.

p. 236 Egbo's reaction to his discovery of Golder's nature is one of physical disgust.

p. 246 Egbo is lost in a reverie of childhood.

p. 248 Dr. Lumoye's raucous levity contrasts (even in her absence) with the unnamed girl's dignity and assurance, and it is clear who has the more valid moral code. His callously improper suggestions to the girl expose the hollowness of his conventional morality. Professor Oguazor's 'meral' stand is no less callous and phoney.

REVIEWS

RUBADIRI & KAYIRA

David Rubadiri, *No Bride Price*, East Africa Publishing House, Nairobi 1967
Legson Kayira, *The Looming Shadow*, Longmans 1968

Determined readers of the African novel soon develop a special faculty for detecting the approach of the *simpliste* hero. This character exists for the sole purpose of falling into every trap that modern Africa can present — and with the minimum of resistance in every case. He is a formula constructed by the author to demonstrate various general propositions about a transitional society. As a fictional creation, however, he is almost invariably shallow, lifeless and dull. We tire of the predictable naïvety of his responses to situations which are the stock of every bar-room conversation, of his insincere nostalgia for the 'simple' life of the village and of his utter lack of tough-mindedness, energy, or resilience.

Unfortunately, there are elements of this figure in Lombe, the hero of David Rubadiri's *No Bride Price*. Mr Rubadiri has sought to place his novel at the nexus of those questions of sexual and personal morality, power and social control, order and freedom, which bedevil a nameless independent state in modern Africa. But this protagonist is too weak for the purpose, because his creator is so concerned with stressing Lombe's essential innocence that he too often appears merely simpleminded.

At the beginning of the book, Lombe has suddenly been promoted to the post of Principal Secretary in a government department. He shies every time his telephone rings and registers general awe at the eminence of his position. His new world is destroyed when the girl he has been sleeping with turns out to be his unknown half-sister from the countryside; and when his Minister, piqued because Lombe fails to procure for him the daughter of the Indian Ambassador, has him framed on a false charge. Both these crucial events, however, suffer from a radical improbability. We are not told how Lombe managed to grow up in the same village without knowing his half-sister's identity. And the most lubricous Minister might hesitate before seducing the daughter of an Ambassador. It is no surprise when these events are overtaken by a military coup, planned by Lombe's closest friends, again without his knowledge.

How much more exciting it would be to have a hero who is alert, complex, self-aware and stuffed with ideas, yet still comes to grief. His fate could teach us something about the real nature of the temptations and moral obfuscations which attend sudden power. Mr Rubadiri has observed these with an eye that is decent and humane, but his hero is too flabby an instrument to expose them fully. The gifts of sympathy and observation that are evident in *No Bride Price* will come into their own when Mr Rubadiri writes a novel of denser and more organized texture, centred upon a hero who is not perpetually surprised by life.

When Lombe's eyes are finally opened to the realities of the world he inhabits, he speaks with a voice that is the author's rather than his own:

'We all saw people like Chozo turning into beasts. They needed our help, but instead we sat down with them, drinking and procuring girls for them, afraid to speak out, watching them destroy themselves and the beautiful things our people stand for. . . .' Lombe's sudden wisdom is too much like a divine visitation. And the military coup which ends the novel is not, as we all know now, the panacea for such evils or the opening of a new milennium. More often it is the opening of a spiral that leads downwards to greater violence and division.

Legson Kayira is another new novelist from Malawi. *The Looming Shadow* is a fairly genial satire upon petty tyranny, superstition and revenge in a small mountain village near Lake Nyasa. The blacksmith Musyani has been persecuted by suspicions that he has bewitched his neighbour Matenda and caused his death. The pompous headman has largely protected Musyani against these suspicions, yet it is he who is imprisoned when Musyani seeks revenge by reporting the whole matter to the white District Officer. Mr Kayira adopts no particular attitude towards his story of village intrigue, but handles everyone with detached amusement and considerable felicity of style. Here Mwenimuzi, the village headman, dismisses his messenger so that he may have a *tête-à-tête* with the native doctor about the witchcraft case: 'In the meantime Mwenimuzi noticed the messenger standing at attention and lifting his braceleted hand, pointed to the door, motioning the messenger to step out. The latter, after an exaggerated salute instead of the usual long low bow, stepped out of the room gracefully. Once outside he actually shouted to himself in a grave and ceremonious pitch "Dismissed!" and walked casually to his barn, where, still wearing his uniform, he attended to the milking of his cow.' Mr Kayira's title may arouse suspicions that we are to be treated to another of those simple juxtapositions of the looming shadow of the past and the shining light of the missionary/administrative present. Fortunately, his poise is too sure to permit that to happen. Malice is exhibited by both sides in this village dispute and to the end we are not certain whether Musyani supposes himself to have practiced witchcraft or not. The disadvantage of this impartial distribution of favours is that we do not greatly care. **Gerald Moore**

Aimé Césaire, *Return to my native land*
Présence Africaine, Paris 1968

It was in 1939 that Aimé Césaire's *Cahier d'un reteur au pays natal* first appeared in an obscure Parisian journal, *Volontés*. It was rescued from possible oblivion by André Breton, the leader of the Surrealist movement, who met Césaire during the war in Martinique, and was so taken by the poem that he arranged its republication in New York in a bilingual edition to which he contributed an enthusiastic and eulogious preface in which he declared the work as 'the greatest lyrical monument of the age'.

In the years that followed the war, and which saw the progressive development of the Négritude movement among French speaking Negro intellectuals, Césaire's long poem became the central piece in the literature of the movement, expressing in a single poetic statement the attitudes and orientation of the new consciousness embodied in Négritude. Césaire revised his poem to an appreciable extent for the definitive edition published by Présence Africaine in 1956, which has now become the standard version of the work. The publication of an English translation of this latter version has been for a long time a pressing need, the more so as the New York edition has been out of print almost since it appeared. Présence Africaine must therefore be congratulated for issuing this new bilingual edition, with an English text based on the earlier New York edition, but brought up to date in conformity with Césaire's revisions as contained in the 1956 Paris edition.

This republication in English of Césaire's

famous work now affords to a wider circle of readers an insight into what constitutes the appeal, and indeed the power, of this singular poem. It is easy to understand André Breton's enthusiastic response to Césaire's work when it is borne in mind that what struck him was first and foremost the technique of *Cahier*, which appeared to him as an exemplary illustration of his own ideas of art, as a work which by its force of expression as well as its purpose bore a particularly striking testimony to the canons of thought and expression which he had been preaching for some twenty years.

Cahier's importance today is due mainly to a basic detail to which Breton's preface paid surprisingly scant attention — namely, its racial theme. Much less than the specific quality of art which Césaire demonstrates in the poem. What gives his work its present status as a classic is obviously the fact that it is the most impassioned statement in all literature of the racial sentiment of the black man in his historical and social relation to the Western world. *Cahier* explicitly communicates the sense of an immediate social reality rather than the perception of a world of the spirit. The declared aim of Césaire is to give voice to a collective agony and to a collective feeling, and he does so with a warmth and energy deriving from personal involvement: 'My tongue shall serve those miseries which have no tongue, my voice the liberty of those who founder in the dungeons of despair.'

It is this public theme, sustained in a single burst of expression by a relentless poetic inspiration, which accounts for the tremendous impact which the poem has had upon the imagination and upon the ideas of a whole generation of French-speaking Negro intellectuals, an impact which has grown with the years to such an extent that it can be righly asserted that no other single work has had so profound an influence in shaping the very spirit and in determining the very movement of contemporary attitudes within the French speaking Negro world. The very fact that the term which designates their specific cultural and ideological movement comes out of *Cahier* is sufficient testimony to the unique

position and role which belong to the work. For if the rational definition of the movement has been the work of L.S. Senghor, to Césaire belongs certainly the merit of having first, in this long poem, given a deliberate and conscious articulation to the upsurge of feelings which remain the basic groundwork of the basic of Négritude.

Yet the historical significance of *Cahier*, as well as the subsequent career of Césaire himself, may obscure for us today the fundamental paradox that governs all his work — that of a consciousness turning wholly against all the prevailing symbols of its own social world. Because over the last thirty years Césaire has consistently developed in all his poetry the implications of the reaction so forcefully announced by *Cahier* and thus accustomed us to the perspective in which his entire work is rooted, the total and dramatic nature of the initial reaction is now somewhat lost on us. Yet the significance of the poem resides precisely in the distinctiveness of tone and vision which it introduced into the self expression and self awareness of the men of his generation, placed in a similar situation like him. The well known problems of assimilation and cultural duality played an important role in this reaction. More pertinent in Césaire's case was his awareness of the absurdity involved in his intellectual conditioning to the system of values of a culture which in its concrete manifestation in social terms represented, as far as the black man was concerned, a total and flagrant contradiction: 'I salute the three centuries which support my civic rights and my minimised blood.'

Poised uncomfortably between the conflicting frames of reference of his social and individual awareness, Césaire's gesture, in this poem, as in this later work, was to work out his own personal redemption by an act of rejection and defiance, which is in reality a refusal of the double consciousness with which he was saddled. Complementary to this is his resolute movement towards the unity of his essential self: 'I force the vitelline membrane which separates me from myself.'

The poetic attitude in *Cahier* is one with its author's conscious choice in the real world, and stems directly from the essential ambivalence implied in his cultural, social and historical (as well as literary) antecedents, both as an individual and as a poet.

As the full title of the poem indicates, the whole programme of *Cahier* involves a return to a clearly defined and stable sense of identity, of which the poet makes his native island the living symbol. This explains the Caribbean emphasis of the poem, for Césaire is concerned with the West Indies not only as a concrete social and political reality, but also as an area of his own mind and sensibility, as a universe involving whole being:

> At the end of the dawn, this most essential country, restored to my inmost greed, not with wide sweetness but with the tormented concentration of fat breasts of hills with an accidental palm-tree like a hardened germ, the abrupt exaltations of torrents and, from Trinité to Grand-Rivière, the hysterical sucking of the sea.

The long evocation of the physical and human misery of the Antilles with which the poem opens is thus an essential part of the unfolding process of self-knowledge and identification which is the fundamental scheme of the poem. It is by exploring the stark reality of his native island which constitutes his immediate human and spiritual universe that Césaire traverses and recognizes the concrete geography of his intimate self.

This means nothing less than that *Cahier* was born out of a compelling inner necessity, to which the historical and ideological implications of the poem must be considered secondary. Its force is that of a personal statement, its enduring strength lies in the fact that Césaire has effected a conjunction of the real and the imaginative in a way which gives to his poetic expression an extension of its meanings, reverberating into the deep layers of experience. Thirty years after it was first written, *Cahier* has lost little of its pertinence, and even when its political references shall have been superseded by historical developments, it will retain its value as the epic record of the spiritual adventure of a singular poetic consciousness. **Abiola Irele**

LETTERS

Ronald Dathorne's analysis of the opening poem of Okigbo's *Heavensgate* in the first issue of this magazine struck me as being that type in which the critic pursues his own inventive pleasure with little regard to the inviolability of context and of what could reasonably be accepted as meaningful within that context – in this case the cultural. I think that in reading a sexual motif into Okigbo's poem Mr Dathorne unwittingly in the process overstretched his imagination to the point of absurdity. Indeed, if the syndrome of 'ritualistic abnormalities' he outlines were valid – 'strong phallic associations'/'goddess as whore'/'sexual conquest'/'insent' – Okigbo's poem would be

utter nonsense, to me at any rate. But it cannot be.

My understanding of Okigbo here is that this is a religious poem pure and simple, of human estrangement from divine guidance, repentance and quest for possible salvation. It is a solemn prayer in a state of contrition and can hardly admit of anything as monstrous as incest. It is also one of the early and most straightforward of Okigbo's poems. Idoto is a water goddess and her 'watery presence' derives directly from this, not from Mr Dathorne's invented 'initial crime' – whatever that is. The oilbean is supposedly the sacred tree of Idoto worship and the logical place for the repentant prodigal to return to. It is there that he can fully feel the awesome power of the goddess, the focal point of the legend in which he is now 'lost'. He is 'leaning' on the sacred tree to demonstrate his recognition of its power to support.

This is a far cry from Mr Dathorne's interpretation:

> 'The familiar image of the tree appears,
> the tree that cannot hope to support him.
> Its relevance is that it suggests strong
> phallic associations which are meant to
> contrast with the suggestion of "lost in
> your legend" or the goddess as whore.'

And one may ask: just what leads Mr Dathorne to all that?

The leaning posture itself seems to be part of the demonstration of humility expressed in 'naked' and 'barefoot' (nothing here points to the conclusion that 'the protagonist only comes in feigned humility') and the two words carry unmistakable religious connotations of a Biblical nature – *naked*[1]: the condition in which the prodigal son returns to his father, the inability to hide anything from an all-seeing divinity, a state of sin or shame; *barefoot*[2]: part of a manifestation of nakedness, also a sign of respect before a sacred phenomenon. I detect nothing here to suggest nudity (in a pornographic sense) which Mr Dathorne sees as 'a pointer towards the ritualistic abnormalities the devoted must undergo – here incest.' What I see is the same kind of invocation of divine powers for protection and salvation that Okigbo expresses with solemn veneration in several poems. An example is the first canto of *Lament of the Drums*:

Antelopes of oilbean groves, cross-country runners.
Swifter than beacon flash, we invoke you.

Hide us, deliver us from our nakedness

Even in the second canto of the same poem where a definite sexual element is present in lines like:

Fold – on – fold of raped, naked water –
What memory has the sea of her lover?

and Palinurus the protagonist is 'alone' and 'naked' and 'resigned,' the poet towards the end calls on

Fishermen out there in the dark – O you
Who rake the waves or chase their wake –

to

Weave for him a shadow out of *their* laughter
For a dumb child to hide his nakedness

(emphases mine) and there is a reference to Palinurus' 'inviolable image.'

Obviously, I have not attempted here anything like a close analysis of this extremely complex poem, just as in the case of the poem that forms the subject of this discussion, for the purpose of this article, I have not considered the subtle artistic devices by which Okigbo obtains his effects. My interest centres on the total meaning those effects contribute to. I am also of course not denying the liberty of individual responses, especially where we are dealing with symbolic art. But I would insist that interpretations of art do have their limits.

Mr Dathorne's misinterpretation of Okigbo raises two grave issues. The first, of a general kind, is the danger inherent in all over-ingenious interpretations of art. The second and more specific, and for my purpose the more serious, has to do with African art – here the literary. How come that Mr Dathorne, a generally competent and versatile critic can make such enormous errors of judgment? The answer is simple: Mr Dathorne has brought to bear on African literature without modification all the concepts belonging to modern Western art, with its belief in desecration and

absurd abstractions of phallic symbolism everywhere. If we accept the dictum that art in spite of its universal applicability first derives from and is an expression of values, concepts and attitudes of a particular cultural group at any one time, it follows then that critical norms cannot be transferred wholesale from the art tradition of one cultural area to another. This is a fact of criticism many of our writers have insisted must be recognized. That some of them – notably Joseph Okpaku in *Journal of the New African Literature and the Arts* (Spring 1967) – have done so with polemical jingoism should not obscure the essential truth. Art is culturally based and the critic cannot afford to ignore this fact. Okigbo may be one of our most Westernised writers but he is at the same time very African. How central the cultural question is in literature was emphasized by E. N. Obiechina in his recent and very enlightening article in Number 1 of this journal. It was in recognition of this that John Povey in the same issue approached certain areas of J. P. Clark's poetry with such caution and such modesty.

I suppose being African, my response to the sacredness of our deity in relation to Okigbo's poem is partly a matter of instinct. It may not come first hand to people whose cultures are different but they can and must be initiated in order to pontificate meaningfully on a lot of African literature – and African critics who have lost their roots to the soil of other cultures will join this age-group – many of us have had to go through such arduous rites to be able to squeak at all about the literature of other lands. If Mr Dathorne's misinterpretation of Okigbo is surprising, it is because he has had a long and close association with this continent. The greatest tribute we can pay to Okigbo's memory is not to trample on but to revere the essence of his message.

Ime Ikkideh
Department of English
University of Ghana.
September 1968
   [1] V. the Bible, *Ex.* 32.25; *Heb.* 4.23; *Rev.* 3.17; 26.25
   [2] *Ex.* 3.5; *Josh.* 5.15

BIBLIOGRAPHY

Compiled by Hans Zell

This is the second in a series of bibliographic listings appearing regularly in this journal.

Its aim is to provide comprehensive and up-to-date information on new and recently published literature by African authors. Unfortunately, at this stage at least, it is by no means complete, and I am particularly anxious to obtain details of 'out-of-the-way' and non-trade publications. Publishers of such material are invited to submit to me details of relevant books so that I may list them in future bibliographies.

The scope of the bibliography is limited to *creative* writing, but also includes critical and reference works, and anthologies. Political, historical, religious literature, etc. are excluded, as are Children's readers and similar material. Individual poems appearing in periodicals are only cited if they are of some considerable length.

Note:

The entire Summer issue (v. 11, no. 4) of *The Literary Review* (Farleigh Dickinson University, Rutherford, N.J.) is devoted to African writing. In addition to the short stories and essays quoted below, it includes poetry by the following authors: Amason, O. O. Amali, George Awoonor-Williams, Jim Chaplin, Joe De Graft, Romanus N. Egudu, Matei Markwei, John Roberts, John Ruganda, Proscovia Rwakyaka, John Ssemuwanga, and Okogbule Wonodi.

Similarly, the Summer issue (v. 1, no. 4) of *African Arts/Arts d'Afrique* (African Studies Center, University of California at Los Angeles) concentrates particularly upon the literature of Africa. There are poems by Cosmo Pieterse, Ismail Choonara, Arthur Nortje, Ishak Mohammed El Khalifa Sherif, Francois-Borgia Marie Evembé, and Khadambi Asalache. Other contributions are included in the bibliography.

PART I: PERIODICAL LITERATURE

AIDOO, AMA ATA
'Other versions'
in: *The Literary Review*, v. 11, no. 4, p. 459–68 (Short story)

ALLEN, SAMUEL
'Two writers: Senghor and Soyinka' in Negro Digest, June 67, p. 54–67

ANDRADE, MARIO DE
'La poésie africaine d'expression portugaise'
in: *Présence Africaine*, 68, no. 65, p. 51–84

ANOZIE, S.O.
'Christopher Okigbo: A creative itinerary 1957–1967'
in: *Présence Africaine*, 67, no. 64, p. 158–61

BAME, K.N.
'Comic play in Ghana'
in: *African Arts/Arts d'Afrique*, v. 1, no. 4, Summer 68, p. 30–1 & 101

CROWLEY, J.
'Symbolism in African verbal art'
in: *African Arts/Arts d'Afrique*, v. 1, no. 4, Summer 68, 1. 14–16 & 116–17

DATHORNE, O.R.
'Tradition and the African Poet'
in: *Présence Africaine*, 67, no. 63, p. 202–6

DATHORNE, O.R.
'Okigbo understood: A study of two poems'
in: *African Literature Today*, v. 1, no. 1, 68, p. 19–23

DESANTI, DOMINIQUE
'Le conflict des cultures et *L'aventure ambigue*'
in: *African Arts/Arts d'Afrique*, v. 1, no. 4, Summer 68, p. 60–1 & 106–10

DIPOKO, MBELLA SONNE
'The first return'
in: *Présence Africaine*, 67, no. 64, p. 159–78
(Short story)

DORSINVILLE, ROGER
'Hinterland Mythology (in
English and French)'
in: *African Arts/Arts d'Afrique*,
v. 1, no. 4, Summer 68,
p. 42–7
(Liberian folk tales)
FREEMAN, R.A.
'Indoro Bush College'
in: *The Literary Review*, v. 11,
no. 4, p. 435–41
(Short story)
GASSEL, ITA
'Poésie dynastique du Rwanda
traditionnel'
in: *African Arts/Arts d'Afrique*,
v. 1, no. 4, Summer 68,
p. 73–98 & 123
GÉRARD. ALBERT S.
'African Literature in Rhodesia'
in: *Africa Report*, v. 13, no. 5,
May 68, p. 41–2
GÉRARD. ALBERT S.
'Bibliographical problems in
creative African writing'
in: *Jnl. of General Education*
v. 19, April 1, 67, p. 25–34
HANNA, JUDITH LYNNE
'Nkwa Di Iche:Dance plays of
Ubakala'
in: *Présence Africaine*, 68, no. 65,
p. 13–38
IKELLÉ-MATIBA, JEAN
Mélancolie et reverie: 12 poems
in: *Jnl. of the New African Lit.
& the Arts*, 67, no. 4,
p. 29–37
JONES, ELDRED
'African literature 1966–67
in: *African Forum*, v. 4,
Summer 67
JONES, ELDRED
'Show me first your penny'
in: *African Arts/Arts d'Afrique*,
v. 1, no. 4, Summer 68,
p. 55–8 & 118–22
(Short novel)
KACHINGWE, AUBREY
'My beautiful Fig'
in: *African Arts/Arts d'Afrique*,
v. 1, no. 4, Summer 68,
p. 62–4

(Short story)
KANE, MOHAMADOU
'Récherche et critique'
in: *African Arts/Arts d'Afrique*,
v. 1, no. 4, Summer 68,
p. 37–9 & 103–4
KASSAM, S.
'The child and the water-tap'
in: *The Literary Review*, v. 11,
no. 4, p. 467–8
(Short story)
KENNEDY, ELLEN C.
'A literary postscript on the
Dakar Festival'
in: *African Forum*, v. 4,
Summer 67
LARSON, CHARLES R.
'Nigerian drama comes of age'
in: *Africa Report*, v. 13, no. 5,
May 68, p. 55–7
LINDFORS, BERNTH
'The palm oil with which
Achebe's words are eaten'
in: *African Literature Today*,
v. 1, no. 1, 68, p. 2–18
McDOWELL, ROBERT E.
'Four Ghanaian novels'
in: *Jnl. of the New African Lit.
& Arts*, 67, no. 4, p. 22–7
(Discusses works by J.W.
Abruquah, Francis Selormey
and S.A. Konadu)
MOORE, GERALD
'The imagery of death in African
poetry'
in: *Africa*, v. 28, no. 1, Jan. 68,
p. 57–70
MOORE, GERALD
'Modern African literature and
tradition'
in: *African Affairs*, v. 66, 264,
July 67, p. 246–7
MOREH, S.
'Free verse (*al-shi r al-hurr*)
in modern Arabic literature:
Abu Shadi and his school,
1926–46'
in: *Bull. School of Oriental &
African Stud.*, v. 31, pt. 1, 68,
p. 28–51
NAIR, S.
'Mrs Kimble'

in: *The Literary Review* v. 11,
no. 4, p. 472–4
(Short story)
NORRIS, H.T.
'Shaykh Ma al-Aynayn
al-Qualqami in the folk
literature of the Spanish
Sahara, I'
in: *Bull, School of Oriental &
African Stud.*, v. 31, pt. 1, 68,
p. 113–36
NWAPA, FLORA
'Idu'
in: *African Arts/Arts d'Afrique*,
v. 1, no. 4, Summer 68,
p. 50–2
(An extract from Flora Nwapa's
forthcoming novel; see book
section, in 'Bibliography'
African Literature Today, no. 1)
NWAPA, FLORA
'My spoons are finished'
in: *Présence Africaine*, 67, no. 63,
p. 227–35
(Short story)
OBIECHINA, E.N.
'Cultural nationalism in modern
African creative literature'
in: *African Literature Today*,
v. 1, no. 1, 68, p. 24–35
OBIECHINA, E.N.
'Transition from oral to literary
tradition; pt. I'
in: *Présence Africaine*, 67, no. 63,
p. 140–61
OBIECHINA, E.N.
'Tutuola and the oral tradition,
pt. II'
in: *Présence Africaine*, 68, no. 65,
p. 85–105
OBUDO, NATHANIEL
'They stole our cattle'
in: *The Literary Review*, v. 11,
no. 4, p. 475–8
(Short story)
OKAFOR, CLEM ABIAZIEM
'The inscrutability of the Gods:
motivation of behaviour in
Chinua Achebe's Arrow of God'
in: *Présence Africaine*, 67, no. 63,
p. 207–14
OKPAKU, JOSEPH O.O.

'Under the Iroko tree'
in: *The Literary Review*, v. 11,
no. 4, p. 481–554
(Novella)
OKPAKU, JOSEPH O.O.
'The writer in politics –
Christopher Okigbo, Wole
Soyinka and the Nigerian
crisis.'
(A brief contemplation of a
fleeting thought and a passing
dream)
in: *Jnl. of the New African Lit.
& the Arts*, 67, no. 4, p. 1–13
PARICSY, PAUL
'A supplementary bibliography to
J.J. Jahn's Bibliography of
Neo-African Literature from
Africa, America and the
Caribbean'
in: *Jnl. of the New African Lit.
& the Arts*, 67, no. 4,
p. 70–82
POVEY, JOHN
'Epitaph to Christopher Okigbo'
in: *Africa Today*, v. 14, no. 6,
Dec. 67, p. 22–3
POVEY, J.
'The quality of African writing
today'

in: *The Literary Review*, v. 11,
no. 4, p. 403–21
POVEY, JOHN
' "Two hands a man has": The
Poetry of J.P.Clark'
in: *African Literature Today*,
v. 1, no. 1, 68, p. 36–47
RAMSARAN, J.A.
'African potential'
in: *Books Abroad*, Winter 67,
p. 39–40
RUORO, P.
'End of a month'
in: *The Literary Review*, v. 11,
no. 4, p. 423–9
(Short story)
SCHMIDT, NANCY J.
'Tutuola joins the mainstream of
Nigerian novelists'
in: *Africa Today*, v. 15, no. 3,
June/July 68, p. 22–7
SONGA, P.W.
'The Intruder'
in: *Jnl. of the New African Lit.
& the Arts*, 67, no. 4,
p. 38–42
(Short story)
THOMAS, PETER
' "Ride me Memories". A

memorial tribute to Christopher
Okigbo (1932–1967)'
in: *African Arts/Arts d'Afrique*,
v. 1, no. v, Summer 68,
p. 68–70
*Tretya konferentsiya pisateley
Azii i Afriki*
Conference of Writers of Asia
and Africa, 3rd, (Beirut,
March 1967)
in: *Inostrannaya Literatura*
(Moscow), 67, no. 6, p. 227–32
TROUT, PAULETTE
'Profile of an African artist:
Jean Ikelle-Matiba'
in: *Jnl. of the New African Lit.
& the Arts*, 67, no. 4,
p. 68–9
TROUT, PAULETTE
'Recent developments in French
African literature'
in: *Jnl. of the New African Lit.
& the Arts*, 67, no. 4, p. 16–7
ULANSKY, GENE
'Caesar crosses the Niger.
Shakespeare and Onitsha
market chapbooks'
in: *Jnl. of the New African Lit.
& the Arts*, 67, no. 4, p. 18–21

PART II: BOOKS

ABRASH, BARBARA; ed.
*Black African literature in
English since 1952. Works and
criticisms*
New York, 1967. Johnson
Reprint Corpt. $ 3.95
*African-Scandinavian Writer's
Conference, Proceedings*
Uppsala, Sweden, 1967.
Scandinavian Inst. for African
Studies 149 p. mimeog.
(Proceedings of conference held
in Stockholm, February 6–9,
1967)
AIDOO, A.A.
Anowa

London, 1968. Longmans ca.
6s. 6d. 64 p.
ANCIAUX, L.
*La femme noire vue par les
écrivains africanistes*
Brussels, 1967. Académie royale
des science d'outre mer 200 p.
APITHY, S.M.
Telle est la vérité
Paris, 1968. Présence Africaine
F 10.00
ARMAH, K.
*The beautyful ones are not yet
born*
New York, 1968. Houghton
Mifflin $ 4.95 215 p.
(London, Heinemann 25s 224 p.)
AYISSI, L.M.

Contes et berceuses Beti
Yaoundé, 1968. Editions C.L.E.
BAKER, S.; ed.
*Cry, the beloved country; the
novel, the critics, the setting*
New York, 1968. Scribners
$ 2.56 221 p. maps.
BALEWA, SIR ALHAJI
ABUBAKAR TAFAWA
Shaibu Umar
London, 1968. Longmans 6s.od.
80 p.
(New York, Humanities Press,
$1.00)
BEBEY, F.
Embarras et Cie
Yaoundé, 1968. Editions C.L.E.
BEDIAKO, K.A.

A husband for Esi Ellua
Accra, 1968. Anowuo Educ.
Publ. 4s.6d. 179 p.
BEIER, ULLI; ed.
Three Nigerian Plays
London, 1968. Longmans 6s.6d.
89 p.
(New York, Humanities Press,
$1.25)
(Contents: 'Moremi' by Duro
Ladipo; 'The Scheme' by Wale
Ogunyemi; and 'Born with the
fire on his hand' by Obotunde
Ijimere)
BREW, KWESI
The shadows of laughter
London, 1968. Longmans
11s.6d.
CALLAN, E.
Alan Paton
New York, 1968. Twayne
$4.50 160 p.
(Biography)
CARTEY, W.
*Whispers from a continent:
Writings from contemporary black
Africa*
New York, 1969. (January)
Random House $8.95
CESAIRE, A.
Return to my native land
(Transl. from the French)
Paris, 1968. Présence Africaine
ca. F 12.00
CISSOKO, S.
Ressac de nous mêmes
Paris, 1968. Présence Africaine
F 12.20 50 p.
CLARK, J.P.
The example of Shakespeare
London, 1969. (in preparation)
Longmans
(Essays)
DADIE, B.
Homme de tous les continents
Paris, 1967. Présence Africaine
F 12.20
DADIE, B.
Legendes et poems
Paris, 1967. Présence Africaine
257 p.
DATHORNE, O.R. &

FENSER, W.; eds.
Africa in Prose
Harmondsworth, 1968. (in
preparation) Penguin Books
DATHORNE, O.R.
*African Poetry for Schools and
Training Colleges*
London, 1968. (in
preparation) Macmillan
DIAKHATO, L.
Temps et mémoire
Paris, 1968. Présence Africaine
F 14.50
ECHERUO, MICHAEL J.C.
Mortality
London, 1968. Longmans
11s.6d. 57 p.
EMANUEL, J. &
GROSS, T.; eds.
*The development of Negro
literature*
New York, 1968. Free Press
$7.95 400 p.
EWANDE, DANIEL
Vive le President!
Paris, 1968. Ed. Albin Michel
F 9.60 224 p.
FALL, MALLIK
La plaie
Paris, 1967. Ed. Albin Michel
F 13.50 256 p.
FARALLA, D.
The straw umbrella
London, 1968. Gollancz 223 p.
*Fonction et signification de l'art
Negre dans la vie du peuple et
pour le peuple*
Paris, 1967. Présence Africaine
F 36.00 656 p.
(Proceedings of 1st World
Festival of Negro Arts, held in
Dakar, April 1–24, 1966)
GATANYU, JAMES
The battlefield
Nairobi, 1967. East African
Publ. House Sh. 3/00 52 p.
GUMA, S.M.
*The form, content and technique of
traditional literature in
Southern Sotho*
Cape Town, 1967. Van Schaik
R 3.50 215 p.

HENSHAW, J.E.
*This is our chance. Plays from
West Africa*
London, 1967. Univ. of
London Press 3s.6d.
JAHN, JANEHEINZ
*A history of Neo-African
literature*
(Transl. from the German)
London, 1968. Faber 50s.od.
(To be published in the USA
by Grove Press, New York)
JOACHIM, P.
Anti-grâce
Paris, 1968. Presence Africaine
JONES, L. & NEAL, L.; eds.
*Black fire: An anthology of
Afro-American writing*
New York, 1968. Morrow
$7.50
JUMINIER, B.
La revanche de Bozambo
Paris, 1968. (in preparation)
Presence Africaine
IPP, C.; ed.
Doris Lessing: a bibliography
Johannesburgh, 1967.
Witwatersrand Univ. Dept. of
Librarianship & Typography
R 1 18 p.
KAYIRA, LEGSON
The looming shadow
London, 1968. Longmans
21s.od. 144 p.
KESTELOOT, L.
*Les écrivains noirs de langue
française: naissance
d'une lettérature* (3rd
rev. ed.)
Brussels, 1968. Ed. de l'Institut
de Sociologie FB 240.–340 p.
KIBERA, L. & KAHIAGA, S.
Potent ash; short stories
Nairobi, 1968. East African
Publ. House Sh. 6/oo 160 p.
KNAPPERT, J.
*Traditional Swahili poetry; an
investigation into the concepts
of East African Islam as reflected
in the Utenzi literature*
Leyden, 1967. Brill Dfl.
45 264 p.

KOELLE, S.W.
African native literature, or proverbs, tales, fables and historical fragments in the Kanuri or Bornu language
(Reprint of ed. London, 1854)
Enlarged by a preface by David Dalby
Graz, Austria, 1968. (in preparation, ready late 1968)
Akademische Druck- und Verlagsanstalt $8.50 pre-publication $10.50 thereafter 460 p.

KONADU, ASARE
Night watchers of Korlebu
Accra, 1968. Anowuo Educ. Publ. 3s.6d. 99 p.

LAYE CAMARA
A dream of Africa
(Transl. from the French by James Kirkup)
London, 1968, Collins 21s.od. 191 p.
(Originally publ. as 'Dramouss', Paris, 1966, Plon)

LEMMA, MENGKISTU
Introduction to modern Ethiopian literature
Uppsala, Sweden, 1967. Scandinavian Institute of African Studies 6 p. mimeog.
(Paper read at African-Scandinavian writers' conference, Stockholm, February 6–9, 1967)

LEROUX, E.
Seven days at the Silbersteins
(Transl. from the Afrikaans by Charles Eglinton)
Boston, 1968. Houghton Mifflin $4.95 205 p.
(London, W.H. Allen, 21s.od.)

LESSING, D.
Golden notebook
New York, 1968. Ballantine Books $1.25 666 p.
(A paperback reissue)

LESSING, D.
Ripple from the storm
New York, 1968. New American Library $0.75

(A paperback reissue)
LESSSING, DORIS
Going home
New York, 1968. Ballantine Books $0.95
(A paperback reissue)

LIENHARDT, P.A.; ed.
The medicine man: Swifa ya nguvumali
By Hasani bin Ismail
London & New York, 1967. Oxford Univ. Press 42s.od./ $6.75 220 p.

LITTO, F.M.; ed.
Plays from black Africa
New York, 1968. Hill & Wang $5.95 ($1.95 pap.)

LUKUMBI, E.T.
Marche, pays des espoirs
Paris, 1967. Presence Africaine

NASSIR BIN JUMA BHALO, A.
Poems from Kenya. Gnomic verses in Swahili
(Transl. and ed. by Lyndon Harries)
Madison, 1967. Univ. of Wisconsin Press $5.00 244 p.

NG'OMBO, C.
Road to Murugwanza
Nairobi, 1967. East African Publ. House Sh. 6/00 150 p.

NWOGA, DONATUS I.
West African verse. An annotated anthology
London, 1968. Longmans 8s.6d. 242 p.
(New York, Humanities Press, $1.50)

OKOLA, LENNARD; ed.
Drum beat
Nairobi, 1967. East African Publ. House Sh. 7/00 160 p.

OGIERIAIKHI, E.
Oba Ovonramwen & Oba Ewuakpe
London, 1968. Univ. of London Press 3s.6d.
(Two short historical plays)

OKPAKU, J.O.O.
The virtues of adultery
Stanford, 1968. (in preparation)

JONALA Publ. $1.25

OYONO-MBIA, GUILLAUME
Three Suitors, one husband & Until further notice
London, 1968. Methuen 7s.6d.

PATON, A.
The long view
Ed. by Edward Callan
New York, 1968. Praeger $5.95 ca. 300 p.

QUILLATEAU, L.
Étude sur Bernard B. Dadie
Paris, Presence Africaine 1967

ROBINSON, C.H.
Specimens of Hausa literature
(Reprint of ed. Cambridge, 1896)
Farnborough, 1969. (in preparation) Gregg Int. Publ. $18.00 pre-publ. $24.00 thereafter 134 p. pl.

RUHUMBIKA, G.
Village in Uhuru
London, 1968. Longmans ca. 8s.6d. 176 p.

SERUMAGA, R.
Return to the shadows
London, 1969. (in preparation) Heinemann

SOYINKA, WOLE
Idanre and other poems
London, 1968. Methuen 16s.od. 88 p.
(New York, Hill & Wang, $3.95)
(Revised entry)

SUTHERLAND, EFUA T.
Edufa
London, 1968. Longmans 6s.6d. 62 p. 4 p. of music
Syracuse University, Maxwell Graduate School of Citizenship and Public Affairs
Onitsha publications
By Andre Nitecki
(Program of Eastern African Studies, occas. paps., no. 32)
Syracuse, 1967. Syracuse Univ. Program of Eastern African Studies $2.00 24 p.

TAIWO, OLADELE
An introduction to West African

Literature
London, 1968. Nelson 9s.6d.
192 p.
(New York, Humanities Press,
$1.75)
THOMAS, PETER; ed.
Poems from Nigeria
New York, 1967. Vantage Press
$2.75 94 p.
THWAITE, A.; ed.
*The stones of emptiness; poems
1963–1966*
London & New York, 1967.
Oxford Univ. Press 18s.0d./
$2.90 67 p.
(Collection of 38 poems,
primarily from North Africa)
TUCKER, MARTIN
*African in modern literature.
A survey of contemporary writing
in English*
New York, 1968. Ungar $7.50
316 p.
TUTUOLA, A.
The feather women of the jungle
London, 1968. Faber & Faber
6s.6d.
London, 1968. (in preparation)
(A paperback reissue)
WACHIRA, GODWIN
Ordeal in the forest
Nairobi, 1967. East African
Publ. House Sh. 6/oo 200 p.
UKOLI, N.M.
Twins of the rain forest
ca. 5s.6d. ca. 64 p.
ZELL, HANS M.; ed.
*Writings by West Africans –
in print at December 1967* (2nd
rev. ed.)
Freetown, 1968. Sierra Leone
Univ. Press Le 0.60/7s.0d./
$1.50 31 p.
(Revised entry. Gives details of
365 'in-print' books by West
African authors. List of
unpublished material now to be
issued separately.)
ZILI, R.
Ifrikya ma pensée
Paris, 1967. Ed. Pierre-Jean
Oswald

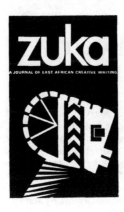

Introduction to Poetry

Desmond Graham

Blake, Lawrence, Senghor, Yeats, Tagore, Marvell, Soyinka, and Jarrell are some of the thirty-one poets represented in this book. Mr Graham introduces the reader whose first language is not English to the simple principles of poetry and shows how an understanding of them deepens appreciation. In the first section of the book he discusses meaning, language, structure, rhythm and the effects of sound entirely through a careful selection of poems which the reader has before him in the text. Mr Graham has included here a section on practical criticism, a glossary and appendices on allusion, tone, irony and scansion as well.

Mr Graham's enthusiasm conveys well the pleasure of poetry, and puts the reader in possession of knowledge which he needs to enjoy poetry of various traditions in a language not his own.

192 pages   paper covers   12/6

New Clarendon Shakespeare

Overseas Edition

Professor Alan Warner has written introductory material for these volumes intended for the student outside Britain. In the light of his teaching experience at Makerere University College in East Africa, he has supplied admirably clear advice to those for whom English is not a native language.

Available are: Julius Caesar, Macbeth, The Merchant of Venice, Romeo and Juliet, Hamlet, As You Like It, Twelfth Night, A Midsummer Night's Dream

each 6/6, containing several plates   prospectus available

Published prices in the UK. Please order through your usual bookseller.

Oxford University Press

Ely House   37 Dover Street   London W1

ALT 3
CONTENTS

1

Editorial Note

The most agreeable feature of a conference on African Literature which brought leading critics from Europe, America and Africa to Ife in December last, was the absence of apology and the devotion to serious criticism. This journal is similarly devoted to the business of serious criticism of African literature.

Already the articles which have been published or submitted are beginning to show that the same work can elicit quite different responses. Dathorne's article on Okigbo which appeared in the first number has had two dissenting replies from Ime Ikiddeh (Number 2), and Edwin Thumboo (this number). In this issue one reaction to Camara Laye is expressed in A. C. Brench's article. A different reaction to one of his works, *The African Child*, is promised by Paul Edwards and Ken Ramchand in the next. Thus we hope it will be possible to see our authors from many angles, and elicit more complete responses to them.

Eldred D. Jones

Corrigenda to No. 1

p. 4: The last sentence should read: It is largely a matter of instinct, but judgement comes into it too.

p. 13: Paragraph 2, second sentence: The following words were left out between 'the' and 'elder': elders together to ask if they think he should heed the summons, one unfriendly . . .

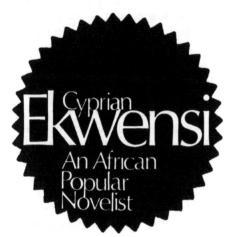

Cyprian Ekwensi
An African Popular Novelist

Bernth Lindfors

Of all the Africans who have written full-length novels in English, Cyprian Ekwensi of Eastern Nigeria (now Biafra) perhaps best illustrates the dictum that practice does not make a writer perfect. At least nine novels, four of them still unpublished, six novelettes for schoolchildren, two collections of folktales, and dozens of short stories have poured from his pen, but not one is entirely free of amateurish blots and blunders, not one could be called the handiwork of a careful, skilled craftsman. Ekwensi may be simply too impatient an artist to take pains with his work or to learn by a calm, rational process of trial and error. When he is not repeating his old mistakes, he is stumbling upon spectacular new ones. As a consequence, many of his stories and novels can serve as excellent examples of how not to write fiction.

2

Part of his problem is that he attempts to write truly popular literature. Unlike other African writers who address themselves to Europe or to an educated African elite, Ekwensi prides himself on being a writer for the masses, a writer who can communicate with any African literate in English. He does not pretend to be profound, subtle or erudite; he would rather be considered entertaining, exciting, sensational. His ambition is to produce thrillers like those that first stimulated his interest in reading and writing. Unfortunately, he seems to have obtained most of his stimulation from third-rate American movies and fourth-rate British and American paperback novels, for these are certainly the most pronounced influences on what he has written. In his favour it may be said that Ekwensi possesses a peculiar talent for imitating bad models well and adapting them to fit into an African setting. He is in this respect an accomplished literary *assimilado*. If his fiction still retains a few vestigial Africanisms, they tend to be all but obliterated under a smooth veneer of slick Western varnish. Nevertheless, these immanent Africanisms should not be over-looked in any evaluation of his writing, for they help to explain some of his idiosyncrasies. This paper will explore Ekwensi's debts to Western popular literature traditions and to indigenous oral traditions and will assess the effects of such influences on his fiction.

Ekwensi's first borrowings were from fairly harmless sources. As a young schoolboy he had been thrilled by his reading of simplified editions of English popular novels: 'I was reading Rider Haggard, Edgar Wallace, Dickens, Sapper, Bates. At Government College in Ibadan we could recite whole chunks of *King Solomon's Mines. Nada the Lily* was a favourite; so was *She*, and *Allan Quatermain . . . Treasure Island* [was] unforgettable.'[1] The impact that these juvenile classics made on Ekwensi can be discerned in one of his first attempts at long fiction, *Juju Rock,* which reverberates with echoes from *Treasure Island* and *King Solomon's Mines.* Though not published until 1966, *Juju Rock* may have been written as much as twenty years earlier. There are references to it in *The Leopard's Claw* (London 1950) and *The Passport of Mallam Ilia* (Cambridge 1960) both of which were written in 1947.

The story of *Juju Rock* is narrated by its hero. Rikku, a young Fulani schoolboy in Western Nigeria who serves as a guide to three

Englishmen on an expedition to mysterious Juju Rock in the northern grasslands. The men are searching for a lost gold mine and for an old sailor who had disappeared on an earlier expedition and was thought to have located the mine. As they near their destination, Rikku, like Jim Hawkins, overhears his companions plotting to kill him as soon as the gold is found. Rikku escapes, disguises himself as a canoe boy, and bravely rejoins the evil three.

When the group arrives at Juju Rock, Robert Louis Stevenson gives way to Rider Haggard. Rikku and his companions come upon a dangerous tribal 'Secret Society' carrying out its rituals, and a fierce battle in a dark cave ensues. The tribesmen overcome Rikku and the three Englishmen and are preparing to sacrifice them when an unexpected rescue party arrives and saves them. Rikku then finds the old sailor in the cave and after a few more scuffles and narrow escapes hears him tell his side of the story. Thus, as in most school readers narrated in the first person, loose ends are conveniently tied up and mysteries efficiently explained so events can be rapidly concluded. As might be expected, the three villains end up in prison and Rikku returns to school a national hero.

If any further proof is required to demonstrate that *Juju Rock* was written in imitation of juvenile adventure fiction, it can be found in the text itself, for Ekwensi, in his eagerness to place his story in this genre, drew very specific parallels for his readers. The first chapter begins as follows:

Now that I have been through it all, and the whole thing seems so distant and remote, I sometimes wonder what it was that lured me into that *Juju Rock* adventure. Boyish curiosity, perhaps; an eagerness to learn more, and the influence of 'Wild West' fiction and very recent reading of *King Solomon's Mines*. In many ways *Juju Rock* was like something out of those romantic days. (p. 7. All page references to *Juju Rock,* Lagos 1966)

Having made this point, Ekwensi apparently did not want anyone to forget it. Later in the story, when Rikku has been captured by the 'Secret Society' and fears he is about to be speared to death by the Chief Priest, Ekwensi has him say:

I could see the eyes of the Chief Priest as he glared at me and I knew he hated me with all his might. This was certainly the end.

4

Never again would I have the joy of reading Wild West stories, or books like *King Solomon's Mines*. (p. 71)

The chapter in which this occurs, it should be noted, is entitled 'Showdown at Juju Rock'. Ekwensi was doing everything he could to ensure that readers would associate his novelette with the 'thrillers' or 'real life adventure stories' that boys enjoyed reading at school.

Ekwensi's familiarity with 'Wild West' stories is most clearly displayed in *The Passport of Mallam Ilia*, another of his early attempts at juvenile adventure fiction set in the cattle lands of Northern Nigeria. Here is a scene borrowed lock, stock and barrel from stagecoach melodramas of the American Southwest:

Mallam Usuman quickly guided his horse up the bank of the stream, and, riding slowly along, studied the transport for a time. Experience told him that they had been travelling for some time and were therefore very tired. He dug his heels into the flanks of his horse. In a moment he had drawn up beside them and levelled his gun.

'Whoever you are,' he snarled, 'you can choose.'

The transport stopped and the driver turned his sun-scorched face towards him. There was anger in his flaming eyes.

'Which do you choose,' Usuman went on, 'your life or your money?'

'There—there is no money,' stammered the driver.

'Don't lie!'

Usuman with his quick eye had already seen the wooden box beneath the driver's seat; but now, as the passengers began to complain and show signs of terror, Usuman noticed that there was a woman in the carriage. She was sitting tightly wedged in between the other passengers, calm and cool. She lifted her black veil for a moment and Usuman's eyes widened at the sight of her face. She was beautiful.

The driver must have been watching him, for he said in Hausa: 'You like her then? Unfortunately, she is not for you ...'

'You rat!' snapped Usuman. 'Throw down the money and drive on.'

The driver glanced from the bore of the rifle into Usuman's face and decided to obey. He got down, fumbled for a moment,

5

and was bringing out something from under the box when Usuman shot him in the hand and a British revolver dropped to the ground.

'Now will you put down the box?'

Cursing, the driver pushed down the box with his left hand and climbed back into his seat.

'Not yet,' said Usuman. He turned and winked at the lady. 'Open the carriage and let her step down!' (*The Passport of Mallam Ilia*, Cambridge 1960, pp. 43-4)

Ekwensi was apparently familiar with all the standard clichés of the Western. Whether he picked them up from fiction or from films cannot be determined, but it is clear that he had no qualms about using them, even if it meant dressing Billy the Kid in the robes and turban of a Hausa Mallam.

Burning Grass, Ekwensi's first attempt at longer fiction,[2] also bears the imprint of the Western branding iron. In *Burning Grass*, there are cattle rustlings, stampedes, galloping horses, saloon confrontations, and ferocious battles galore. Here is an archetypal ambush:

Hodio's gallop out of New Chanka quickened as his temper mounted. He dug his heels hard into his horse's flanks, cursing the while, slashing cruelly down with his cane. Lying close to his horse's mane, his eyes darted keenly into every nook and crevice of the scrub . . .

His horse twisted and turned as it followed the crooked path before him. Shehu and his men had had too much of a start. At this rate, he might never catch up with them . . .

He slowed down. The large rock ahead of him would bear no prints. But something else seemed imminent. He could almost feel a third presence. He got down, climbed the large rock. From the top he commanded a grand view of the country behind him. It was a dead end, true enough. But somewhere behind this rock should be another path. It might take long to find, perhaps too long.

He decided to search. He turned. Like a flash, the arrows whizzed past his ear. He threw himself flat down. His horse broke away, yelping with pain. He could see the butts of at least three arrows in its flank. Slowly the horse would die of the poison in the iron tips.

6

He looked down the bottom of the rock and saw three men labouring up towards him. The biggest of them all was Shehu, the man he sought. (*Burning Grass*, London 1962, pp. 59-60)

What is most remarkable about these quoted excerpts is that they are very accurate imitations. Ekwensi has an uncommonly good ear for narrative style, a gift for mimicry, and a knack for transplanting un-African events onto African soil. He can make Nigerian schoolboys imagine an impossible treasure hunt or feel at home on the range because he has mastered the conventions and commonplaces of foreign juvenile adventure fiction and knows how to domesticate them. His is a literature of imitation and adaptation, not a literature of imagination and original invention. So long as he continued to address an adolescent audience, his fiction remained as innocuous and unobjectionable as the material upon which it was modelled. It was when he began to try to reach an older audience that he turned to less innocent models and descended from the highroads of classic juvenile literature to the more pedestrian paths of earthy popular fiction.

Ekwensi's first tentative step in this new direction was taken in 1947, when he published a forty-four page pamphlet novel entitled *When Love Whispers*. This was one of the first inexpensive paperback novelettes, now commonly called chapbooks, to be issued in Nigeria. Three substantial survey articles have been written on this literature: Ulli Beier, 'Public Opinion on Lovers. Popular Nigerian Literature Sold in Onitsha Market', *Black Orpheus*, No. 14 (February 1964), pp. 4-16; Donatus I. Nwoga, 'Onitsha Market Literature', *Transition*, vol. 4, No. 19 (1965), pp. 26-33; Nancy J. Schmidt, 'Nigeria: Fiction for the Average Man', *Africa Report*, vol. 10, No. 8 (August 1965), pp. 39-41. Like so many that have followed since, *When Love Whispers* was essentially the story of a maiden in distress. Beautiful, pure-hearted Ashoka, whose fiancé has just left for engineering studies in England, finds herself in continual difficulty. She is kidnapped, almost sold to an odious white man in a neighbouring French territory, and eventually seduced by her fiancé's best friend. Unable to abort her pregnancy, she marries a third man whom she doesn't love. The wages of sin are sorrow.

Appropriately enough, *When Love Whispers* is written in a style which closely approximates that found in much drugstore pulp magazine fiction. Ekwensi must have known this type of literature quite well, for he was able to echo it very faithfully. The following passage is taken from the first few pages of the novelette:

> She loved him. She had promised to marry him. She was waiting now, hoping and praying for that great day when both of them would stand before the priest and say those age-old words . . . And then they would walk down arm in arm, she in her white bridal dress, he in his starched collar. (*When Love Whispers*, Onitsha, p. 5)

It must be remembered that at this early stage in his literary career Ekwensi was accustomed to addressing his fiction to a young audience so he had had little experience in writing passionate love scenes. This may explain why love-making is described with such reticence in *When Love Whispers*. In later novels Ekwensi grew much bolder and seemed to relish going through all the motions of a seduction scene, but during his apprenticeship he didn't dare treat sex too explicitly. Here, for example, is how Ashoka loses her virginity:

> She turned her face towards him in the moonlight, and there were points of fire in his eyes.
> 'You're just too beautiful for words,' he said. 'Is that not how the song goes?'
> She said nothing.
> She felt his hand on her cheeks, and then he was touching soft parts of her, and still she said nothing. Then his lips were hot on hers and she was sighing.
> 'Leave me!' she shouted suddenly, pushing him back. 'Let me go: you thief! You thief! I—I shall never see you again.' (*When Love Whispers*, p. 33)

In Ekwensi's later novels there was never any doubt about what the thief had stolen or which soft parts he had touched.

Perhaps it was the enormous popular success of *When Love Whispers*[3] that prompted Ekwensi to write two full-length novels about the misadventures of liberated Nigerian women. *Jagua Nana*, probably his most successful work, records the ups and downs of an ageing Lagos prostitute who is in love with her work. In describing her affairs Ekwensi sometimes cannot suppress a vulgar smirk:

8

He was beginning to regard himself as the rightful lover, always jealous. She got around him by mothering him. She went over now and sat on his knee, rubbing her thinly clad hips into his thighs. She threw one arm over his shoulder, so that her left breast snuggled close to his lips. Presently she felt his thick, rough lips close on the nipple. 'A dog with food in his mouth does not bark,' went the proverb. (*Jagua Nana*, London 1961, p. 126)

In *Iska*, his most recent novel, another city girl falls into a life of sin and later comes to rue her misspent youth. Ekwensi again spices the narrative with racy details;

He came over, gripping the body of her breasts. She did not resist. Instead she took off her clothes and stood revealed before him.

He gazed at her with his eyes nearly coming off their sockets. There she was on offer, the flesh of black woman, pale and bleached by a thousand cosmetic creams, completely devastating. (*Iska*, London 1966, pp. 123-4)

Because his sinful heroines usually come to bad ends, Ekwensi can be viewed as a serious moralist whose novels offer instruction in virtue by displaying the tragic consequences of vice. But it is always quite clear to the reader that he is far more interested in vice than in virtue and that he aims to titillate as well as teach.

As Ekwensi moved from romantic love to torrid sex he also developed an interest in crime. The hero of his first full-length novel, *People of the City,* was both a crime reporter and a part-time band leader, a man in an excellent position to observe both lowlife and highlife in a Nigerian metropolis. Here is a typical scene from this stereotypical novel:

The phone rang. Sango went over.
'*West African Sensation* . . .'
'May I speak to the editor, please?' The voice was tinny, strained, very excited.
Sango could feel the tension.
'The editor is not here.'
'Any reporter there?'
'Yes . . . who's speaking, please?'
The office became silent. Over the wires, Sango could smell news. It always gave him a kick to smell news. Even Lajide and

his debtor had frozen and were looking at him, listening intently. Sango felt proud to impress Lajide with his importance.

'Never mind who I am. If you want something for your paper, come out to the Magamu Bush, and you'll get it.'

'Where are you speaking from? Hello . . . Hello . . . Hello . . .! Oh! He's hung up.' (*People of the City*, London 1964, p. 50)

Ekwensi was obviously still operating under the influence of Hollywood and popular pulp fiction.

It was perhaps inevitable that Ekwensi should eventually try his hand at detective fiction. *Yaba Roundabout Murder*, a chapbook he published in Lagos in 1962, relates how a clever police inspector catches a murderer by pretending to make advances to the murderer's wife. Many of the standard ingredients of detective fiction—the anonymous telephone tip, the trail of clues, the interrogations, the newspaper headlines, the cool-headed police inspector—can be found here, the only novelty being the African setting in which they appear. What detective novel does not have a scene something like the following:

Inspector John Faolu walked up to the door and knocked. But he found the door open. There was no one in the room. He pressed the switch. There was no light. His torchlight showed him that there was a bulb in the ceiling, but apparently it had not been connected to the mains. The house was a new one.

The room was in disorder. There was every sign that the occupants had left in a great hurry. Clothes were carelessly strewn on the bed.

The books on the table had been disarranged, and beneath this was a box which though closed, had a number of clothes sticking out of it.

Faolu took in the scene with deep interest. (*Yaba Roundabout Murder*, Lagos 1962, p. 17)

This passage and others like it reveal that Ekwensi was familiar with the whodunit genre, knew its stock situations and cliches, and had not lost his flair for imitating bad models well.

Given Ekwensi's extraordinary susceptibility to influences from Western popular literature, what, if anything, could he possibly be said to owe to indigenous oral traditions? Can it be seriously suggested that there is something characteristically African or,

10

more precisely, something characteristic of African oral narrative art in his fiction? The answer to this question is a tentative yes. There are at least two features of Ekwensi's novels and novelettes that resemble and perhaps derive from features of oral narrative art. Whether these are exclusively African characteristics is doubtful, but it seems more likely that Ekwensi assimilated them from traditional African narratives than from traditional European or American tales. In the late nineteen-forties and early fifties, when he was just getting started as a writer, he avidly collected and translated Ibo folktales, publishing them in local magazines and later in booklets designed for use in schools.[4] In 1947 he also collected a long traditional tale of vengeance from 'an aged Hausa Mallam' who offered it as a story that 'would keep [his] readers awake all night'.[5] Ekwensi published this tale fifteen years later under the title *An African Night's Entertainment*. Thus it may be said that both early and late in his writing career Ekwensi demonstrated an active interest in African oral narratives.

One of the features that Ekwensi's fiction shares with African folktales is a tendency to moralise, a tendency to use action and character to illustrate a thesis or underscore a point. Ekwensi's heroes and heroines sometimes seem like cardboard personifications of virtue or vice. They are more complex and better individualised than folktale heroes, but they give the same impression of having been created for a specific didactic purpose. They are like wooden puppets clumsily manipulated to spell out a conventional message. Ekwensi does not ordinarily state his moral explicitly at the end, as do many traditional storytellers, but he gives the reader enough nudges and winks along the way to make the moral known.

Good examples of Ekwensi's heavyhanded moralising can be found in one of his most recent novels, *Beautiful Feathers*, the title of which is based on an Ibo proverb: 'However famous a man is outside, if he is not respected inside his own home he is like a bird with *beautiful feathers*, wonderful on the outside but ordinary within.' (p. 1. All page references to *Beautiful Feathers*, London 1963.) The hero of the novel is a Pan-Africanist politician who is just beginning to win a reputation and following when his marriage starts to collapse. His neglected wife not only refuses to prepare his meals but spites him by brazenly taking a lover. Ekwensi has his hero recognise the mordant irony of his situation:

11

Solidarity, where does it begin? Here, in my own home? I am the leader of the Nigerian Movement for African and Malagasy Solidarity. Wilson Iyari, good looking, famous outside. At home I am nothing. I am like a fowl with beautiful feathers on the outside for all to see. When the feathers are removed the flesh and bones underneath are the same as for any other fowl. I am not really different from other men. In fact, if only they knew how I am spited in my own home they would despise me. They would never again listen to me talking about solidarity. (p. 20)

Throughout the novel Ekwensi plays upon the proverbial image of the ordinary fowl with beautiful feathers by continuing to contrast sharply Wilson's successful public life with his steadily deteriorating home life. For example, there is a splendid scene in which Wilson, while addressing a group of political leaders in his home, sees his wife go out to meet her lover.

As he mentioned the word 'solidarity' Wilson saw the door of the bedroom open. His wife, resplendent, came out, passed through the sitting-room, and before they could rise to greet her she was outside, leaving a bewitching trail of *Balmain*. (p. 48)

The contrast between Wilson's public and private life is presented with graphic clarity here, but Ekwensi is not content to leave it at that. A few lines later he firmly underlines the message so no one will miss it.

She is going to meet her lover, Wilson thought. *I talk about solidarity. There it is! My own family split. But how can Africa be united when such a small unit as my family is not united?* (pp. 48-9)

Such heavy-handedness ruins some of Ekwensi's best effects. Even the ending of the novel is spoiled by a lack of subtlety. After having Wilson retire from politics and reunite with his wife, Ekwensi concludes:

They had truly come together now. It could be said of him that he was famous outside and that at home he had the backing of a family united by bonds of love. Wilson's beautiful feathers had ceased to be superficial and had become a substantial asset. (p. 160)

12

Ekwensi simply cannot resist the temptation to tell his readers what the action signifies. Like a traditional storyteller, he frames his tale to illustrate a proverb.

Another feature that Ekwensi's fiction shares with many African oral narratives is a circular structure. To use Joseph Campbell's terms in *The Hero with a Thousand Faces* (New York 1949) the hero undergoes a sequence of adventures involving a departure, an initiation and a return. In the end he is usually back where he started, older and wiser for his experiences and purged of all personal excesses. He has accomplished his tasks, liquidated his lacks, and achieved a state of emotional equilibrium. Sometimes he completes his cycle of adventures by repudiating new Western ways and affirming old African values. He returns, in other words, to his African essence, to his roots, abandoning deviant foreign patterns. He is, in a sense, a modern African culture hero.

A few examples of Ekwensi's reliance on circular structures will suffice. In three of his juvenile novelettes—*Juju Rock, The Leopard's Claw,* and *The Drummer Boy*—a boy-hero rejects school life, enters a corrupt adult world where he encounters and overcomes evil, and then, having proven his courage and integrity, turns eagerly to the very life he had earlier rejected. In *Beautiful Feathers* the hero becomes embroiled in European-style politics but quits in order to save his marriage. He decides his family means more to him than fame, so he gives up his Westernised, individualistic pursuit of personal glory. In *People of the City* a young man leaves his village in the Eastern Greens for the glamour and easy money of the big city, but after being exposed to some of the city's ills, temptations and tragedies, he yearns for a cleaner life and departs for the Gold Coast to make a fresh start. In *Jagua Nana* a childless middle-aged woman leaves her idyllic village, turns to a life of prostitution in the city, and then returns home to bear an illegitimate child. In his article '"Rebushing" or Ontological Recession to Africanism' Austin J. Shelton has persuasively argued that her return to the village is 'more than a symbol of the rejection of westernisation,' that it is in fact an act of 'rebushing' or ontological recession, 'showing that [her] very Africanism, *despite her Europeanisation*, militates against her remaining permanently in the city where she has been separated from all the truly vital forces of her people and culture.' Following 'the cyclic principle of African personality,'[6] she first proceeds outward from

13

the village and tradition and then returns to her African heritage. Her return is thus psychologically and philosophically fulfilling. It is perhaps significant that in his article 'The Dilemma of the African Writer' (*West African Review*, July 1956, p. 703) Ekwensi once defined African writing as 'that piece of self-expression in which the psychology behind African thought is manifest; in which the philosophy and the pattern of culture from which it springs can be discerned.' In Ekwensi's fiction it is often by means of a circular structure that the psychology behind African thought and the philosophy and African pattern of culture from which it springs are made manifest.

All this said, Ekwensi's novels are still failures. They combine some of the worst features of Western popular literature with some of the least subtle techniques of African oral narrative art. It seems that when Ekwensi is not trying to get by with cheap effects borrowed from shoddy sources, he is labouring to make an obvious point. Thus, rather like his heroes, he vacillates between complete Westernisation and reversions to his African heritage. There would be nothing wrong with mixing foreign and native narrative traditions in a literary work, if it were artfully done. But Ekwensi lacks artistic discretion, and for a popular novelist there is no more fatal flaw.

NOTES

1. Cyprian Ekwensi, 'Literary Influences on a Young Nigerian', *Times Literary Supplement*, 4 June 1964, p. 475.
2. Though not published until 1962, *Burning Grass* had been completed before 1950. See the unpublished dissertation (Northwestern 1966) by Nancy J. Schmidt, 'An Anthropological Analysis of Nigerian Fiction', p. 73.
3. In an interview published in *Afrique*, No. 24 (May 1963), p. 49, Ekwensi said, 'for some people [*When Love Whispers*] has become a kind of classic. Today it is still in circulation, and people still read it before going to bed.' I am grateful to Mrs. Sandy Barkan for this translation.
4. *Ikolo the Wrestler and Other Ibo Tales* (London 1947) was later reissued under the title *The Great Elephant-bird* (London 1965). Ekwensi also published *The Boa Suitor* (London 1966) another collection of Ibo tales.
5. Cyprian Ekwensi, 'Outlook for African Writers', *West African Review*, January 1950 p. 19.
6. Austin J. Shelton, 'The Cyclic Principle of African Personality', *Présence Africaine*, English edition vol. 17, No. 45 (1963), pp. 145-50.

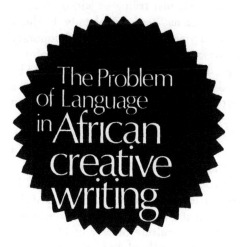

The Problem of Language in African creative writing

B. I. Chukwukere

What I intend to do in this article is twofold. First, I am going to pose a few general questions on the achievement of African novelists writing in English, but this may apply to French as well, or for that matter any language besides the author's native tongue. Secondly I will refer to two Ibo-speaking novelists, Cyprian Ekwensi and Chinua Achebe, first to explain the nature of the fundamental problem, as I conceive it, facing this pioneer generation of African literature and further to illustrate the weakness and the strength of attempts to grapple with it.

I might mention here in passing Mr. Wali's article in *Transition* five years ago which sparked off lively debates and sharp comments in subsequent issues. He claimed that 'educated African writing' in English and French was 'an extremely difficult and illogical situation'. Pointedly Wali added: 'any true African literature must be written in African languages', otherwise the writers and their 'western midwives' [critics or publishers?] 'would be merely pursuing a dead end, which can only lead to sterility, uncreativity and frustration'.

However, I am not in this article just trying to add by way of amplification or refutation to what has been said already. Rather I have chosen a different angle of view which places contemporary African literary art as a whole in the broader context of the educational system that produced the artists themselves. The system, if I may be allowed to state the obvious, is one of the cultural imports from western Europe, and from England and France in particular. It is necessary to approach the subject from this viewpoint because there is such a close relation between literature and society that it would be methodologically unsound to divorce them in an intelligent discussion of literature alone. Socio-cultural factors, that is to say, must be taken into account in literary criticism. Thus, this article is a preliminary appraisal of the inevitable conflict resulting from the impact of formal education, which is an integral part of western culture or way of life, on its African recipients, specifically the novelists' and in this context their experiment with the foreign language which was the chief medium of instruction at school and is the medium of their fiction-writing today.

Let us focus attention on three basic questions. One, should the African novelist write in English or his own native language? The problem implicit in this question is not so facile as it might seem at first sight. In any case it lies at the very heart of the matter. Two, if English is desirable or indispensable what form or variety of it should the author employ? In other words, should the English of the African novel be the 'standard' form spoken and written in the parent country, England, or the variety common in the author's own country? The rub here is that there may be no agreement on what 'standard' is, even if empirically one can establish such a phenomenon. But I can only beg the question in this article since I am not concerned with the problems of morphology and semantics in English. Three, since communication in the novel proceeds by means of various techniques, including straightforward and oblique narration, dialogue (direct or re-ported) and what they call, with reference to a twentieth-century school of novelists, 'stream of consciousness', how should the African novelist's language reflect the various behavioural levels of the characters he assembles on his wide canvas, as well as the

16

nature of the world he creates for them and into which his readers would like to get a clear insight? This question evokes a number of corollaries which I hope will crystallise in the course of the argument.

Meanwhile, let us try to establish a sort of analytical framework in which the above questions and our answers, implied or expressed, could be placed in proper perspective. It is pertinent for us to emphasise the nature of the relation between the artist's sensibility and that of his public on the one hand, and on the other between the artist and his medium of communication—human language in the present context. There is such an affinity between the novelist's idiom of feeling, experience or thought and the actual expression of these, that a loss of vital touch between the two would result in what T. S. Eliot has termed a 'dissociation of sensibility'. Used strictly in Eliot's original sense, to define a general decline in the quality of late seventeenth century English poetry, the phrase is not applicable to contemporary African fiction. But I simply wish to adapt the word 'dissociation' to denote the sloppy, incoherent literary creation which results from a novelist's failure to grasp fully and articulate skilfully those almost indefinable aspects of socio-literary phenomenon which we have epitomised by the word 'sensibility'. At the opposite end is what one might call (reversing Eliot) 'association of sensibility', which implies an integration, in this particular case, of the diverse aspects of the novel, i.e. character, plot, story, language or style in general. Such an association yields high quality results—a novel rich in texture, artistically coherent and therefore enjoyable. In either case, it seems to me the crux of the matter is not whether the language is foreign or native but how efficiently it is manipulated to depict differences in levels of characterisation, narration and speech-processes as a whole. That is to say, the acid test for our African writers in English is the degree to which each proves himself a real master of his medium, for such is the gateway to entertainment—a prime object of literature.

Nevertheless, I think it would be just as preposterous for any serious reader or critic to under-rate the inherent difficulties in writing in a foreign language as to unduly exaggerate this problem and use it as an apology for poor creative writing. One could, for example, logically argue that a fundamental 'dissociation' exists between the language of African writers' experiences or thoughts and their expression in English. It is a cultural discrepancy between the language of 'the home' and 'the school'. In spite of this, I believe the African novelist can be successful if firstly he is sufficiently sensitive towards his reading public, and employs themes that either have a significant bearing upon real life or give a clear insight into the nature and the general spirit of the age or society he is writing about; and secondly if he shows evidence of full realisation of, and presents convincingly consistent pictures of, the changing situations in which we find his characters. The language is 'the thing', by which we will judge the success of the author. For literature, to use Cardinal Newman's words, is 'the personal use or exercise of language. That this is so is further proved from the fact that one author uses it so differently from another.'

In the above sense we, the readers, expect to recognise, without an iota of ambiguity, the moments when the writer himself is talking to us, and when he makes his characters converse with one another or just talk to us, the audience. The most accurate indicator of these levels of speech is the author's own handling of his medium, language—idiom, vocabulary, imagery, syntax: in short all that goes to make up his style. The extent to which he has fully conceived his story, theme, plot and characters reveals itself in his style. To stress this point finally, one might reiterate that the manipulation of any artistic medium is a crucial touch-stone for determining the overall effect and success of the finished product.

Therefore, when Okonkwo of *Things Fall Apart* is with his friend Obierika we expect the proverbial flavour of the conversation of people in such circumstances of life. 'Proverbs', Achebe says in reference to the Ibo characters in the book, 'are the palm oil with which words are eaten.' But when we meet Obi Okonkwo, the grandson and hero of *No Longer At Ease,* we expect Achebe to paint a clear picture of a highly-educated young African. This ought to be evident in Obi's thought- and speech-processes, especially when he is with his fiancée Clara, also educated, or his friend Christopher, like himself a university graduate. And when Ekwensi's Jagua Nana (in the novel of the same title) confronts her partners in the Lagos sex-market one would expect some sharp, business-like, often staccato, dialogues. But when she returns to her native village home it is absurd to hear her speak to her own mother in the same manner in which she speaks to her city-friends unless one takes the rather extreme view that Jagua is an absolutely alienated person, which she is not in the novel anyway.

Part of the greatness of Achebe, part of the pleasure we get from reading him, lies in the very fact that he has a sure and firm control of his English, exemplified particularly in his rendering of Ibo language-processes—idiom, imagery, syntax and so forth—into English. He effortlessly, as it appears, leaps across an enormous gulf dividing the two basic sources of literary creativity: feeling or thought, the stimulus of vision, and expression, the externalisation in words of the vision. His achievement in *Things Fall Apart* deserves emphasis and emulation. The characters speak in a manner any Ibo or allied language-speaker would easily recognise as *natural* to them—in rhythm, verbal nuances and the like. The most admirable feature of this *tour de force* is that Achebe neither rudely shocks nor seriously wounds the basic English sentence-pattern or sentence-structure, and at the same time he does not reduce the fundamentals of Ibo language idiom, sound and flow, to obscurity. Consequently a non-Ibo, or to be more precise any native English speaker, would have no good ground for antagonism. It would be wrong for him or her to grumble that the English of the novel is un-English. A native Ibo speaker, on the other hand, would acknowledge the fact that although the conversations or narrations are in English, yet Ibo speech-patterns and speech-flow are evident. To look for the planning and effort that went behind the erection of this almost indescribable bridge across a wide cultural gap is a step towards discovering what one might call *the essential Achebe*.

A close examination of a few passages from *Things Fall Apart* will, I hope, elucidate the above point further. The village wrestling scene comes readily to mind. There is tension in the air as the contestants, warming up in the rather exuberant and robust fashion of traditional wrestlers, in the background of ballad-keyed drum beats, draw to the arena eager-eyed and loquacious spectators from different directions. The latter converge, eloquent in their forecasts reminiscent of rival local football fans. The first match of the tournament, regarded as a sort of prelude, is just over. Achebe narrates:

The drummers stopped for a brief rest before the real matches. Their bodies shone with sweat, and they took up fans and began to fan themselves. They also drank water from small pots and ate kola nuts. They became ordinary human beings again, talking and laughing among themselves and with others who stood near them. The air, which had been stretched taut with excitement, relaxed again. It was as if water had been poured on the tightened skin of a drum. Many people looked around, perhaps for the first time, and saw those who stood or sat next to them.

'I did not know it was you,' Ekwefi said to the woman who had stood shoulder to shoulder with her since the beginning of the matches.

'I do not blame you,' said the woman. 'I have never seen such a large crowd of people. Is it true that Okonkwo nearly killed you with his gun?'

'It is true indeed, my dear friend. I cannot yet find a mouth with which to tell the story.'

In the first part of this extract it is clear that it is Achebe himself: educated, well-spoken (in English). Nevertheless, he is sensitive to the vitality of local imagery. He seems to remind us that metaphors, similes and other figures of speech are most graphic if drawn from the characters' environment; hence he introduces that image of 'water poured on the tightened skin of a drum'. This is appropriate, simple, straightforward, and also vivid and lucid. The theme of relaxation in the tensed atmosphere around the arena is thus tellingly enacted not by the use of a *pure* English metaphor but by 'translating' a local Ibo one into English. In the dialogue of the passage we might recognise what William Wordsworth, in his Lyrical Ballads, calls 'the language of real life' namely the type spoken by simple countryfolk: 'I cannot yet find a mouth . . .'. This is how a native Ibo speaker would express himself in such circumstances, but not a native English speaker who might say something like 'words fail me . . .' But one has no good ground to doubt that the end result of Achebe's delineation is English all the same—I mean *respectable* English.

Later on in the story, Okonkwo and his friend Obierika are conversing when the latter's son drops in. Okonkwo immediately switches to praising the young man for his last wrestling feat and general manly abilities, and in contrast bemoans his own son's feminity, as he sees it:

'I am worried about Nwoye. A bowl of pounded yams can throw him in a wrestling match. . . . But I can tell you, Obierika, my children do not resemble me. Where are the young suckers that will grow when the old banana tree dies?'

Presently the topic changes to the sad incident of Ikemefuna's death. Okonkwo defends his active role:

' "The Earth cannot punish me for obeying her messenger. A child's fingers are not scalded by a piece of hot yam which its mother puts into its palm".'

The point I wish to spotlight is that the reader cannot mistake Okonkwo's voice. The full picture we get of him in the novel confirms this ever-recurring resort to proverbs—the epitome of traditional maxims and morality, the chief seasoner of Ibo conversations and speeches. The greatness of *Things Fall Apart* derives partly from this skilful manipulation by the author of the various strata of speech utterances indicative of himself and his various characters. In the end, one is left with a feeling of finality, of organic conception and creation of plot, characters, theme and story. Achebe does not use pidgin English for the characters, because in normal life they would speak locally-rooted, correct Ibo. The English 'translation' should at least, since it cannot recapture all of the original local flavour, be grammatically correct, not pidgin. In *No Longer At Ease,* where the world is that of contemporary, urban Nigeria, we find no fault with the use of pidgin; it is true to life, and shows how the author realises very well the dimensions of his work. But whereas *Things Fall Apart* owes its rich texture to this fact of artistic 'association' or integration of the sensibility of the various participants in, and aspects of, the tragic drama, *No Longer At Ease,* on the other hand, flags and slackens in places because, I think, Achebe does not seem to know fully what to do with the characters and how to do it on particular occasions. A typical situation is the so-called love of Obi and Clara. The idiom of their relationship is at times ridiculously naive; banal, one might say. In some of their confrontations the two lovers hardly come to life—they seem just like skeletons: no flesh and blood. For example, Clara in the following passage is asserting the modern African woman's expectation of companionate relationship with her man.

'Why didn't you tell me?' she asked when he had told her about the overdraft.

'Well there was no need. I'll pay it easily in five monthly instalments.'

'That's not the point. You don't think I should be told when you're in difficulty.'

'I wasn't in difficulty. I wouldn't have mentioned it if you hadn't pressed me.'

'I see,' was all she said. She went across the room and picked up a woman's magazine lying on the floor and began to read.

After a couple of minutes, Obi said with synthetic light-heartedness: 'It's very rude to be reading when you have a visitor.'

'You should have known I was very badly brought up.' Any reflection on her family was a very risky subject and often ended in tears. Even now her eyes were beginning to look glazed.

'Clara,' he said putting his arm round her. She was all tensed up. 'Clara.' She did not answer. She was turning the pages of the magazine mechanically. 'I don't understand why you want to quarrel.' Not a sound. 'I think I had better be going.'

'I think so, too.'

'Clara, I'm very sorry.'

'About what? Leave me, *ojare*.' She pushed his arm off.

Obi sat for another couple of minutes gazing at the floor.

'All right.' He sprang to his feet. Clara remained where she was, turning the pages.

'Bye-bye.'

'Good-bye.'

In the above scene it looks as if Achebe is being a faithful pupil of the school of squeamish true-romance magazines fostered by Hollywood.

Weakness of characterisation as a result of inadequate grasp and control of relevant levels of language is most pronounced in Cyprian Ekwensi's writings. *Jagua Nana*, in my opinion his best novel, has this flaw, a corollary of which is the author's failure to give a consistent picture of Jagua, the principal character, vis-à-vis the minor ones. I shall clarify this criticism by mentioning some of the instances in which Jagua interacts with them. My main

22

objection stems from the use or non-use of pidgin English. Why does a character speak in pidgin at one time and in grammatically correct, or what I prefer to call here 'formal', English at another? Or why does a character use the one when his or her partner in conversation is using the other? I must stress that I am not against the use of pidgin English *per se*, not in any case in a novel dealing with urban life in Nigeria, or West Africa for that matter. But any critical reader would expect a systematic and consistent employment of this *acculturated* form of English.

On the first page of *Jagua Nana*, Ekwensi inadvertently—one can only conclude it is so—gives one strong reason why many town-dwellers prefer pidgin English to their own native or local language: 'Like Freddie, she was an Ibo from Eastern Nigeria, but when she spoke to him she always used pidgin English, because living in Lagos City they did not want *too many embarrassing reminders of clan or custom.*' (Italics mine.)

Following the logic of the above statement let us see how Jagua speaks to other characters in circumstances, places and contexts remote from city environment. One scene comes to mind: Jagua with her brother Fonso who has come to Lagos to announce their father's approaching end:

'So will you get ready and come now,' Fonso said with finality.

'Now? Leave Lagos . . . now?'

'Yes, now . . . If you like, you stay. Papa will die. Is an ol' man awright; but he jus' wan' to see you before . . .'

Jagua began to cry 'But I have nothin. Them seize all my thin' . . . How I can come without money! Is a shame! . . .

'No money—all these years?' His voice was biting. 'Not you tell me when you come Onitsha that you got cloth business?' He laughed . . .' (What a sense of humour! Joy or sorrow?)

The dialogue, in my opinion, is a piece of contrivance in the bad sense of the word. It is unrealistic, in the context, that a brother and his sister expressing filial feelings for their dying father should use a form of speech so artificial and far-removed from the commonplace idiom of home life. One might be tempted to defend this by saying that Jagua is a broken and unhomely person. However, Ekwensi himself negates such a view of his heroine; she is not completely degenerate and alienated: 'Her father's love was a

23

great prize and after ten years of having betrayed it, she knew she would go back to him and still be welcome.' I should have thought that 'formal' English—the structural equivalent of the Ibo in which the brother and sister must have spoken—would have gone far to erase, or at least mitigate, the touch of triviality which their dialogue lends to the occasion.

Pidgin English, one must bring home to readers ignorant of it, is usually the *spoken* language of the majority of urbanised and urban dwellers in Nigeria and some other West African countries, but hardly ever that of village-born, village-bred and village-resident people. Even when the latter come to live in town and adopt this typically urban trait of speech, they quickly revert to their local dialects for familiar, homely circumstances or topics.

The major criticism I am levelling against *Jagua Nana* here is not that the author uses pidgin English where good artistic sense would counsel otherwise, but that he fails to draw a consistent, convincing and realistic picture of his characters in this medium. One asks, for example, why Uncle Namme and Chief Ofubara, the two political enemies reconciled by Jagua's sexual potency (another example of Ekwensi's sensationalism) use 'formal' English all the time in their encounters with an unmistakable prostitute from Lagos who continues to address them in 'broken' English.

Leaving this aside, one asks further why the rustic night-watchman who first welcomes Jagua on her first home-visit speaks thus: 'Your father is not a young man anymore. If he can get someone to stay with him and look after him, he will feel better. Your mother is sickly too. *Them both them needs young people about them!*' (Italics mine). One wonders if Ekwensi had any clear idea of the social relationship between Jagua and this simple rural fellow.

Further still, Jagua's electioneering speech is rightly reported in 'formal' English, rightly because she spoke originally in Yoruba. We are therefore forced to ask: why does Ekwensi not keep to this pattern when Jagua and other characters must be speaking in their native tongue? A deducible answer is that the author is either too careless or does not conceive his heroine in her total situation—that is in relation to the whole story, the plot and the other characters. A muddle of the various levels of speech appropriate to different persons and situations is one of the bad results of the writer's negligence or artistic weakness.

24

I take my last example from the very end of the book—a conversation between Jagua and her mother. Now a widow, she is apprehensive that her daughter may soon desert her again after the death of her (Jagua's) baby. (The birth itself is another piece of the author's characteristic surprises.) Here is the conversation:

'When you are strong again, Jagua, what you goin' to do?'
'Mama, I don't know yet. But I wan' some place—not too far to Ogabu. Dere [i.e. 'there'] I kin trade.
I kin come here when I like for look you. Ah wan' try Onitsha whedder I kin become Merchant Princess. I already got experience of de business . . . I goin' to join de society of de women an' make frien' with dem. I sure to succeed.'
Her mother replies: 'Is good. I fear before whedder you wantin' for go back Lagos. Now is good I got me daughter on dis side of de Niger.'

This, I believe, is the sort of dialogue appropriate to Jagua and her 'business' comrades or customers. Even if it could pass for a frivolous occasion between a mother and her daughter, it can hardly suit the serious situation the author undoubtedly creates, for according to him there was 'fear in her mother's eyes, that she [Jagua] would forsake her.'

That Ekwensi writes in such a careless manner is indicative of some missing links in his conception of his characters and their role in the story. I dare claim that a novelist's totalistic conception of the various aspects of his book is necessary for its success, which in turn ensures sustained pleasure for at least the critically-perceptive reader.

To conclude, what emerges from this rather cursory discussion of two West African authors, both well educated and both native Ibo speakers, is this: the problem of the language of literary art, as it exists in Africa today, is first and foremost that creative writers should try to master their medium, English or French or any African language. Writing in one's native tongue does not solve the issue overnight. As much bad writing could be produced in Ibo by a native Ibo as by the same person in English. This applies to good writing as well. The core of the matter lies in effective control of the levels of utterance appropriate to the author, to the different persons of the story, and to the diverse occasions and contexts in which they encounter one another. And here the artist has got somewhat of a trump card: he can make his characters do whatever he likes, unfettered by the facts of history or incidents of actual life. However, he should be consistent and present a verisimilitude of life. If, however, he chooses to create a topsy-turvy world, he should at least *convince* his readers of its persistent grotesqueness.

The disadvantages of writing in a foreign language are real enough and are not being underrated; but these initial setbacks, if we may so call them, are not permanent and should not be made an excuse for sloppy, skill-less fiction writing. Language, undoubtedly, is the gateway to success in literary art. But this success cannot be achieved unless all other aspects of the genre in question—novel or play or poem—are harmoniously brought together. Language is the only vehicle for assembling these, but it is the artist's task to organise them in accordance with his total conception of the particular work in hand.

PRESENCE AFRICAINE

NEW BILINGUAL REVIEW   No. 70–2nd Quarterly 1969

CONTENTS

For details concerning free catalogues, subscription rates, availability of back-numbers etc., please write to:

'PRESENCE AFRICAINE',
25 bis, Rue des Ecoles, 75 PARIS 5e

26

An Interpretation Mongo Beti's Mission to Kala

Eustace Palmer

Readers of Mongo Beti's *Mission to Kala* tend to react in one of two ways. On the one hand are those who applaud the author's single-minded glorification of the 'native' African rural values and his corresponding denigration of modern 'city' traditions, associated as these are with an alien (in this case French) colonialist influence. These readers see Mongo Beti as a rebel reacting against the French educational system which has moulded him and calling for a revitalisation of pure native African traditions as the only means of achieving an independence which would be more real than the already realised political independence. On the other hand are those who, while acknowledging the idealisation of African tribal life in the novel, are inclined to see this idealisation as phoney, bogus and affected. They see Mongo Beti as one of those gallicised Africans who, while basking contentedly in Parisian elegance and splendour, feel periodically called upon to pay lip service to the superiority of African values. This article intends to demonstrate, *inter alia*, that both views are wrong and stem from a failure to respond to the complexity of the novel's texture and the ironic experience it offers.

The misconception, in fact, stems from too facile an identifi-

27

cation of the author, Mongo Beti, with the narrator—hero, Jean-Marie Medza, that silly, posturing, opinionated schoolboy, with his class-room clichés and inflated sense of his own self-importance. It is of course quite easy to see what kind of a boy Jean-Marie is, but we must be equally clear about what he is not. He is not necessarily Mongo Beti. No doubt this identification has been fostered by the assumption that *Mission To Kala* is an autobiographical work. Yet apart from the fact that both Jean-Marie and Mongo Beti were born in the Cameroons and attended lycées there, there is very little evidence in the work itself and the details of Mongo Beti's life as we know them, from which we could make a watertight deduction that the novel is autobiographical.

The relationship between the author of a first person narrative and the narrator could vary from one of complete identification to one of complete hostility, in spite of the fact that the story is being told in the first person. The author of a first person narrative might wish to inform his readers that a gap exists between his point of view and the narrator's, and that the narrator's interpretation of the significance of events should not be accepted as the meaning or the message of the work. Now if the author of a third person narrative wishes to point to the gap between his point of view and those of his characters, if, in other words, he wishes to comment adversely on them, there are several technical resources available to him. He could, if he wishes, comment directly in his own person, or he could get other characters to comment on the characters concerned, or he could make use of irony. But the resources available to the author of a first person narrative who wishes to point to this authorial distance, are more limited. He is precluded from commenting in his own person since the story is being told by a narrator, not by the author himself; since few people are likely to report the adverse comments made on them, the author hardly makes use of other characters to comment on the narrator. By the same token he hardly allows the narrator to comment on himself. The technique most readily available to the author, therefore, is that of irony.

A careful reading of *Mission to Kala* ought to reveal that there is a gap between the author and the narrator-hero. Either there is this gap, or we must be forced to conclude that Mongo Beti is as irresponsible, as snobbish, as short-sighted and as deluded as his school-boy hero. For in spite of his endearing wit, there are several reasons why readers might tend to dislike Jean-Marie. He is stupid, condescending, and a fraud. Surely Mongo Beti must wish to distance himself from Jean-Marie and to expose these qualities in him. And this is precisely what he does in the novel. Accordingly the hero, Jean-Marie, becomes not so much a spokesman, as a mouthpiece or *persona* or mask, to be manipulated at will, to be deliberately put in all sorts of embarrassing situations and laughed at, and at times even he himself will join in the laughter at his own expense. Irony, indeed, becomes the dominant mode in *Mission to Kala*.

The irony is primarily reflected in the nature of the language the hero uses; an even superficial analysis of Jean-Marie's style reveals that he is very much addicted to clichés and stockphrases:

> My god, how lovely she was! Her cheekbones stood out just far enough; her nose was small and pert, her mouth proud as well as sensual. Her whole personality breathed that air of calm, detached assurance which is only to be found in those girls who know what they want and can reflect on many past occasions when they got it. . . .
>
> She seemed to be waiting for something; but the longer I watched her, the less certain I became of just what it was. All women spend their lives waiting for something, I thought—probably I'd read that somewhere—and they only differ in the degree of their foreknowledge. (p. 70)[1]

This cannot be Mongo Beti speaking, or writing in the way he normally writes. If it is, then he must be condemned for indulging in a style reminiscent of tenth-rate American 'sex-and-crime' fiction. But in fact he ought to be applauded for a very subtle use of language. To take another example:

> My heart began to beat violently. I was as nervous as a partisan about to raid a strongly held enemy position. (p. 93)

The truth is that Jean-Marie's style is infiltrated with a lot of jargon from his reading of cheap fiction and his uncritical assimilation of bits and snippets from his masters' lessons and conversation; hence the clichés and stockphrases. Mongo Beti is very deliberately and subtly moulding the style to suit the

29

[1] All page references to *Mission to Kala* (translated by Michael Green), African Writers Series, Heinemann 1964.

character. But he is not merely interested in suiting language to character, he is also using these clichés to expose the essential hollowness of Jean-Marie's mind, a point which will be of great significance as we follow the movement of the story. This is all part of Beti's ironic technique; he is quite surely conditioning and manipulating the reader into reacting against Jean-Marie, although Jean-Marie is himself telling the story.

Of course irony does not entirely depend upon the infusion of clichés into the character's speech; it could be just as effectively indicated by the tone of voice, the vehemence of the speakers arguments or the illogicalities in what he says. Mongo Beti shows himself quite capable of deploying all these. For instance, Jean-Marie describes a meal:

> This was, according to custom, an enormous meal chiefly because they only had two meals a day. The women went to work in the fields early in the morning, and only returned late in the afternoon. . . .
>
> The table was loaded with food. My uncle was distinctly lacking in table manners: he crammed his mouth so full that a great bulge appeared in each cheek, and I was afraid he might burst. I trained myself not to catch his eye during meals so as to avoid betraying my astonishment at his feeding habits. His son, on the other hand, shot constant glances of shame and reproach at him. (p. 57)

This is Jean-Marie at the height of his condescension towards the people of Kala and it is a condescension that the author does not share. It is surely exposed in Jean-Marie's contemptuous reference to their 'two meals a day' and in the obvious exaggeration about his uncle's table manners. To take another example:

> Is there, as I am inclined to suspect, a kind of complicity, an unspoken agreement between even the severest examiner and any candidate? And if so, does this complicity not rest on the implied assumption (which the professor at least is consciously aware of) that all they both know is, in differing degrees, illusory and insubstantial? Pursuing this sour train of thought, I asked myself how many geography teachers in Western Europe and the areas under European influence, such as Central Africa, had any real or precise information about contemporary conditions in Russia? It was a depressing state of affairs if countless

30

poor little bastards were forced to sacrifice their youth in assimilating a lot of fairy tales (p. 68)

Failure to see the aesthetic distance between Mongo Beti and his hero in a passage such as this leads to the notion that Mongo Beti is a rebel against European values. Jean-Marie here is merely inventing face-saving formulae for his incompetence as a lecturer on Russian conditions. The passage is a tissue of illogicalities and non-sequiturs. Jean-Marie assumes he would have passed an oral in Russian geography simply because he got away with it in this 'extra-mural' session in Kala. He furthermore implies that in this event his lecturers would have demonstrated, not only their incompetence, but the general complicity which exists between examiner and examinee, caused by the ignorance of the examiners themselves. From this he goes on to imply that most European geography teachers are ignorant of Russian conditions, and refers to the facts of geography as 'fairy tales'. All this he deduces from the fact that he was able to hoodwink the people of Kala with lies about Russia. We the readers, know all too well, that Jean-Marie has not only not passed his oral, but has failed his entire baccalauréat. It is not college learning which is called into question here, as Jean-Marie assumes, but his own imperfect assimilation of the facts his teachers have been trying to drill into his head.

Mongo Beti is looking at Jean-Marie with a critical eye and so should we. These two passages have been analysed in some detail, because it is important to establish at the outset that there is a difference in point of view between author and narrator, and that Jean-Marie's statements and judgements should neither be accepted at face value, nor relied upon. We can now proceed with a detailed examination of the novel.

The first point to note is that *Mission to Kala* is not about a mission to recover anyone's delinquent wife. In the deepest sense it is a mission of growth and discovery during which the hero is forced to acknowledge many truths about himself, his upbringing, his education and his so-called rustic cousins. As is usually the case with the picaresque novel, interest lies not so much in the adventures the hero encounters during his travels, as in his moral, emotional and psychological development. Like all picaresque heroes Jean-Marie starts off in a state of innocence in spite of his airs, and therefore has to be thrown into the world and exposed to external experiences, so that he may learn more about life.

31

It is important to realise that at the start Jean-Marie is himself under no illusions about his actual position and achievement. He is fully conscious of himself as a failure, and this is the reason for his depression. It is his fellow Vimilians who persist in regarding him as an idol, as the educated man with his learning, certificates and knowledge of the white man's secrets: 'He only has to make the trip there and put the fear of God into those savages'. And so we have the beautiful paradox that a sixteen-year-old boy is about to be sent on an errand to recover the wife of a thirty-five-year-old man. The situation has tremendous comic potential; Mongo Beti rises to the occasion and exploits it to the full, and the comedy is partly at the expense of the Vimilians.

At this stage of the proceedings there are only two sane people. The first is aunt Amou, that self-effacing but very perceptive widow. She is the voice of reason and sanity, and she sees with amazing clarity that the Vimilians are attributing to Jean-Marie a whole scale of values that he quite patently does not possess. 'Aren't you ashamed to drag this poor boy into your dirty lies? He's just a child—' The second is Jean-Marie himself. He is quite properly appalled at the prospect of the task he is being asked to undertake, and we and Mongo Beti are solidly behind him, and we endorse his judgements at this stage.

But then a very strange thing begins to happen to Jean-Marie. As soon as it becomes clear that the Vimilians are determined to send him on this mission he becomes infected with their spirit of enthusiasm for the task and condescension towards the people of Kala: 'An *easy* adventure, among comparatively simple people, is the secret wish and aim of every adventurer. When you come to think of it, the very existence of adventurers is only made possible by the survival of primitive simple-minded tribes.' Jean-Marie is already demonstrating a marked readiness to accept the values of other people, a readiness which will manifest itself later in the work. He is thus revealed as an unreliable narrator and guide through the tortuous mazes of his Kala experiences, and he has already moved quite some distance from Mongo Beti, from us the readers, and aunt Amou who, we are told, could not get over the decision to send him.

Jean-Marie is already having delusions of grandeur. He regards himself not just as a missionary taking light to the barbarous people of Kala, but also as a conquistador about to engage on a

32

mission of conquest. When he thinks of a means of transport he dreams of a richly caparisoned horse and he refers to his bicycle as a 'splendid machine', an 'aristocrat among bicycles':

> Occasionally, I stopped, and with one foot just touching the ground while the other remained, as it were, in the stirrup, I gazed at this vast panorama lying open to my future exploits. (This vast panorama was for the most part restricted to a seedy vista of tree-trunks lining the road, oppressive in the most literal sense.) Then there was this strange name of mine, Medza. If I added one tiny syllable, only one, it would be transformed into a real Conquistador's name. Medzaro!—just like Pizarro or near enough anyway. (p. 20)

Jean-Marie comes to Kala with a whole set of preconceptions about the people of Kala and about himself, but he is gradually going to be forced to change them. In the first place he does not get the hero's welcome proper to a conquistador, since the village is preoccupied with its own pastimes and no one notices him. Here is how he reacts to the game he finds in progress:

> I was astonished by the whole thing, though in the end, I remembered that when we were about six or so we used to play a similar sort of game at home. But in our case it was a childish pastime, a mere survival from former times, and not taken in the least seriously. At Kala, to judge by this match it was still going very strong indeed. (p. 22)

It is Jean-Marie's overweening condescension and arrogance that strikes the reader in this passage. In his view, the people of Kala are at the emotional and mental state of children of 'six or so'; they are not only mentally retarded as it were, they are also technologically regressive—living in a bygone age. Subsequently his eyes light on Zambo:

> Having first taken a bird's eye, panoramic view of the scene, I now began to examine it in detail. The first thing that caught my eye was a great hulking devil in the Kala team, who had such enormous muscles that I concluded he must have bought them on the instalment system. There was simply no other explanation possible. He was tall and flat-footed, with a dispro-

33

portionately lengthy torso, which, nevertheless he carried very badly. His buttocks were incredibly slender, yet he retained the country native's slight pot-belly due to a habitually rough and meagre diet. He was like a kind of human baobab tree. . . .

I found it hard to believe that this monster was really my cousin, the young man from whom old Bikokolo had promised me so wonderful a reception. By what miraculous process, I asked myself, could this man be related to me in any way? (p. 23)

After Jean-Marie's description Zambo emerges as a horrible monster. But as the novel progresses we begin to entertain doubts about the accuracy of the description, for Zambo as we experience him, does not look like a brute; indeed, all the girls seem to be in love with him. A little later in the novel, when he is being forced to shed his air of superiority as a result of his set-backs in Kala, Jean-Marie himself refers to Zambo as his handsome cousin, and on yet another he calls him a Greek demi-God. It must surely be that the picture Jean-Marie presents of Zambo is a hopeless distortion, and we can see that this is the case if we look again at the passage. What happens here is that in the first half of each statement Jean-Marie gives an account which is to Zambo's credit, but in the next half he proceeds to denigrate him; he takes away with one hand, what he gives with the other. Zambo's enormous muscles are not to be despised, but in the second half of the first statement Jean-Marie proceeds to ridicule them. In the first half of the next statement we are informed that Zambo was tall, and anyone can see that this must be an asset, especially to a muscular man, but in the next half Jean-Marie quashes this favourable impression with the contemptuous 'flat-footed'. Zambo seems to Jean-Marie to have a disproportionately lengthy torso; and in spite of the denigratory 'disproportionately', the implication is that a lengthy torso is an advantage, since its owner will almost certainly carry it elegantly, but we are told in the next breath, that, nevertheless, Zambo carried his very badly. Zambo's incredibly slender buttocks are certainly an asset in a man, yet we are told of his country-native's pot-belly. We may well ask how Jean-Marie knows about the country-native's rough and meagre diet seeing he has never been in Kala before? Moreover we ourselves are soon to see that the Kalans' diet is anything but rough and meagre.

34

The point is that Jean-Marie is deliberately forcing Zambo to fit the preconceived mould he has brought with him of the rustic Kalan. However, from now on the tables will be turned, and Jean-Marie will be forced to laugh at himself as he discovers his inferiority to the Kalans in many respects. His first surprise comes with the warmth and hospitality which are extended to him on his arrival at Kala. His cousin Zambo, from whom he expected nothing but savagery and uncouthness, behaves to him with such marked courtesy and sophistication that he almost faints with shock.

At Kala Jean-Marie discovers what had been so conspicuously lacking in Vimili—the strength and warmth of personal relationships. Those four 'irresponsibles'—Zambo, Petrus-Son-of-God, Abraham the Boneless wonder, and Duckfoot Johnny, cling to each other with an almost religious devotion. It is not for nothing that their names have religious connotations. Zambo enjoys the most cordial relations with his father who even allows him to keep his mistress in the house. We can imagine how Jean-Marie's father would react to his son's girl-friend living underneath the same roof with him. Indeed the Zambo-Niam relationship is the exact antithesis of that between Jean-Marie and his father. Jean-Marie's father ruled his household with a mailed fist and hardly communicated with his sons. It was a family, moreover, in which squabbling and bullying were the order of the day; 'there was never any peace or sense of security; nothing but rows, reproaches and fear'. The father scolded everyone, the mother scolded the children, the boys took it out on the girls, and the elder sister told off the younger. It was a home exactly calculated to produce juvenile delinquents, and it is hardly surprising that both Jean-Marie and his elder brother become something like delinquents in the end.

In Kala Jean-Marie discovers a freedom and spontaneity he never thought existed. When they go swimming in the river and the other boys take off their clothes and plunge in naked, without any feelings of shame or guilt, Jean-Marie, conditioned as he has been by the restrictive morality of his environment, rather self-consciously keeps on his pants until he is shamed by the others into removing them.

It is in Kala that Jean-Marie is first introduced to the pleasures of drinking alcohol. It happened most opportunely at one of the 'extra-mural' sessions when Jean-Marie, bombarded from all angles by questions he was unable to answer, felt hot under the collar and called for water. Some bright chap guessed that nothing but strong spirit would be good enough for the 'city slicker' and he obliged with a bottle of American whisky. So, even while commenting contemptuously on American whisky Jean-Marie discovers that 'there is nothing like alcohol for putting you at your ease in any surroundings'. Later the condescending youth, who had earlier drunk palm wine only because he had to, is to discover that 'there is nothing like palm wine for adding a special edge to your sophistication'.

But by far the most important of all Jean-Marie's discoveries in Kala is sex. We have already seen that in this novel interest lies in the process whereby the hero's eyes are opened to new vistas of experience as a result of which he changes and grows. Now sexual experience is one of the foremost indicators that anyone has passed the watershed between youth and manhood. It is therefore not surprising that much of the novel is taken up with attempts to get Jean-Marie to go to bed with a girl. It is here in 'primitive' Kala that the supposed 'city slicker', the superior youngster with experience and savoir-faire is initiated into manhood. At the start, Jean-Marie is a virgin and he is scandalised by his cousin's proposals to find him a girl. However, the urge takes hold of him and he becomes desperate for sexual experience. Yet, when he is confronted by the most beautiful, sophisticated and proudest girl in the village he is so overwhelmed by a sense of his own inexperience and inadequacy, and his suspicions of the girl's expertise, that he withdraws into frigid impotence. Later, still pretending to be the city slicker with lots of experience, he braves it out by making the most scandalous allegations about the girl's purity and health as an excuse for his failure to ask her for the greatest favour. However, his interest has been aroused and he is finally able to 'make it' with the equally inexperienced Edima, the chief's daughter.

Increasingly, Jean-Marie the conquistador finds himself at a disadvantage and is forced to admit his inferiority to the other boys; 'I'd have given all the diplomas in the world to swim like Buckfoot Johnny, or dance like the Boneless wonder; or have the sexual experience of Petrus-Son-of-God.'

However, in spite of his set-backs on the swimming, dancing, sex and athletics fronts, there is one area of experience in which

Jean-Marie ought to be incontestably the champion. This is the field of learning or education. After all he is the only person in Kala with any education worth talking about, and he had been deliberately selected by Vimili for this mission because of his learning and his certificates. Moreover, the main reason why the Kalans revere him as they do is their conviction that he is the educated man who knows the white man's secrets. Yet it is in this area of activity that Jean-Marie's inferiority is most glaringly exposed. He had intended to bring light to the barbarous savages, but finds out that he is much less than a match for them, for his own lack of basic facts manifests itself, and the Kalans, moreover, in spite of their lack of formal education, have a strong native intelligence.

The Kalans, like the Vimilians wrongly attribute a whole scale of values to Jean-Marie because they regard him as the scholar. Therefore, they organise 'extra-mural' sessions at which he is supposed to answer their questions and talk to them about the white man's secrets. Before the first of these sessions Jean-Marie behaves with his characteristic condescension and conceit. His hostess asks him what he has been taught at school and he says:

> I wanted to be kind to this woman; she meant well enough; but how on earth was I to give her the most elementary notion of such things as geography, advanced mathematics or the social sciences?
> ... I honestly believed that the old lady was suffering from the effects of senility. (p. 48)

Jean-Marie later has reason to wish he had not been so condescending and conceited:

> Scarcely was dinner over when my hostess began to fire a whole fusillade of questions at me. She sat next to me and went on absolutely ruthlessly, dragging detailed explanations out of me, and going back over muddled points with needle-sharp clarity. She obviously was aware of all my weaknesses and shortcomings; she was equipped to give me the most humiliating oral I had ever been through in my life. To think that there are people like me whose job is passing exams all their life. (p. 62)

But the woman is no exception; the entire audience fire the most penetrating questions at Jean-Marie, probing his weaknesses and exposing his essential ignorance. He becomes increasingly embarrassed, but at the next session the torture continues, and he wants 'to yell for mercy, to throw in the sponge, anything'. He had even gone to the extent of preparing 'bright definitions' as possible answers to possible questions, but this does not help him in the least. He has to fabricate over Russian Geography, falsify New York's problems and is completely unable to articulate his own prospects and those of other members of his generation.

But this is not all. For Jean-Marie does not merely fail to educate the Kalans; it seems as if in certain matters he is going to be educated by them. It has already been seen that he completes his sex-education in Kala; it is also quite obvious that he has to be taught lessons in village economics and tribal customs during his stay there. Moreover, he is hardly what one might call a bright student. Indeed, on many occasions Zambo and his father almost throw up their hands in despair at the impenetrable thickness of this boy. For instance, after a characteristic howler from Jean-Marie during the celebrated discussion on blood relationships this is how his uncle reacts:

He stooped down to his work again, his face twisted into a kind of despairing grimace. It was just such an expression as is common among classics masters in the provinces, indicating that their pupils are incurably third-rate and will never be any use at anything, let alone classics. Then he stood up once more, with an air of conscientious determination. *Nil desperandum* was written all over him. (p. 89)

And on one occasion Zambo is forced to exclaim:

'Don't you know anything in your part of the country?'

What we are witnessing is a process whereby Jean-Marie's initial position relative to the people of Kala is being completely reversed. This reversal is particularly marked in his relationship with Zambo. At the start Jean-Marie is quite convinced not only of Zambo's barbarity, but also of his dumbness and stupidity. As far as he is concerned Zambo is a creature of complexes; and of mule-headed stubbornness with no imagination and no critical faculty whatever. But increasingly the would-be conquistador is forced to rely on the dull-witted savage for security and support. Moreover, as we get to know Zambo, we fail to see any evidence of dullness or complexes; on the contrary he seems a highly imaginative and resourceful young man who is really more quick-witted and perceptive than his educated cousin. It is Zambo who first realises that the whole episode in which Edima and Jean-Marie are discovered in bed together is a carefully planned farce, designed to bolster the ego of the mother and improve Edima's matrimonial chances. When Niam's delinquent wife returns and treats Jean-Marie with studied indifference, it is Zambo who points out that she must have deliberately behaved in this manner 'in order to run him around a bit'. Jean-Marie is eventually forced to admit:

> There was a good deal of commonsense in Zambo's remarks: he was more level-headed about the whole thing than I was. (p. 145)

Although, in many ways, the Kalans treat Jean-Marie as a superior person, it seems clear that in other ways they behave to him as if they were conscious of his basic inferiority. There is little doubt that Jean-Marie is used and exploited by all the various age groups in Kala. Even Zambo uses him to bolster his prestige. When Jean-Marie, in his simplicity, supposed that the four friends, Zambo, Duckfoot Johnny, Abraham the Boneless wonder, and Petrus-Son-of-God had invited him on their shady, groundnut-scrounging enterprise as a mark of friendship, it is revealed that he was merely being used as a mascot: 'you've got to admit it, we've our little city mascot to thank for this haul. If he hadn't been there, no one would have taken any notice of us at all. . . . That's why we invited him to come along.'

But it is his uncle Mama who exploits Jean-Marie most of all. He farms him out every evening to any takers, with complete lack of consideration for his health or convenience. In one section of the novel (page 109) Jean-Marie speaks contemptuously of these people who were 'entirely innocent of modern notions concerning economics and capitalism', but his uncle demonstrates he has a very good notion of both modern and village economics. He knows quite well he has a commodity which is very much in demand and he is determined to provide the supply. So Jean-Marie has to go to these 'extra-mural' sessions whether he likes it or not. In the meantime the collection of sheep and poultry (the fee for hiring out Jean-Marie) goes on increasing, and subsequently his uncle, after cleverly luring him into a false sense of security by a pretended affability and tenderness, and hoodwinking him into a specious discussion on blood-relationships, calmly proceeds to appropriate half the sheep and poultry for his own use.

By this time any notion we had of Jean-Marie as the competent negotiator who could put the fear of God into those Kalans and recover Niam's wife, has disappeared. It is therefore not at all surprising that the negotiations are largely conducted by Mama and Zambo, and Jean-Marie, the real emmissary, hardly plays a significant role in them at all.

Finally, in those brilliantly comic scenes towards the end of the novel, the 'city slicker' is duped into marrying Edima, the chief's daughter. The dream sensation which pervades the work at this point is appropriate, for Jean-Marie is carried away by forces that have proved too strong for him. And so we have the supreme irony that the educator becomes the educated and the conquistador becomes the conquered.

In the meantime Jean-Marie has himself been fully conscious of what has been happening to him. Bullied, exploited, duped and exposed, faced with the superiority of these rustic Kalans and fully aware of his own inadequacies, he becomes a rebel against his background, against the educational system which has reared him and against his father. As far as Jean-Marie is concerned it is these factors, not any defects in his own character and personality, which are to blame for his débâcle at Kala:

Looking back, I suspect Eliza had become my symbol of absolute liberty, the freedom enjoyed by country boys like Duckfoot Johnny, the Boneless wonder, Son-of-God, and the rest. I saw this freedom as the most precious possession I could acquire, and realized at the same time that in all likelihood, I should never have it. Without being aware of it, I was no more than a sacrifice on the altar of Progress and Civilization. My youth was slipping away, and I was paying a terrible price for—well, for *what*? Having gone to school at the decree of my all powerful father? Having been chained to my books when most children of my age were out playing games? (p. 63)

The same sentiments are expressed towards the end of the novel with much greater vehemence:

Fathers used to take their children to school as they might lead sheep into a slaughterhouse . . .

40

We were catechized, confirmed, herded to communion like a
gaggle of holy-minded ducklings . . .
What god were we being sacrificed to, I wonder? (p. 165)

Now it is easy to take statements such as these literally as part
of the message of the novel, and to see Jean-Marie-Medza as the
white man's 'representative' who, having been exposed from an
early age to Western education and Western civilisation is at a loss
in his own tribal culture. It seems as if Mongo Beti is suggesting
that to expose a boy to an alien system of education is to cut him
off from his roots in the tribe, to rob him of all that is good and
beautiful and valuable, and render him unfit, not only for tribal
life, but for any kind of life at all.

But to make this kind of judgement is to simplify Mongo Beti's
meaning, to identify him much too facilely with Jean-Marie, to do
less than justice to the subtlety and complexity of his technique,
and to fail to see passages such as those quoted above as the
culmination of the ironic process which has been going on all
along.

We have already seen that in many ways Jean-Marie is an
unreliable narrator whose judgements must be viewed with a
certain amount of scepticism. We have already seen irony operating in another passage in which he discusses education with
characteristic vehemence. The irony operates no less in these
passages. It is their general vehement tone that is the indication.
How true is it anyway that Jean-Marie's youth is slipping away?
Does he not exaggerate when he calls this freedom the most
precious possession he could ever acquire? Does he not falsify
when he describes himself as a sacrifice on the altar of progress
and civilisation? Jean-Marie is merely wallowing in self-pity and
giving vent to his personal antagonism for his father whom he sees
lurking behind all his troubles. Mongo Beti must not be identified
with him here and certainly does not give him his endorsement.

No doubt there are valuable things in Kala society and Jean-
Marie is the worse for not possessing them. But to go on from this
and suggest that Mongo Beti is decrying education or Western
civilisation is to make a judgement that is not warranted by the
text. In the first place, Jean-Marie is not really the symbol or
representative of the white man. It is the Kalans and the Vimilians,
not Mongo Beti, who regard him as the white man by attributing

41

values to him that we can see he does not possess. On one occasion one of the Kalans says to him, 'for *us* you are the white man, you can explain these mysteries to us.' But what Mongo Beti demonstrates is Jean-Marie's complete inability to explain these or any other mysteries. He does not possess the white man's secrets. In the second place, Jean-Marie is not really the embodiment of Western education. In spite of all this talk about his learning and certificates we know he has failed his baccalauréat and is only partially educated. Indeed at Kala his inability to respond to and assimilate his teachers' lessons is all too clearly revealed. At best, Jean-Marie's attitude to his studies has been merely perfunctory; he tell us so himself:

> I had really only applied myself to my studies at all because my father was ambitious on my behalf. He wanted me to get more and more diplomas and certificates, without bothering his head overmuch as to where they would get me. In short I had been made to go to school, and then arranged things as best as I could to suit myself. I had turned the whole thing into a game, something to pass the time away and amuse me (p. 79)

This is Jean-Marie's attitude to his education. How then can we blame his education for his reverses at Kala? How can we say he is rendered impotent at Kala because he has been transformed by Western education into the 'white man's representative'.

Jean-Marie, partly because of his antagonism to his father, and partly because of his discomfitures, comes to regard Kala society as the ideal. It has already been seen that one of the reasons for his unreliability is his readiness to accept other people's values quite uncritically. We must surely question these Utopian values that he attributes to Kala. In the first place the Kala freedom he becomes so nostalgic about can easily degenerate into licentiousness as is shown by the case of Zambo himself, who cannot go to sleep 'so long as there is a girl to screw somewhere in the world'. Moreover, death is ever-present in this world as the case of Elias Messi proves, and there is something rather pathetic about the 'togetherness' which binds Zambo and his three friends. Endongolo and his sister are orphans and Jean-Marie himself admits that the lives of most of the Kalans was miserable: 'It is extraordinary how different lives resemble one another, superficial details apart: they all seem to be miserable.'

Mongo Beti is much too intelligent to idealise the Kalans. They are very much like ordinary human beings, not the ideal. They can be vulgar like Petrus-Son-of-God, or the girls who watch the boys bathing in the river, generous like Zambo, self-effacing like Zambo's mother, petty like the chief, mean and calculating like Zambo's father, friendly like Endongolo, flirtatious like Edima and sluttish like Niam's wife. They are, in fact, very much like the rest of us. Jean-Marie's mistake is to regard them as the ideal and therefore to rebel so violently against his education and background, with the result that he becomes a juvenile delinquent and a vagrant.

Mission to Kala then is neither an attack on education nor on Western civilisation; rather it is a brilliant satire directed at all those half-educated chaps who feel, that because of a partial exposure to Western ways they have a right to feel superior to those of their brethren who still live the tribal life. It is Jean-Marie's personal weaknesses, his condescension, arrogance and stupidity which Mongo Beti subjects to rigorous criticism by means of his comic art.

Edwin Thumboo

A response to 'Okigbo understood: a study of two poems',
African Literature Today, No. 1 (1968), p. 19

The objections to Dathorne's opening remarks are two-fold. It
does not take us very far to say for instance that all of Okigbo's
poems are concerned with 'archetypal experience', and 'that in all
cases the protagonist's [Okigbo or the *persona* he adopts] view of
the world is essentially a religious one'. We anticipate—for
Dathorne is usually perceptive and sensible—some quick illuminating remark which will reduce the good intentions of his key
phrases to manageable proportions. But Okigbo's poetry, with its
enormously attractive complexity, proves irresistible: 'There is no
single accepted ethic that dominates it; it sums up the variety of
human experience and distils it in enigmatic form.' And the
reference to the 'the religious density of meaning that the poet
intends' does not clear the air.

It is difficult to see a poet's work simultaneously as archetypal
in character and possessing 'enigmatic form'. Dathorne is com-
pressing his arguments and no doubt has in reserve the modifi-

44

cations necessary to eliminate these and other difficulties. But the paragraph is misleading.

If Okigbo's poetry is essentially religious, it is only so in a special sense. Dathorne is right in noting that no 'single accepted ethic' dominates it. The poetry is not prescriptive, not directly concerned with moral interests. It deals with the individual behaviour, 'the variety of human experience', Okigbo's experience. When we call it religious we are merely recognising the poetry's intensity, and the extent to which it reflects the profound and almost total exploration of the individual's sensibility as it evolved in a ferment compounded out of the confrontation between traditional interests and modernity. Okigbo's language in *Heavensgate*, *Limits* and the *Laments*, is religious and ritualistic, drawn from Christianity and traditional sources. But these resources are utilised to establish the protagonist's journey into himself, towards self-understanding, a psychological rather than religious undertaking. There is a process of growth and integration, an assimilation of experience.

Because his poetry has a powerful impact we tend to think of it as religious in origin. We should recognise instead that Okigbo exploits the potential of a language normally identified with religion to work for a secular purpose, though that purpose is nothing less than the birth of a personal identity, the personalisation of his contacts and so forth. To some extent the confusion results from a failure to recognise in Okigbo that rare bird, a lyrical poet with a strong sense of drama, of large structural organisations. The development of his themes, the images and symbols that shape and establish the themes, meant careful orchestration. Dathorne himself may have had this in mind when he said in his review of 'Limits' (*Black Orpheus*, No. 15 (1964), p. 59) that 'Christopher Okigbo's poetry is all one poem: it is the evolution of a personal religion. The poet is a messiah, suppliant, apostle etc.' The poetry therefore includes a close network of inter-relationships within which a symbol—Idoto is an obvious example—grows in the body of poetry so that it has affinities throughout the poetry. Okigbo is a craftsman of a high order and keeps a tight control on this growth. The result is that he usually succeeds in investing his lines with a 'telegraphic precision'.

But, as I said earlier, Okigbo is basically a lyric poet. We must guard against uncovering complexities on those occasions where

45

the lyric impulse is not accompanied by large, or elaborated purposes. See for example, Section 1 of the 'Lament Of The Silent Sisters', noting especially the counterpointing of the Sisters' lament and the words of the Chorus, and also how the lyrical quality of some of the lines is exploited in a poem predominantly dramatic in tone.

Dathorne mistakes the first poem to be about 'two lovers who have achieved physical proximity, even though emotional nearness is denied them.' This, and much of the subsequent analysis, is an unnecessary complication. The comments on 'between' and 'us' from the first two lines of the poems are a fair example of the dangers.

The lovers are denied fulfilment, are kept separate: this is the whole point of the poem. Clearly, 'between' serves to emphasise this separation and also to provide a brief verbal structure—'between us/between two pines'—that will identify the lovers and the two pines. It enables the emblematisation of the lovers' predicament. Okigbo is providing an imagistic, physical embodiment of their separation. Once the transition is made, he proceeds to develop his poem by exploiting the narrative power latent in the descriptive possibilities.

> We are now shadows
> That cling to each other
> But kiss the air only.

The moon, drawn from the 'encyclopaedia of the poetic experience', plays its conventional role. Because the lovers are separated,

> Love with the moon has ascended
> Has fed on solitary stems

Love has departed with the moon and the lovers are thwarted, i.e. have had to feed on solitary stems.

The claim that 'pines' 'suggests both the tree and the archaic, meaning of the sufferings of hell' seems far-fetched. If one is inclined to spot ambiguities, it is surely closer to the tone and general import of the poem to take the simpler alternative of 'pine: to languish, waste away, from grief, disease etc; long eagerly . . .' This, however, may have been rejected as disadvantageous because it would deny any reference to the fall, and 'man's consequent separation from God'.

46

Dathorne has a tendency to press the lines too hard. For instance 'bow' in 'pines/That bow to each other'—a gesture of futility, a withdrawal of energies—is interpreted as follows: 'the bowing is not ritualistic; it suggests the worship of false gods that have taken the place of the truth in which he lived before'. The text, the poetry is left far behind with interpretation free to yield a series of statements that support some unusual conclusions or conclusions that can only be formulated from a study of other poems by the same poet:

> Not only is the poem just considered indicative of Okigbo's technique of meaning-accumulation but it also shows something of his interests. There is an assumption in all of the poetry that the primordial rift between matter and essence, earth and sky, man and his gods has to be atoned for. There is as well the assumption that the rift is not a complete break but a severance that can be bridged by expiation.

Like the generalisations I made earlier on the pre-occupation of Okigbo's poetry the technique of meaning-accumulation can only be properly examined and documented by looking at the whole body of his work. The poem under discussion is too fragile to bear the weight of interpretative comment. Nor is it easy to see how the lines give some idea of Okigbo's interest: Dathorne's remark has the benefit of hindsight and his special interpretation. And the assumption he makes of fundamental rifts that have 'to be atoned for' and expiated, really amount to a double misunderstanding. Okigbo's poetry is too buoyant with energy, with life, is not guilt-ridden and can have little to do with atonement. It does not seek to heal rifts, but does seek to reconcile opposites and the many disparaged areas of experience. This activity is a pretty normal one and is part of the function of ordinary minds all the time. Any suggestion of a 'severance' that requires expiation before being 'bridged' is artificial. Such divisions are inherent in the material, in life itself. Okigbo's subject-matter, the material of his poetry, is normal—how else can we claim that his work is archetypal?—except that *his* perceptions and their embodiment in language are sharp and particular. They differ from ours *qualitatively*. It is more accurate to see the 'expiation', the ritualistic elements which are boldest in *Heavensgate* and *Limits,* as really

47

part of Okigbo's technique which adopts Christian and traditional resources for the purpose of articulating his salvation as a person.

Dathorne's comments on the Invocation to *Heavensgate* are more to the point although one might not agree with what he has to say at the further limits of his interpretation. Moreover, the emphasis he gives to the sexual elements in the poem is questionable.

> The posture is one of abject humility; indeed 'naked' and 'barefoot' suggest humiliation. These are the two key-words of this section and they introduce a sexual element in the quest. Like the cannibalistic love which fed on its own stems, in the poem considered before, this nudity is a pointer towards the ritualistic abnormalities the devoted must undergo—here incest. The 'mother'—Eve, Mary, a minor river goddess, the mother of the protagonist—is the sexual means through which the heavenly connection can be made.

We forget that the language of religious adoration has frequently had recourse to the language of love. The tone of the lines, their very drift and gravity, compel us to see the language of the invocation as sacred and not profane. It cleverly sets the mood for a meditative and serious frame of mind:

> Before you, mother Idoto,
>   naked I stand,
> before your watery presence,
>   a prodigal,
>
> leaning on an oilbean;
> lost in your legend. . . .

The gravity so dominant and all-embracing lies in the incantatory quality and the deft touches that are both Christian and traditional as in:

> Under your power wait I on barefoot,
> Watchman for the watchword at heavensgate

or phrases such as 'naked I stand', 'prodigal'. The nudity here is that of a novice, exposed and expectant, remote from any brutal sexuality. Okigbo meditates on his theme to bring it alive in a

48

series of related pictures; but while this is one intention of the poetry we notice hints of a gradual withdrawal from external circumstance into an inner world of being where Okigbo will develop the drama, the tensions and resolutions in terms of images, linked phrases, and symbols. But this withdrawal is clearer when you look at the rest of *Heavensgate*. The point we need to stress is that if we listen to the poetry, attend to it without preconception, we will likely avoid any exaggeration of its parts:

> Therefore the opening lines of the *Heavensgate* sequence begin not with humility but with a certain braggadocio; the protagonist only comes in feigned humility for his nakedness vaunts his powers of procreation and his boast suggests that the male in him preceded the female in her.

These gestures are just not there. We fall into the error of shaping our response according to suggestions outside the lines and risk diminishing the power of the poetry. And in so doing we mar that other function of criticism, the need to help others to the poems in accordance with their understanding.

49

FERDINAND
OYONO

Ferdinand Oyono, *The Old Man and The Medal* (a translation of *Le Vieux nègre at la medaille,* 1956, by John Reed), African Writers Series, Heinemann 1969

The Old Man and The Medal has the quality, so rare in modern African writing, of bringing together both the comic and the sad elements in the situation of pre-independence Africa.

Meka is an old and respected member of the village Doum in an unspecified French colony. He is to receive a medal from the French regional Governor. Informing him of the good news, the Commandant tells Meka:

> 'You have done much to forward the work of France in this country. You have given your land to the missionaries, you have given your two sons in the war where they found a glorious death. You are a friend.'

Kelara's joy at having this honour bestowed on her husband is later marred by a youth's comment. 'To think he has his land and his sons just for that. . . .' But Meka's own happiness and sense of importance are strong enough to take him through the agonies and frustrations of the presentation ceremony. When he wakes up late at night from the drunken sleep into which he had fallen after the reception, he tries to find his way home, is arrested for loitering in the 'white section' of the town and imprisoned. He is subsequently released the following day, but his illusions have been cruelly destroyed. He says to the interpreter:

> 'Tell him (The Police Officer) I am a very great fool who yesterday still believed in the white man's friendship. . . .'

For the reader too, the laughter aroused by Meka's ridiculous clothes, by his prayers as he waits for the Governor's arrival:

> 'Almighty God . . . Thou seest that my dearest wish at this moment is to wait

for the medal and for the white Chief
... that my dear wish and great longing
is to take off these shoes and to have a
piss ...'

This laughter too, is clouded by an increasing awareness of the deeper issues involved. We are reminded of the colonial tragedy underlying this one incident around which the story is woven.

The tragedy, however, does not seem, except in a minor way, to obscure the charm of this true, vivid and lighthearted panorama of African village life; just as in Oyono's previous novel *Houseboy*, the sadder aspects of the houseboy Toundi's life are lightened by the very funny and convincing account of his experiences.

Here to my mind lies the chief value of *The Old Man and The Medal*. Informative without being tedious, the novel is free of invective, polemic or whining self-pity. It contains all the elements so familiar to the African novel: the social gap between whites and blacks, coloniser and colonised, with the exploitation of the latter by the former, the African mistress carefully kept out of sight, and adequate criticism of a powerful and hypocritical church. But these are all etched in to provide sufficient background to a funny story.

Here are people (blessed perhaps?) with the ability to raise a laugh out of even the most difficult situations. Here is Meka, disillusioned and dispirited after his imprisonment bursting into hoots of laughter at the thought of the Governor having to pin the medal on his 'bila' (underpants) had he gone to the presentation with nothing on!

The author's easy use of the local turn of phrase also contributes to the freshness of the novel. After the first few pages the reading is no longer delayed by sentences like this:

'Meka, you are now somebody among men. Since I came to their country I have never seen cocoa as well dried as yours.'
'For good cocoa, yours is certainly that,' put in Ntua.

Furthermore, neither here nor anywhere else does Oyono intrude either to explain a saying, comment on a character's motive or criticise his action: nothing but minutely detailed narrative:

Solemnly he took down his ancient pith-helmet, now black with smoke. It hung by the chin strap which had broken and been mended. Some cockroaches and a small centipede came out of it and ran over to Kelara who stamped on them with the back of her heels. Meka gazed at the inside of the helmet, tapped it, gazed inside again and put it on. Then he put the finishing touch to his attire by slipping the strap underneath his chin.
'You look very nice,' said his wife, 'like an American missionary.' Meka smiled back at her and sat down on an old sardine packing case.

The absence of exoticism or sentimentality is characteristic of Oyono's writing. There are moments when even the best literature of 'commitment' bores.

From the sociological angle though, I found one aspect particularly interesting. In the course of the change between the traditional African values and new French standards, the emphasis on the virtues of a 'real' man or even on the meaning of manhood are seen to have shifted. Is this not the heart of the racial anxiety from which have a sprung the notions, 'Négritude', 'Africanité' and 'African identity?' Or as an unsympathetic critic once put it, 'négritude, or the philosophy, the uglier it is, the better'. Whatever it is called, this is certainly the result of an effort to acquire recognition and gain equal status within the new society.

Meka is vaguely aware of the need to assert himself, as he waits for the Governor to arrive. Hot, bothered by the desire to 'satisfy a need', suffering a million agonies from the new shoes into which he has managed to squeeze his feet, he says to himself:

'I am a man, just as my ancestors made me and left me. They are watching me now, in this situation. . . . I must not let them be ashamed of me. I was circumsized with the knife and the doctor spat out pimento onto the wound. I did not cry out. . . .'

And later:

'In all my life I have never cried. A man, a real man, never cries. . . .'

Surely in the eyes of the Governor, the Police Officer 'Gullet' and the French community Meka is not a 'real' man! while to the villagers at Doum, he is a respected dignitary, descendant of the 'Great Mekas' to whom the villages around had belonged. That the recognition of his fellow villagers is not enough, can be deduced from Meka's pathetic eagerness to receive the medal, symbol of the white man's favour. But he soon realises that the medal is of little significance, since on the same night he is arrested, like any other African, for being in the white section of the community at night without a good reason. His wife, Kelara, also comes to feel that a medal is paltry recompense for the loss of her sons and his land. Engomba too, in the last two chapters becomes acutely aware that Meka has been humiliated, that men like Meka and himself have been diminished in stature by the white man and his culture.

Oyono's story ably illustrates this much, but lightly. His chief aim has always been to entertain and, like *Houseboy*, this novel makes thoroughly enjoyable reading.

The translation from the original French by John Reed is excellent.

Jeannette Kamara (Mrs)

JOHN MUNONYE

John Munonye, *The Only Son*, African Writers Series, Heinemann 1966

If one considers Africa continent-wise—and few nowadays will object—then clearly English is a good thing for Africa. English, and in its degree, French. Given expression in Mende, in Yoruba, or in Twi, the Pan-African sentiment is necessarily less resonant and less uniting: inaudible beyond the confines of the tribe, let alone the nation. Woe betide the Englishman who says so, perhaps, yet the political fact is inescapable. Much less straightforward, however, are the advantages of English to the African writer, that is to the novelist or playwright or poet. Between politics and literature, it would seem, there is a distinction of the first order. Literary preoccupations are complex where political issues are simple. Literature is essentially local; politics, on the other hand, is an interest in its nature migratory from the local to the national, from the national to the international. The politician cannot get as far down as the individual; even the small group is liable to rebuke for being small, for being therefore low in voting power. The writer, on the contrary, begins with the individual and all that is individual about him. He never indeed departs from this personal level: his persons remain persons however numerously they throng his works. The group, the class, are political abstractions to which he cannot have access in his work.

Of course this distinction is in the last analysis artificial. If we are at all concerned with politics as vital art, and not as gross miscalculation, then the politician is bound to take account of the individual. Neither can the writer neglect the political and social roles in which his characters appear in his books—without which indeed they scarcely can appear, no matter how determined he is to divest them of these appearances—if he is to present an undifferentiated human nature.

Nevertheless for the writer there is a difficulty. It is still through a foreign language that he must present his most intimate sense of the reality of things. There would doubtless be no problem if an African writer's reality were much the same as an English writer's. But it is not—the interest of the matter lies there as well as the awkwardness. For example, the English language contains as yet no convenience of idiom for describing a polygamous state of affairs. Every language has its armoury of casual reference for things accustomed: in English 'our elder mother' simply raises eyebrows. One might be tempted after too prolonged a diet of African novels to such locutions as 'Woman, are you preparing food for me?'—rather is it to our knowing it principally as debased idiom, as the pseudo-language to such language does not unfortunatley owe simply to a departure from the norm; rather is it to our knowing it principally as debased idiom, as the pseudo-language to which English writers have resorted in writing about 'natives', 'savages' and others of that ilk. The problem of securely idiomatic diction, of writing dialogue that sounds entirely native to the speakers, of writing about people in such a way that action, behaviour, custom all strike one as normal—again as native, and so scarcely needing to be described—this problem is naturally at its most acute in those African novels that deal with tribal Africa, novels which are naturally numerous when so much of Africa is, or has been, tribal. The day-to-day life of the village, a matter at once of total ignorance and—due to the sentimental or hostile glossing of missionaries, travellers and administrators—partial familiarity to the English reader, has to be rendered from scratch, with little in the way of idiom to draw upon except that which I already suspect. Requirements for a successful rendering are also pretty severe: anyone's 'interesting account of life in an African village' will not really do, for an interesting account is not what we are after. In a novel the place of day-to-day life is after all in the background of attention, not the foreground; and whereas in an English novel for English readers there is no difficulty, the details of this life being known to the reader and therefore, except for the most casual reference, left unrendered by the writer, in an African novel the details do have to be rendered and the problem of doing this without making them intrusive does exist. Given that the language is English, this appears to apply whether the reader is African or English. It would, however, be interesting to know how Chinua Achebe would have written *Things Fall Apart* if consciously he had been writing only for Ibo readers, as inward that is to say as himself concerning things Umuofian, yet equally literate with him in English. Might it not have been more elliptical, more sophisticated in its dealings with the reality, more productive of literary elbow-room?

Things Fall Apart has come, deservedly, to be regarded as a kind of standard expository text, but after reading a more recent novel, *The Only Son* one wonders whether Achebe's place has not in this regard been challenged, and by a fellow Ibo, John Munonye. Munonye has, to begin with, offered the reader an immediately compelling relationship, that of a mother—a widowed mother—with her only son. It is as though he had said, 'Let us take something that will not be conditioned—or not crucially so—by the African experience, something I shall not have to explain, however discreetly.' The relationship of Chiaku and Nnanna has its reality independent of the context of tribe and village; Okwonko, on the other hand, in *Things Fall Apart,* seemed a shade programmatic, the tribal hero evincing tribal virtues then tragically failing to adapt: he was not as Chiaku and Nnanna convincingly are, on the scene before the book begins, human nature pushing its way onto a scene that turns out to be an African village but might not have been. One must keep the platitude that human nature is everywhere the same, well to the fore: glee inhabits the reader of this novel when he discovers that it is about nothing more desperately circumstantial than a mother and son—she protective and anguished, scolding and ear-clouting, fatuously fond and exploit-reciting, prudently seeing about a wife, scandalised by a defection from the honoured pagan ways (of course, but it's managed very well), finally, sensibly and rather socratically, finding another man for herself and Leaving the Boy to Go His Own Way; he, indolent and complacent, *enfant terrible* with bow and arrow, disgrace of the neighbourhood and delinquent gang leader, by smooth transition then to village hero as wrestler in his age-group, sustains his mother with perfectly gauged grudgingness, thoughtful in late adolescence, succumbs (he does not prissily lead the way though) to school and church, these upstarts conceived very practically as ways out of the tribal rut. These characterisations are not, needless to say, substitutes for the author's; so very accurate is his placing that they come ready to hand, but coming so to speak at second hand are much nearer to stereotype than his. The great point of course is that human nature everywhere *is* the same; it's the flash of familiarity that delights, the classical human gestures descried where all else is unfamiliar and foreign. An almost casual sense of this truth pervades Munonye's novel: it is what prevents him from being bemused by what is indigenous, local and specifically African, by what therefore has to be *conveyed.* He does indeed at points simply explain, guide-book-wise; but his explanations are lightly charged with humour and with irony: being defections from the narrative vein, they are ironically proffered as such.

A nice point: the very first sentence of the book is, 'Her steps were quick and forceful and her face was cloudy, like one on an errand of grief.' Not 'but'? And the fifth sentence, 'The chickens were coming out of the pen then and the palm of the hand was only faintly visible.' comes under stricture for being 'poetic', African village style. But there is not much of this and the proverbs, when they come, do not really sound like proverbs but like witty rejoinders, sharp things said in conversation. An altogether successful first novel.

Don Carter

AYI
KWEI
ARMAH

Ayi Kwei Armah: *The Beautyful Ones Are Not Yet Born* Heinemann 1969 (African Writers Series, Heinemann to be published late 1969)

Only hours after a coup to oust a corrupt regime, a bus driver has just secured the release of his bus at a road block by discreetly bribing a policeman; the bus moves on, revealing the quaintly misspelled slogan painted on its back: 'The beautyful ones are not yet born'. The episode which culminates in the slogan is another of the many sharp symbols or symbolic situations with which Ayi Kwei Armah punches home his theme of continuing corruption.

The dominating mood of the novel is one of hopeless despair. This is emphasised by an image pattern organised around filth, corruption, decay, and defecation. From the opening page of the novel when the conductor of the decaying bus spits out 'a generous gob of mucus against the tire', to the flight of the ousted Party man, Koomsoon, through the filth and the smell of a lavatory box, we are never far away from these images of filth and putrefaction. Armah displays an almost Swiftian preoccupation with bodily secretion. The spiritual rottenness of the part man takes physical form when in his downfall he is surrounded by the foulness that he emits:

His mouth had the rich stench of rotten menstrual blood. The man held his breath until the new smell had gone down in the mixture with the liquid atmosphere of the Party man's farts filling the room. At the same time Koomsoon's inside gave a growl longer than usual, an inner fart of personal, corrupt thunder which in its fullness sounded as if it had rolled down all the way from the eating throat thundering through the belly and the guts, to end in further silent pollution of the air already thick with flatulent fear. (pp. 191-2)

This is a specimen of the deliberately coarse language that Armah has chosen to express the coarse corruption the novel treats. Somehow it is unpleasantly apt. (Wole Soyinka was after a similar affect in *The Interpreters* when he too descanted on lavatory matters and invented a 'Voidante' philosophy for one of his characters.)

The main character is a strange mixture of ordinariness and a miserable unacknowledged heroism; the sort of man who in Biblical language would be called a fool for Christ's sake. He does not even have a name, being referred to throughout as 'the man'. In his anonymity he represents the millions of victims of political organisation in Africa. His life is drab and totally frustrating without the slightest glimmer of hope at the end of the dark tunnel. At the beginning of the novel he is dribbling on to the seat of a half dark bus as he sleeps on his way to his flat, colourless, ill-paid job at the Railway Administration. He meekly bears the insults of the bus conductor, and even the spray of contemptuous spit that the latter jets in his direction. Throughout the novel he suffers the taunts of his wife, the contempt of his mother-in-law, the silent accusations of his underfed children, and even the curses of a timber merchant whose unnecessary bribe he refused to accept. The man behaves in this way not out of any unassailable certainty of rightness. Everything around him is an attack on his position. It is almost as if he is sustained by his doubts. Why should not a man look after his own? Why must he doom his children to the same dull cycle he was himself caught in? The man turns these thoughts over in his mind:

> It would be the same for the children. They would grow up accustomed to senseless cycles, to cleaning work that left everything the same, to efforts that could only end up placing them at other people's starting points, to the damning knowledge that the race would always be won by men on stilts, and they had not even been given crutches to help them. (pp. 138-9)

For all his honesty (which is consistently called folly by everyone except Teacher, another anonymous symbolic character) the man too has to crawl through the filth with the corrupt Party man, thus sharing in the contamination of a man whose corruption he had himself painfully avoided.

There is certainly no false optimism in this novel. The man having left the fleeing Koomsoon and taken his symbolic cleansing bath in the sea, wakes up after a long sleep to a picture as depressing as before; a picture of decay, corruption, and despair. He sees Maanan, last seen bright with hope and the gleam of salvation in her eyes, now aimlessly muttering to herself and letting the sand run through her fingers as the dreams and hopes had run through her life. He sees the policeman taking bribes as usual, and the prospect before him as he walks back is:

> Oyo [his wife], the eyes of his children . . . the office every day, and above all the never ending knowledge that this aching emptiness would be all that the

remainder of his own life could offer him. (p. 215)

The novel starts with a deliberate lack of definition; it is dark, the location is uncertain, the characters are unnamed and the whole impression is one of Everyman in a field of folk. There is a parabolic quality here and indeed all over most of the novel. Towards the end, the author becomes more particular. Names become more common. We are explicitly in Ghana, and it is clear that the redeemer-betrayer is Nkrumah.

The earlier vagueness and anonymity combine to give the earlier part a peculiar effectiveness. If this was a deliberate effect sought by the author it is difficult to see why he chose to become increasingly particular. The character of the novel changes as a result, without seeming to gain much by the change. The strange anonymity of the man himself remains throughout however.

Armah drops the third person narrative half way through the novel (pp. 72-106) as he gives in a series of flashes the background which has left Teacher a detached, rather cynical observer of the political and social scene, after which the resumes the third person narrative to the end. This concentrated middle section carries a good deal of the satirical comment of the novel. It is here that we see, mainly through Teacher's eyes—sometimes it is difficult to tell whose mind we are being shown—the degeneration of the Messiah:

> How could this have grown rotten with such obscure haste?

(The word rotten and its cognates occur with great frequency.) The answer seems to be in the nature of power itself:

> It is possible that it is only power itself, any KIND of power, that cannot speak to the powerless. . . . He was good when he had to speak to us, and liked to be

with us. When that ended, everything was gone. (p. 103)

The language Armah has chosen will be a stumbling block for many people. For those who can keep their feet (or hold their stomachs in) the resulting novel is strikingly effective.

Armah has taken the predicament of Africa in general, Ghana in particular, and distilled its despair and its hopelessness in a very powerful, harsh, deliberately *unbeautyful* novel.

Eldred Jones

SHORT NOTICE

Baratte, Thérèse. *Bibliographie: auteurs africains et malgaches de langue française* (Second edition, revised). OCORA (Office de Cooperation radiophonique), Paris, 1968
This is an accurate, convenient and up-to-date list including practically every title by African and Malagasy authors writing in French. Except for a first section, devoted to anthologies, congress reports, and other

general works, the authors' names are listed country by country, with a complete alphabetical list appended. In addition to the usual information, this bibliography tells the price of many volumes, and consigns others to the melancholy category of *épuisé*, (out of print), or sometimes more hopefully, 'printing' or 'to be re-issued in 1968'. Any such indication is, of course, ephemeral, and when dealing with fast-moving Africana, it seems doubly so. It is gratifying, therefore, to see such detailed information delivered in such a legible, attractive form.

BIBLIO-GRAPHY
Compiled by · Hans Zell

This is the third in a series of bibliographic listings appearing regularly in *African Literature Today*.

The present listing provides details of material published late in 1968 and during 1969. A number of forthcoming publications are also included.

The scope of the bibliography is limited to *creative* writing, including critical works and anthologies. Political, historical, religious literature, as well as children's readers and similar material, is excluded.

This third listing appears in a somewhat different and improved form. Periodical literature is no longer listed separately, and the bibliography is now arranged in four major parts—covering both books and periodical articles—as follows:

I. BIBLIOGRAPHIES.
REFERENCE WORKS
II. CRITICAL WRITINGS
III. ANTHOLOGIES
IV. WORKS

In section four, poetry and plays are especially identified as such, whereas all prose appears without an annotation. Indivual poems not exceeding a minimum of at least two pages are not cited. Nationalities of *African* authors are now also given.

Works by a number of Caribbean writers are included, as are books and. articles on 'Négritude'.

Publishers of African literature are invited to submit to me, c/o Africana Publishing Corporation, 101 Fifth Avenue, New York, N.Y. 10003, regular information on relevant new and forthcoming publications. April 1969

I. BIBLIOGRAPHIES, REFERENCE WORKS

ASSMUS, URSULA; comp.
Léopold Sédar Senghor. Bibliographie des Friedenspreistraegers 1968
in: *Boersenblatt fuer den Deutschen Buchhandel,* v. 24, no. 62, 2 Aug. 1968, p. 1789-93

EAST, N. B.; comp.
African theatre: A checklist of critical materials
in: *Afro-Asian Theatre Bulletin,* v. 3, Fall 1968, 15 p.
LINDFORS, BERNTH; comp.
Additions and corrections to Janheinz Jahn's 'Bibiliography of Neo-African Literature' (1965)

in: *African Studies Bulletin,* v. 11, no. 2, Sept. 1968, p. 129-48
LINDFORS, BERNTH
American University and research library holdings in African literature
in: *African Studies Bulletin,* v. 11, no. 3, Dec. 1968, p. 286-311
WOLF, PAMELA GAIL; ed.

An index to the programmes of the Johannesburg Repertory Players from 1928 to 1959
Johannesburg, Univ. of the Witwatersrand, Dept. of Bibliography, Librarianship and Typography, 1968. 99 p. R 1.00

II. CRITICAL WRITINGS

ACHEBE, CHINUA (Nigeria)
Chinua Achebe on Biafra. (Talking to TRANSITION) in: *Transition*, v. 7, no. 36, July 1968, p. 31-8
AKYEA, E. OFORI (Ghana)
'The Atwia-Ekumfi Kodzidan—an experimental African theatre' in: *Okyeame*, v. 4, no. 1, Dec. 1968, p. 82-4
ASALACHE, KHADAMBI (Nigeria)
'The making of a poet: Wole Soyinka' in: *Présence Africaine*, no. 67, 1968, p. 172-4
AWOUMA, JOSEPH (Cameroun)
'Le conte africain et la société traditionelle' in: *Présence Africaine*, no. 66, 1968, p. 137-44
CARTEY, WILFRED
Whispers from a continent. The literature of contemporary black Africa
New York, Random House, 1969. 397 p. $8.95
CHADWICK, H. M., and CHADWICK, NORA, K.
The growth of literature Vol. 3, The Tatars, Polynesia, Some African Peoples, General Survey. (Reprint of ed. London, 1940)
London & New York, Cambridge Univ. Press, 1969. ca. 900 p. ca. $22.50
COLLEGE OF CAREERS, CAPE TOWN
Notes on Afrikaans short stories
(College of Careers, study-aid series, no. 717) Cape

Town, College of Careers, 1968. 38 p. R 0.50
COOK, MERCER, and HENDERSON, STEPHEN E.
The militant black writer in Africa and the United States
Madison, Wisc., Univ. of Wisconsin Press, 1969. 112 p. $5.00 ($1.95 pap.)
CRUSE, HAROLD
The crisis of the Negro intellectual
London, W. H. Allen, 1969. 512 p. 63s.
DE ANDRADE, MARIO
La poésie africaine d'expression portugaise
Rouen, P. J. Oswald, 1969 (in preparation)
DIAKHATÉ, LAMINÉ (Senegal)
'Valeurs de la Négritude et convergence' in: *Présence Africaine*, no. 68, 1968, p. 149-52
DIPOKO, MBELLA SONNE (Cameroun)
'Cultural diplomacy in African writing' in: *Africa Today*, v. 15, no. 4 Aug./Sept. 1968, p. 8-11
ETHERTON, MICHAEL J.
'Christopher Okigbo and the African tradition. A reply to Professor Ali M. Mazrui' in: *Zuka*, no. 2, May 1968, p. 48-52
(A reply to Ali M. Mazrui's article 'Abstract verse and African tradition', that appeared in *Zuka*, no. 1, September 1967, p. 47-50)
FISCHER-BARNICOL, HANS
'Zu Verleihung des Friedenspreis des Deutschen Buchhandels and Léopold Sédar Senghor' in: *Der Junge Buchhandel* (Suppl. to Boersenblatt fuer den Deutschen Buchhandel), v. 21, no. 9, 1968, p. 129-34
FOUTCHANTSE, VINCENT
'Promouvoir une littérature Africaine' in: *Présence Africaine*, no. 67, 1968, p. 124-56

HANF, I.
Léopold Sédar Senghor—ein afrikanischer Dichter franzoesischer Praegung
Munich, Wilhelm Fink, 1969 (in preparation). ca. 256 p.
JONES-QUARTEY, K. A. B. (Ghana)
'The problems of language in the development of the African theatre' in: *Okyeame*, v. 4, no. 1, Dec. 1968, p. 95-102
KANE, MOHAMADOU (Senegal)
'Naissance du roman Africain francophone' in: *African Arts/Arts d'Afrique*, v. 2, no. 2, Winter 1969, p. 54-8
KEDJANYI, JOHN (Ghana)
'Masquerade societies in Ghana' in: *Okyeame*, v. 4, no. 1, Dec. 1968, p. 85-90
KENNEDY, ELLEN CONOVER
'Aimé Césaire: an interview with an architect of négritude' in: *Negro Digest*, May 1968, p. 53-61
KENNEDY, SCOT
'Language and communication in the Ghanian theatre' in: *Okyeame*, v. 4, no. 1, Dec. 1968, p. 103-9
KESTELOOT, LILYAN
Négritude et situation coloniale
(Collection Abbia, 10) Yaoundé, Ed. C. L. E., 1969. 93 p. CFA 300/$3.25
KHATIBI, ABDELKABIR
Le roman maghrébin
Paris, Maspero, 1968. 152 p. F 15.40
KUNENE, DANIEL P. (South Africa)
'Deculturation—the African writer's response' in: *Africa Today*, v. 15, no. 4, Aug./Sept. 1968, p. 19-24
KUNENE, DANIEL P. (South Africa)
'A. C. Jordan 1907-1968'

in: *African Arts/Arts d'Afrique*, v. 2, no. 2, Winter 1969, p. 24-6
(An obituary)
KUNENE, MAZISI
'Background to African literature'
in: *Sechaba*, Aug. 1968, p. 14-15
LAHBABDI, MOHAMED-AZIZ (Morocco)
'La Nouvelle au Maroc'
in: *African Arts/Arts d'Afrique*, v. 2, no. 2, Winter 1969, p. 28-9 and 70-1
LARSON, C. R.
'The search for the past; East and Central African writing'
in: *Africa Today*, v. 15, no. 4, Aug./Sept. 1968, p. 12-15
LAURENCE, MARGARET
Long drums and cannons
London, Macmillan, 1968. 208 p. 32s. 6d.
(Examines the work of Nigerian dramatists and novelists)
LEWIS, PRIMILA
'Politics and the novel. An appreciation of "A wreath for Udomo" and "This Island now" by Peter Abrahams'
in: *Zuka*, no. 2, May 1968, 41-7
LINDFORS, BERNTH
'Achebe's African parable'
in: *Présence Africaine*, no. 66, 1968, p. 130-6
LINDFORS, BERNTH
'A decade of *Black Orpheus*'
in: *Books Abroad*, October 1968, p. 509-16
LINDFORS, BERNTH
'Robin Hood realism in South African English fiction'
in: *Africa Today*, v. 15, no. 4, Aug./Sept. 1968, p. 16-18
MAZRUI, ALI A. (Kenya)
'Meaning versus imagery in African Poetry'
in: *Présence Africaine*, no. 66, 1968, p. 49-57
MAZRUI, MOLLY
'Religion in African fiction: a consideration'

in: *East Africa Journal*, Jan. 1968, p. 32-6
McDOWELL, ROBERT E.
'African drama, West and South'
in: *Africa Today*, v. 15, no. 4, Aug./Sept. 1968, p. 25-8
MENSAH, ATTA ANAN (Ghana)
'The popular song and the Ghanaian writer'
in: *Okyeame*, v. 4, no. 1, Dec. 1968, p. 110-19
MOHOME, PAULUS M. (South Africa)
'Négritude: Evaluation and Elaboration'
in: *Présence Africaine*, no. 68, 1968, p. 122-40
MORRISEAU-LEROY, FELIX
'African National Theatre'
in: *Okyeame*, v. 4, no. 1, Dec. 1968, p. 91-4
MOSER, GERALD M.
'Castro Soromenho, an Angolan realist'
in: *Africa Today*, v. 15, no. 6, Dec./Jan. 1969, p. 20-4
MPHAHLELE, EZEKIEL (South Africa)
'Realism and romanticism in African literature'
in: *Africa Today*, v. 15, no. 4, Aug./Sept. 1968, p. 4
NKOSI, LEWIS (South Africa)
'Can Themba'
in: *Transition*, v. 7, no. 34, Dec./Jan. 1968, p. 40
(Obituary)
OBIECHINA, E. N. (Nigeria)
'Growth of written literature in English-speaking West Africa'
in: *Présence Africaine*, no. 66, 1968, p. 58-78
PIETERSE, COSMO, (South Africa) and MUNRO, DONALD; eds.
Protest and Conflict in African Literature
London, Heinemann, 1969. 192 p. 25s. 0d. (12s. pap.)
New York, Africana Publishing Corp., 1969. 192 p. $4.50 ($1.75 pap.)

POVEY, JOHN
'West African poetry: Tradition and change'
in: *Africa Today*, v. 15, no. 4, Aug./Sept. 1968, p. 5-7
SCHMIDT, NANCY
'Nigerian fiction and the African oral tradition'
in: *Jnl. of the New African Lit. and the Arts*, no. 5/6, Spring/Fall 1968, p. 10-19
SHELTON, AUSTIN S.
'The problem of Griot interpretation and the actual causes of war in "Sondjata" '
in: *Présence Africaine*, no. 66, 1968, p. 145-52
SILVEIRA, ONESIMO DA
'Prise de conscience dans la littérature du Cap-Vert'
in: *Présence Africaine*, no. 68, 1968, p. 106-21
TROUT, PAULETTE, and KENNEDY, ELLEN, CONROY
'David Diop: Négritude's angry young man'
in: *Jnl. of the New African Lit and the Arts*, no. 5/6, Spring/Fall 1968, p. 76-8
VAN NIEKERK, B. V. D.
The African image (Négritude) in the poetry of Léopold Sédar Senghor
Cape Town, Balkema, 1969 (in preparation)
WÄSTBERG, PER; ed.
The writer in modern Africa. The Afro-Scandinavian writer's conference
Stockholm, 1967
Stockholm, Almqvist & Wiksell (for Scandinavian Inst. of African Studies), 1969. 123 p. SwKr. 15.
WEINSTOCK, DONALD J.
'Achebe's Christ-Figure'
in: *Jnl. of the New African Lit. and the Arts*, no. 5/6, Spring/Fall 1968, p. 20-7
WILSTRAND, CARL GOSTA
Lyrics of social protest in East Africa
(Scandinavian Inst. of African Studies, research reports, no. 2)

Uppsala, Scandinavian Inst. of African Studies, 1969 (in preparation)

III. ANTHOLOGIES

DATHORNE, O. R.; ed.
Africa in prose
(Penguin African Library, AP 24)
Harmondsworth, Middx., Penguin Books, 1969. 6s. 0d.
(Revised entry, see ALT, no. 1, 1968)

IKIDDEH, IME (Nigeria)
Drum beats; an anthology of African narrative prose
Leeds, E. J. Arnold, 1968. 155 p. 8s. 6d.

IRELE, ABIOLA; ed. (Ghana)
Lectures Africaines: A prose anthology of African writing in French
London, Heinemann, 1969. 118 p. ca. 10s. 6d.

JAHN, JANHEINZ; comp.
Afrika lacht. Sinnliche, freche und witzige Geschichten, Pointen und Songs aus Afrika, Westindien und Nordamerika
Frankfurt/M, Baermeier & Nikel, 1968. 296 p. DM 20.00
(Anthology of short stories, poetry and plays)

JAHN, JANHEINZ; comp.
Schwarzer Orpheus. Neue Sammlung. Moderne Dichtung afrikanischerv Voelker beider Hemisphaeren. Mit vier Gedichten von Léopold Senghor.
Munich, Hanser, 1968. 320 p. DM 11.00
(Re-issue in cheap edition.)

JAHN, JANHEINZ; ed.
Vierunddreissigmal schwarze Liebe. Erotische Erzaehlungen aus Afrika, Westindien und Nordamerika
Frankfurt/M, Baermeier & Nikel, 1968. 350 p. DM 20.00

KESTELOOT, LILYAN
Anthologie negro-africaine. Panorama critique des pro-
sateurs, poetes et dramaturges noirs du XXe siècle
(Coll. marabout université, 129)
Verviers, Belgium, Gerard, 1968. (Paris, l'Inter) 432 p. F 7.50

LITTO, FREDRIC M.; ed.
Plays from black Africa
New York, Hill & Wang, 1968. 316 p. $5.95 ($1.95 pap.)

MEMMI, ALBERT
Anthologie maghrebine, vol. 2
Paris, Présence Africaine, 1969 (in preparation)

MILLAR, CLIVE; ed.
Sixteen stories by South African writers (New ed.)
Cape Town, Maskew Miller, 1968. 174 p. R 1.50

MOORE, GERALD, and BEIER, ULLI; eds.
Modern poetry from Africa
(New rev. and enlarged ed.)
(Penguin African library, AP 7)
Harmondsworth, Middx. & Baltimore, Penguin Books, 1968. 268 p. 3s. 6d./S1.25
(Originally publ. 1963)

PACKMAN, BRENDA
Etoiles africaines: morceaux choisis de la littérature de l'Afrique noire
London, Evans, 1968. 72 p. 6s. 0d.

PIETERSE, COSMO (South Africa)
Seven South African Poets
(African Writers Series, 64)
London, Heinemann Educ. Books, 1970. 96 p. 8s. 0d.

ROBINSON, C. H.
Specimens of Hausa literature
(Reprint of ed. Cambridge, 1896)
Farnborough, Gregg Int. Publ., 1969 (in preparation)
$24.00 134 p. pl.

SHELTON, AUSTIN J., Jr.; ed.
The African Assertion: A critical anthology of African literature

New York, Odyssey, 1968. 288 p. $2.45

SKINNER, NEIL; ed. and transl. *Hausa tales and traditions* 3 vols.
(An English translation of 'Tatsuniyoyi na Hausa'. Originally compiled by Frank Edgar)
London, Frank Cass, 1969 (in preparation)

SKINNER, NEIL
Hausa Readings. Selections from Edgar's 'Tatsuniyoyi'
Madison, Univ. of Wisconsin Press, 1968. 278 p. $5.00

IV. WORKS

AIDOO, AMA ATA (Ghana)
'Anua'
in: *Okyeame*, v. 4, no. 1, Dec. 1968, p. 41-50

AMADI, ELECHI (Nigeria)
The Great Ponds
(African Writers Series, 44)
London, Heinemann Educ. Books, 1969. 228 p. ca. 6s. (hardback ed. 30s.)

AMALI, SAMSON O. O. (Nigeria)
The downfall of Ogbuu
Ibadan, Author, n.d. (1968?). 43 p. 7s. 6d.
(distr. by Nigerian Book Suppliers, Ltd., Ibadan)

ANSAH, KWAW (Ghana)
'Mother's tears'
in: *Okyeame*, v. 4, no. 1, Dec. 1968, p. 61-9

ARMAH, AYI KWEI (Ghana)
'An African fable'
in: *Présence Africaine*, no. 68, 1968, p. 192-6
(Short story)

ARMAH, AYI KWEI (Ghana)
The beautyful ones are not yet born
Boston, Houghton-Mifflin, 1968. 215 p. $4.95
New York, Macmillan Co., 1969. pap.
London, Heinemann Educ. Books (African Writers Series, 48), 1969. ca. 224 p. 8s. (hardback ed. 25s.)

ASARE, BEDIAKO (Ghana)
Rebel
(African Writers Series, 59)
London, Heinemann Educ.
Books, 1969. 160 p. 6s.
(hardback ed. 25s.)
AWOONOR, KOFI and
ADALI-MORTTY, G.
(Ghana); eds
Poems from Ghana
(African Writers Series, 42)
London, Heinemann Educ.
Books, 1969. ca. 96 p. ca.
8s. 6d.
BALOGUN, OLA (Nigeria)
*Shango, suivi de Le roi-
éléphant*
(Collection 'théâtre africain',
4)
Rouen, P. J. Oswald, 1968,
96. p. F 9.00
(Play)
BEBEY, FRANCIS
(Cameroun)
*Embarras et Cie. Nouvelles
et poemes.*
(Collection Abbia, 2)
Yaoundé, Ed. C. L. E., 1968.
117 p. CFA 240/$2.75
BEBEY, FRANCIS
(Cameroun)
'Un vaudeville africain'
in: *Jeune Afrique*, no. 417,
Dec. 30 through Jan. 5
1969, p. 54-6
BEIER, ULLI; ed. *Political
Spider and other stories*
(African Writers Series, 58)
London, Heinemann Educ.
Books, 1969. 128 p. ca.
6s.
BOUKMAN, DANIEL
(Martinique)
*Chants pour hater la mort du
temps des Orphée*
(Collection 'théâtre africain',
2)
Rouen, P. J. Oswald, 1968.
128 p. F 12.00
(Play)
BRUTUS, DENNIS (South
Africa)
Letters to Martha
(African Writers Series, 46)
London, Heinemann Educ.
Books, 1969. 64 p. 5s.
(Poems)

CÉSAIRE, AIMÉ (Marti-
nique)
'Une tempête'
in: *Présence Africaine,* no.
67, 1968, p. 3-32
(Play)
CÉSAIRE, AIMÉ (Marti-
nique)
An Afrika. Gedichte
(Transl. from the French by
Janheinz Jahn)
Munich, Hanser, 1968. 198
p. DM 25.00
(Poems; bi-lingual ed.
German/French)
CHOONARA, I. (South
Africa)
'The Stone'
in: *Jnl. of the New African
Lit. and the Arts*, no. 5/6,
Spring/Fall 1968, p. 50-4
(Short story)
CLARK, JOHN PEPPER
(Nigeria)
America, Their America
(African Writers Series, 50)
London, Heinemann Educ.
Books, 1969. 224 p. 6s.
New York, Africana Publish-
ing Corp., 1969. 224 p.
$1.50
(Originally publ. London,
Deutsch, 1965)
DADIÉ, BERNARD (Ivory
Coast)
La ville ou nul ne meurt
Paris, Présence Africaine,
1969 (in preparation)
DEI-ANANG, KOFI (Ghana)
'Yaa Asantewa'
in: *Okyeame*, v. 4, no. 1,
Dec. 1968, p. 70-81
DERVAIN, EUGENE
(Cameroun)
*La reine scélérate, suivi de
La langue et le scorpion*
(Collection Abbia, 13)
Yaoundé, Ed. C. L. E., 1968.
105 p. CFA 300/$3.25
(Two plays)
DIOP, DAVID (Senegal)
'Ten Poems' (Transl. by
Paulette Trout and Ellen
Conroy Kennedy)
in: *Jnl. of the New African
Lit. and the Arts*, no. 5/6,
Spring/Fall 1968, p. 28-49

DIPOKO, MBELLA SONNE
(Cameroun)
Because of Women (African
Writers Series, 57)
London, Heinemann Educ.
Books, 1969. 176 p. ca. 6s.
(hardback ed. 21s.)
DOGBEY, RICHARD
(Cameroun)
Cap liberté
(Collection Abbia, 19)
Yaoundé, Ed. C. L. E., 1969.
80 p. ca. CFA 200/$2.50
(Poems)
EASMON, R. SARIF (Sierra
Leone)
'Genevieve'
in: *African Arts/Arts
d'Afrique*, v. 2, no. 2, Winter
1969, p. 30-2 and 72-6
FULTON, ANTHONY
(South Africa)
The dark side of mercy
Cape Town, Purnell, 1968.
233 p. R 2.50
GBADAMOSI, BAKARE
and BEIER, ULLI; eds.
(Nigeria)
Not even God is ripe enough
(African Writers Series, 48)
London, Heinemann Educ.
Books, 1969. 64. p. 5s.
(Collection of Yoruba
myths)
GREEN, LAWRENCE
GEORGE (South Africa)
*Full many a glorious
morning*
Cape Town, Timmins, 1968.
238 p. illus. R 2.50
HONWANA, LUIS
BERNARDO (Mozambique)
*We killed mangy-dog and
other stories*
(African Writers Series, 60)
London, Heinemann Educ.
Books, 1969. 128 p. 6s.
(Short stories)
JONKER, INGRID (South
Africa)
Selected poems
(Transl. from the Afrikaans
by J. Cope and W. Plomer)
London, Cape, 1968. 52 p.
21s.
JORDAN, A. C. (South
Africa)

'Nomabhadi and the Mbulu'
in: *African Arts/Arts d'Afrique*, v. 2, no. 2, Winter 1969, p. 26-7 and 62-9
KAHIGA, SAMUEL (Kenya)
'Face to face'
in: *Zuka*, no. 2, May 1968, p. 5-11
KARIARA, JONATHAN (Kenya)
'The highroad'
in: *Zuka*, no. 2, May 1968, p. 12-13
KARIARA, JONATHAN (Kenya)
'Grass will grow; Vietnam; Song; A girl's lament'
in: *Zuka*, no. 2, May 1968, p. 12-16
(Three poems)
KASSAM, SADRUDIN (Uganda)
'I, and Peter'
in: *Zuka*, no. 2, May 1968, p. 33-7
KAYIRA, LEGSON (Malawi)
Jingala
New York, Doubleday, 1969. (August) $4.95
KIBERA, LEONARD (Kenya)
'The potent ash'
in: *Jnl. of the New African Lit. and the Arts*, no. 5/6, Spring/Fall 1968, p. 68-75
(Play)
KINTEH, RAMATOULIE (The Gambia)
Rebellion. A play in three acts
New York, Philosophical Library, 1968. 79 p. $4.00
KONADU, S. A. (Ghana)
Ordained by the Oracle
(African Writers Series, 55)
London, Heinemann Educ. Books, 1969. 160 p. ca. 6s.
(hardback ed. ca. 25s.)
LADIPO, DURO (Nigeria)
Three plays
(African Writers Series, 65)
London, Heinemann Educ. Books, 1969. 120 p. 6s.
LESSING, DORIS (Rhodesia)
The four-gated city
London, MacGibbon & Kee,

1969. 712 p. ca. 50s.
LIYONG, TABAN LO (Uganda)
'Two stories'
in: *Transition*, v. 7, no. 36, July 1968, p. 60-1
MAIMO, SANKIE (Cameroun)
Sov-Mbang the Sooth Sayer
(Collection Abbia, 17)
Yaoundé, Ed. C. L. E., 1969. CFA 100/$1.50
(Play)
MENGA, GUY (Cameroun)
La palabre sterile
(Collection Abbia, 12)
Yaoundé, Ed. C. L. E., 1969. 220 p. CFA 300/$3.25
MPHAHLELE, EZEKIEL (South Africa)
'The Wanderers. A novel of Africa'
in: *African Arts/Arts d'Afrique*, v. 2, no. 2, Winter 1969, p. 12-15 and 59-61
MULIKITA, FWANYANGA M. (Zambia)
The point of no return
London, Macmillan, 1968. 112 p. 21s.
(Short stories)
MUNONYE, JOHN (Nigeria)
Obi
(African Writers Series, 45)
London, Heinemann Educ. Books, 1969. ca. 224 p. 6s.
MYOMO MEDOU, REMY GILBERT (Cameroun)
Africa BA'A
(Collection Abbia)
Yaoundé, Ed. C. L. E., 1969. 184 p. ca. CFA 250/$3.00
NDAO, CHEIK A. (Senegal)
L'exil d'Albouri, suivi de La décision
(Collection 'théâtre africain', 1)
Rouen, P. J. Oswald, 1968. 136 p. F 12.00
NG'ETHE, RALPH (Tanzania?)
'The yellow river'
in: *Zuka*, no. 2, May 1968, p. 17-22
NGUGI, JAMES (Kenya)
The Black Hermit

(African Writers Series, 51)
London, Heinemann Educ. Books, 1969. 96 p. 5s.
(Play)
NKAMGNIA, SAMUEL (Cameroun?)
Le femme prodigue: comedie en deux actes
(CLE theatre, 1)
Yaoundé, Ed. C. L. E., 1968. 41 p. ca. CFA 150/$1.75
(Play)
NKOSI, LEWIS (South Africa)
'Muzi'
in: *Présence Africaine*, no. 66, 1968, p. 181-96
(Short story)
NOKAN, CHARLES (Ivory Coast)
Les malheurs de Tchakô
(Collection 'théâtre africain', 3)
Rouen, P. J. Oswald, 1968. 100 p. F 9.00
(Play)
NWAPA, FLORA (Nigeria)
Idu
(African Writers Series, 56)
London, Heinemann Educ. Books, ca. 200 p. ca. 9s.
(Revised entry; see ALT, no. 1, 1968)
NWANKO, NKEM (Nigeria)
Danda
(African Writers Series, 67)
London, Heinemann Educ. Books, 1970. 208 p. 7s.
OCULI, OKELLO (Uganda)
Prostitute
Nairobi, East African Publ. House, 1969. $5.00
OCULI, OKELLO (Uganda)
Orphan
Nairobi, East African Publ. House, 1968. 104 p. Shs. 6/00, $1.80
OGOT, GRACE (Kenya)
Land without thunder
Nairobi, East African Publ. House, 169. ca. $5.00
OKARA, GABRIEL (Nigeria)
The Voice
(African Writers Series, 68)
London, Heinemann Educ. Books, 1969. 160 p. 6s.

OKIGBO, CHRISTOPHER
(Nigeria)
*Labyrinths and Path of
Thunder*
(African Writers Series, 62)
London, Heinemann Educ.
Books, 1969. 88 p. 8s.

ONIORORO, NIYI (Nigeria)
Lagos is a wicked place
Ibadan, Author (P.O.B.
151), 1968. 3s. 6d. 76 p.

OUOLOGUEM, YAMBO
(Mali)
Lettre à la France Nègre
Paris, Edmond Nalis, 1968.
220 p. F 12.00

OUOLOGUEM, YAMBO
(Mali)
Le devoir de violence
Paris, Ed. du Seuil, 1968.
208 p. F 15.00

OUSMANE, SEMBENE
(Senegal)
God's bits of wood
(Transl. from the French by
Francis Price)
(African Writers Series, 63)
London, Heinemann Educ.
Books, 1970. 288 p. ca. 8s.
(Originally publ. New York,
Doubleday, 1964)

OWUOR, CHARLES
(Kenya)
'The negro; I see a road;
Those dark days; Your
cigarette burned the
savannah grass; Vietnam'
in: *Zuka*, no. 2, May 1968,
p. 8-11

OWUSU, MARTIN (Ghana)
'The story Ananse told'
in: *Okyeame*, v. 4, no. 1,
Dec. 1968, p. 51-60

OYONO, GUILLAUME
(Cameroun)
*Trois prétendants ... un
mari* (2nd ed.)
Yaoundé, Ed. C. L. E., 1969.
128 p. CFA 200/$2.25

PALANGYO, PETER (Tan-
zania)
Dying in the Sun
(African Writers Series, 53)
London, Heinemann Educ.
Books, 1969. 136 p. 5s. 6d.
(hardback ed. 18s.)

PIETERSE, COSMO (South
Africa)
Ten One-Act Plays
(African Writers Series, 34)
London, Heinemann Educ.
Books, 1968. 304 p. 7s. 6d.

RABIE, JAN (South Africa)
A man apart
New York, Macmillan, 1969.
$6.95

RUBADIRI, DAVID
(Uganda)
'Christmas '67; Yatuta
Chisiza'
in: *Zuka*, no. 2, May 1968,
p. 30-1

SALIH, TAYEB (Sudan)
*Season of Migration to the
North*
(African Writers Series, 66)
London, Heinemann Educ.
Books, 1969. ca. 160 p. ca.
8s. 6d. (Hardback ed. 25s.)

SERUMAGA, ROBERT
(Uganda)
Return to the Shadows
(African Writers Series, 54)
London, Heinemann Educ.
Books, 1969. 176 p. 6s.
(hardback ed. 21s)

SCHIFFRIN, ELINOR
(Nigeria?)
'The river'
in: *Jnl. of the New African
Lit. and the Arts*, no. 5/6,
Spring/Fall 1968, p. 55-67

SCHREINER, OLIVE
(South Africa)
Olive Schreiner; a selection
edited by Uys Krige
Cape Town, Oxford Univ.
Press, 1968. 214 p. R 5.40

SELLASSIE, SAHLE
(Ethiopia)
The Afersata
(African Writers Series, 52)
London, Heinemann Educ.
Books, 1969. 96 p. 5s.

SENGHOR, LÉOPOLD
SÉDAR (Senegal)
Ansprach anlaesslich der
Verleihung des Friedens-
preises des Deutschen Buch-
handels am 22. September
1968 in der Pauluskirche zu
Frankfurt am Main.
Frankfurt/M, Buchhaendler

Vereinigung GmbH (Box
3914), 1968. 73 p. DM 4.00

SENGHOR, LÉOPOLD
SÉDAR (Senegal)
*Botschaft und Anruf. Saemt-
liche Gedichte*
(Ed. and Transl. from the
French by Janheinz Jahn)
Munich, Hanser, 1968. 229
p. DM 25.00

SOYINKA, WOLE (Nigeria)
Le lion et la perle
(Transl. from the English)
(Collection Abbia, 16)
Yaoundé, Ed. C. L. E., 1968.
93 p. CFA 300/$3.25
(Play)

TATTY-LOUTARD, J. B.
(Cameroun)
Poems de la mer
Yaoundé, Ed. C. L. E., 1969.
ca. CFA 300/$3.25

TSHIAKATUMBA,
MATALA MUKADI (Congo
Republic)
'Héritage; Dans les méandres
de l'enfer rythmique'
in: *Présence Africaine*, no.
66, 1968, p. 126-9
(Two poems)

UMEASIEGBU, REM NNA
(Nigeria)
The Way We Lived
(African Writers Series, 61)
London, Heinemann Educ.
Books, 1969. 160 p. illus. 7s.
(Introduction to Ibo cus-
toms and stories)

U TAM'SI, TCHIKAYA
(Congo-Brazzaville)
Legendes africaines
Paris, Seghers, 1968. 264 p.
F 12.00

ZAHAN, DOMINIQUE
(Senegal?)
'Le viande et la graine'
Paris, *Présence Africaine*,
1969 (in preparation)

Note: *Okyeame*, v. 4, no. 1,
December 1968, contains
poetry by the following
Ghanaian writers: *Kofi Sey,
Patience Henaku Addo, Ivan
Annan, John Okai, Kofi-Dei
Anang,* and *Mohammed Issa
Chambah.*

ALT 4
CONTENTS

Editorial Note

African Studies, whether retaining its
old autonomy or subsumed into its
precocious relative Black Studies, is
enjoying a boom particularly in the
United States of America. So long as
these studies are soundly based they
can do nothing but good. The rehabilitation of the black man's self-
respect, large though it may loom
because of its historical urgency, is in
true perspective a by-product of the
fuller study of man and his activities.
Thus ideally whites stand as much to
gain from black studies as blacks.

Black study courses should thus
have a sound academic basis if they
are to survive, add to the sum of
man's knowledge of himself, and
quicken his sensibility. The alternative is the quick catch-penny course
which glitters like tinsel and is
equally undurable.

In the prevailing state of ignorance of Africa and of its peoples
both at home and abroad, it is easy
for even the only slightly informed
to be mistaken for experts. Acade-
mics should approach this field as
they should all others with true
scholarly humility.

Eldred D. Jones

1

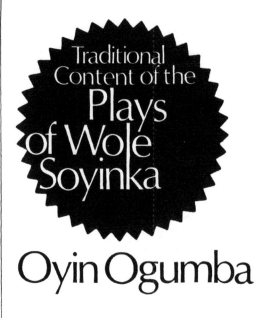

Traditional Content of the Plays of Wole Soyinka

Oyin Ogumba

Although critics of Wole Soyinka's plays have usually recognised the author's indebtedness to traditional African forms and ideas, the precise nature of his borrowing has not been determined. In this article I shall endeavour to perform this function and thus place the traditional material within the context of the playwright's dramatic art.

First, there are obvious elements like the use of traditional African (mostly Yoruba) expressions and pseudo-traditional songs

2

and chants. The traditional expressions are mostly wise sayings and are woven-in in a kind of translation. In *A Dance of the Forests* Agboreko, of the Elder of Sealed Lips (whatever that means), who has a way of excusing his colourful language by saying 'proverbs to bones and silence', habitually uses ponderous Yoruba expressions typical of his kind to convey rather commonplace thoughts. For example in talking to Old Man about the identity of one of the town dwellers (really Forest Head posing as Obaneji, the Chief Clerk) Agboreko says:

> The eye that looks downward will certainly see the nose. The hand that dips to the bottom of the pot will eat the biggest snail. The sky grows no grass but if the earth called her barren, it will drink no more milk. The foot of the snake is not split in two like a man's or in hundreds like the centipede, but if Agere could dance patiently like the snake, he will uncoil the chain that leads into the dead . . .

All he wants to do is to advise Old Man to be patient, and assure him that the mystery will be unravelled. This kind of exuberant, verbose eloquence, far from being out-of-place in the play, is, in fact, integral to it as a pointer to the nature and character of the speaker, and by giving a certain quality to the scene.

As may be expected, Baroka, the *bale* (village head) of Ilujinle is the one character who most frequently resorts to traditional expressions in *The Lion and the Jewel*. One such, and perhaps the most felicitous of these expressions, is the one he utters in the process of 'wooing' Sidi, the village belle:

> The monkey sweats
> It is only the hair upon his back
> Which still deceives the world . . .

He explains that, contrary to Lakunle's (the school-teacher's) opinion, his life is not just a pleasure-loving, lascivious one. Rather, he too undergoes a crisis of experience inevitable in these new times. The traditional image of the monkey as used here brings out the essential ambivalence, the foolish-wise character, of this animal and thus tends to show off Baroka as a 'traditional modernist' seeking to reconcile in himself the opposing thoughts and dual world-views of contemporary Africa.

3

Sidi, too, makes use of traditional expressions. In the scene in Baroka's room, she has been watching the wrestling between Baroka and his man and then a conversation ensues:

SIDI: I think he will win.
BAROKA: Is that a wish, my daughter?
SIDI: No, but–(*Hesitates, but boldness wins*)
             If the tortoise cannot tumble
             It does not mean that he can stand.

Sidi here uses the image of the tortoise that cannot stand to taunt Baroka about the so-called impotence. She will, of course, find later to her dismay (and paradoxically also to her joy) that the tortoise can in fact stand. But meanwhile Sidi's point catches and Baroka, 'seemingly puzzled', begins to understand her 'discourteous' intrusion into his privacy.

Kongi's Harvest is, up to now, the Soyinka play that is most replete with traditional expressions. Here one may almost quote at random. The very opening lines read:

> The pot that will eat fat
> Its bottom must be scorched
> The squirrel that will long crack nuts
> Its footpad must be sore.

which is a Yoruba traditional, poetic way of expressing Kongi's self-imposed, herculean assignment. In the same way, when Sarumi tries later in the play to intervene between Oba Danlola and the Superintendent he finds himself saying:

> Oba Danlola, don't be angry
> With your son. If the baobab shakes
> Her head in anger, what chance
> Has the rodent when
> An ear-ring falls
> And hits the earth with thunder?

This is a way of saying that the king's words carry a divine efficacy and that Oba Danlola should be restrained in his anger lest he pours doom on the world. In another typically traditional expression Oba Sarumi says:

4

Let the dandy's wardrobe
Be as lavish as the shop
Of the dealer in brocades
It cannot match an elder's rags.

This too is a way of emphasising the inscrutable dignity of the elder or the king whom age or divine association has given a supernatural aura.

All the traditional expressions quoted above are translations of commonplace sayings of the Yoruba. They are put in the plays for various reasons and with differing significance. In some of them, like the pot on fire, the idea is to demonstrate the truth of the saying as transcending time and place; in others, like the import-ance of the elder's rags, the idea is to ridicule the illusion of the naïvety of conservative tradition.

The songs and chants in these plays are only pseudo-traditional, that is, they merely wear a traditional appearance. They fall into two groups, namely, those which are taken from popular disc records of modern commercial musicians who work in the tra-ditional mode and those which, starting off in a truly traditional mode are, half-way through, deliberately given a satirical twist by the author. Two examples of the first group will suffice. One of the layabouts in *The Road* strums his guitar and sings a popular Nigerian disc song of the 1950s:

Ona orun jin o eeeee
Ona orun jin dereba rora
Ee dereba rora
Ee dereba rora
Ona orun jin o eeeee
Eleda mi ma ma buru
Esin baba Bandele je l'odan
Won o gbefun o
Eleda mi ma ma buru
Esin baba Bandele je l'odan
Won o gbefun o.

It's a long road to heaven
It's a long road to heaven, Driver
Go easy a-ah go easy driver
It's a long long road to heaven
My Creator, be not harsh on me

Bandele's horse galloped home a winner
But the race eluded him.
My Creator, be not harsh on me
Bandele's horse galloped home a winner
But the race eluded him.

This casual song is inserted ostensibly to provide some comic relief. But in fact it is closely linked with the idea of the road to death which is the central preoccupation of the play. In the course of the play the 'driver' fails to heed the warning and so drives humanity to destruction. This is the way some of these songs and chants behave in this playwright's art. They are introduced in a seemingly irrelevant or indifferent context, but on closer examination they prove to be structurally significant and closely connected with the dominant idea of the play.

The second example of this group of songs and chants is to be found in *The Lion and the Jewel*. The prisoners working under a white surveyor on a road that would have passed through Ilujinle, sing an old Nigerian pub song of the 1940s as they work:

N'ijo itoro
N'ijo isisi, emu ni.
Nba ti l'aya keregbe ni o je o

Whenever I have threepence
Whenever I have sixpence, it is palm wine.
I would have been married, but for the gourd.

This song too has more significance than being merely a 'low' prisoners' song. It is concluded in the same spirit of regret and anger which provokes Lakunle to accuse Baroka of extreme conservatism. Ilujinle would, in his thinking, have become a modern community but for Baroka's selfish lasciviousness.

The second type of songs and chants, that which sounds purely traditional but is tampered with by the author, may be exemplified from *Kongi's Harvest*. Most of 'Hemlock' is in this mode but a much better example is to be found in the Second Part. Daodu's attempt on Kongi has failed and the latter is well on the road to his 'inevitable apotheosis'. Meanwhile, there is 'a real feast, a genuine Harvest orgy of food and drink that permits no spectators, only celebrants'. The dance song that follows is substantially traditional, especially the second section:

6

Mo ti d'ade egun
Pere gungun maja gungun pere

I have borne the thorned crown
Rashly, enthusiastically, thoughtlessly.

But in the other two verses of the song (that is, verses one and three) the author has woven in an important contrast. The first verse deals with the First Coming of a Messiah:

Ijo mo ko w'aiye o
Ipasan ni.
Igi lehin were o
Kumo lehin were o

At my first coming
Scourges all the way
Whips to my skin
Cudgels on the madman's back.

The Messiah wanted to redeem mankind through his own personal sacrifice by demonstrating to man a magnificent altruism—giving himself up to torture and death. But how can this work when all that man seems to understand is a fierce opportunism and self-interest? In the Second Coming (verse three) he is going to change his tactics—no self-immolation, no high ideals. Rather, he is going to forget all noble principles and turn Epicurean:

Adeyin wa o
Igba ikore ni
Aiye erinkeji
Iyan ni mo wa je
Ayo a b'ori
Aiya ni mo wa fe
Ayo a b'ori
Aiye erin ni mo wa
Ayo a b'ori
Emu ni mo wa mu

Now this second coming
Is time for harvest
This second coming
Is for pounding of yams
Peace is triumphant

I have come wife-seeking
Peace is triumphant
I am borne on laughter
Peace is triumphant
I have come palm-wine thirsting.

This playwright does not seem to like Messiahs—whether they are ascetic or Epicurean—for each kind indulges in some ridiculous excess which undermines the very principle on which the idea is based. Kongi is in the ranks of the new kind of Messiah, resolute in his voluptousness and unmindful of whatever pains he inflicts on others. But the real interest in this passage is the way the author has used the framework of a traditional song to produce unexpected results so that one is plunged not only into a particular incident but into a new thought of the universal pattern of the notion of Messiahs.

But by far the most significant traditional element in these plays is the overall design of a festival. This is particularly true of three of the plays, namely, *Kongi's Harvest, The Strong Breed* and *A Dance of the Forests*. In each of these plays, the prevailing mood is that of the preparation for or celebration of a great event which produces so much excitement or tension in the whole populace that everybody thinks of nothing else but the great event. This is, in fact, the atmosphere that prevails when important ceremonies are performed in traditional Africa and Soyinka in these plays very often catches the essence of the festival mood with the drumming, bustle and other manifestations of a holiday.

In *Kongi's Harvest*, the design is that of a king's festival, especially a Yoruba king's festival. The king in Africa is still God's deputy on earth and so he combines both spiritual and political functions. Hence his festival is not a private celebration but one that has meaning for the whole community and in which everyone is expected to participate with interest. As the first citizen, the ideal figure around whom the whole tradition is woven, the king's dance is the dance of the community by its divine leader, a re-enactment of the whole living tradition of the people. It is thus a life-giving ritual which has to be done in epic style to demonstrate the higher aspirations of the community.

Thus when *Kongi's Harvest* opens with a roll of drums and the traditional characters, led by Oba Danlola, break into their special

8

'anthem', they are in effect uttering a version of the pre-sacrifice invocatory chant to the founder and past executors of the royal tradition. This is an indispensable opening to such celebrations. The difference, of course, is that instead of the usual fulsome praise in magnificent poetry, this chant is a complaint against 'isms', the 'new race' of leaders and their mass media of false propaganda like the 'penny newspaper' and the radio. The traditional characters express despair, for they can no longer cope with nor effectively challenge the means of mass communication of the new race. When they chant:

> . . . Who but a lunatic
> Will bandy words with boxes
> With government rediffusion sets
> Which talk and talk and never
> Take a lone word in reply

they are in effect giving up the struggle, virtually accepting the inevitable triumph of modernism over traditional sanctions. The image of the impersonality of the rediffusion boxes thundering proclamations to the people is the symbolic manifestation of the new administration which levels the people with the authority of the wireless.

This sad strain is continued in the latter part of 'Hemlock' as the king's men begin a dirge of *ege*. Here again the dirge has a different significance, for it quickly becomes a dance of the death of tradition itself since the king's umbrella no longer gives shade. The Ogbo Aweri put the point summarily when they chant:

> This is the last
> That we shall dance together
> This is the last the hairs
> Will lift on our skin
> And draw together
> When the *gbedu* rouses
> The dead in *Oshugbo*.[1]

The important point is that the traditional dramatic device of invocation and the poetic form of *ege* (a funeral dirge of the Yoruba) are being used here to proclaim the death of tradition itself instead of the death of a particular leader. So, instead of the king's men chanting of the glorious dead in the usual flattering manner, they are chanting of imminent death that will destroy completely all traditional ways—the very blackout of tradition.

It is no wonder, then, that all this is taking place in Kongi's Detention Camp, with Oba Danlola and his troupe in prison, the whole ceremony being nervously supervised by the Superintendent of Isma Camp. Soyinka's satirical point comes through as one gradually realises that the atmosphere of merriment and royal splendour is only one of make-believe, a thin cover under which the real meaning of the situation hides itself. So that, although the moment of the glorification of the royal tradition is celebrated, with junior Oba Sarumi paying homage as if to an Alafin at the Bere festival[2] in the glorious days of the Oyo empire, the pomp and revelry soon lapse into a slow, mournful dance which is truer to the essence of the occasion.

In this section, Soyinka makes an important structural point. He reverses the normal sequence of events in a Yoruba king's festival, making the triumphal dance precede the ritual dance and is thus able to emphasise the more the imminent extinction of tradition. The whole idea of the royal dance in tradition is to show in symbolic terms the process by which a régime passes through toil and occasional tragedies to the glory of the present. In so doing, the royal tradition is presented to the populace as a triumph of civilisation. Almost invariably, such a dance features a progress through ritual reminiscent of the trials of state-building, to eventual success.

In *Kongi's Harvest*, by contrast, the trials continue, and extinction is in sight; merriment evaporates, and despair and death descend on the traditional characters. The attempt to revive the dance and re-enact the mood of joy and royal splendour in the Second Part, therefore, becomes an anti-climax and so warrants Daodu's tearing of the royal drum which gives a finale to the royal make-believe.

Oba Danlola appraises the event of the tearing of the drum well when he says:

> When the next-in-line claps his hand
> Over the monarch's mouth, it is time
> For him to take to the final sleep
> Or take to drink and women.

10

In this case the next-in-line is both Daodu and Kongi. Each of them from an opposite end will scramble for what Danlola has combined in himself. At the meeting point the struggle will be fierce and protracted, for they represent the two main trends of modernism in contemporary Africa. On the one hand is Kongi the ultra-modernist who cultivates a deliberate contempt for tradition and will seek to 'replace the old superstitious festival by a State ceremony governed by the principle of Enlightened Ritualism,' as the Fourth Aweri so eloquently enunciates. But the author's satirical point comes to the fore as we realise that this is merely a convenient appearance. Deep down Kongi likes acting roles just as much as the Kabiyesi, Oba Danlola. Daodu, on the other hand, is a rugged realist, who still wants to succeed to the traditional throne of Oba Danlola and from this pedestal work hard to make tradition accommodate modernism.

Whatever the future holds, Oba Danlola's pure tradition, for long moribund, has to die. The traditional god on earth has to be superseded by a greater, more contemporary god who is better able to comprehend the complexities of modern life. But meanwhile the king's predicament is given a two-fold satirical touch. One is his resistance to the historic system of which he is a part and which was the very foundation of the authority he has wielded so far. This inevitable process of growth and decay must eventually bring about the extinction or at least modification of the royal system just as it has vigorously brought it to life. The second is the delusion and falsehood which modernism generates, especially in Kongi's mind, leading him, in his arrogant ambition, to think that he can be absolutely iconoclastic and new, as if it is such an easy task to make a clean break with tradition. The sharp point of the satire is the author's picture of the amount of human suffering and needless labour that goes into merely regrouping or renaming traditional structures which masquerade as modern forms. Thus Kongi's Reformed Aweri Fraternity wants to be called 'a conclave of modern patriarchs'—a revealing phrase, pinpointing the fact that the element of change or modernism in the new formation is quite insignificant.

One important detail in the overall structure and design of a festival in *Kongi's Harvest* is the symbolism of the New Yam. In traditional Africa, the New Yam signifies the life-giving spirit, the fruit of the fertility and the diligent cultivation of the land. It can also be a sexual symbol, the manifestation of the virility and fertility of the citizens of a community. The presentation of the New Yam to the head of the community is thus a ritual action, an evidence of the realised principle of continuity of the tribe. It is a collective sacrifice to the living spirit of the tribe which is also the spirit of harvest.

It is therefore essential for Kongi in his bid to acquire power in his modern state to lay claim to the title of the 'spirit of Haar-vest' in the grand tradition of master 'state-builders'. But the really explosive point is that Kongi is a Spirit of Harvest almost in contrast to the spirit of diligent cultivation and growth. In this he may appear unique, for other master 'state-builders' have usually pretended some interest in cultivation and growth before becoming harvest-mongers.

In a way the whole satirical point of the play hinges on this, that Kongi, the new man, the iconoclast with fresh ideas still wants, with startling inconsistency, the New Yam as a ritual symbol of his new authority. It is a way of exposing the hypocrisy of the new breed of rulers with a surface impression of thoroughgoing modernism and individualism but a reality that completely belies the apparent impression.

But Kongi is also typical and the image of the New Yam in the play touches off a universal point, showing Kongi using familiar tactics to achieve his end. In this particular case the setting is in Africa and Kongi is probably a dictator of the sixties exploiting the African predilection for ritual sanctity to obtain power for personal gain rather than for altruistic purpose. The universal element is that it exemplifies the career of the dictator put outside time and place, craving for deification as an essential ingredient of power that aspires to be perpetual.

The full significance of a harvest by Kongi is that conveyed in one of the speeches of the Secretary: 'This year shall be known as the year of Kongi's Harvest. Everything shall date from it.' Kongi thus suddenly steps out of nowhere into the sphere of the immortal and takes a place in the planetary system. The bizarre antics of this Jesus of Isma, an ordinary man masquerading as a mystic and a divine, may well provoke scornful laughter. But its crude and fierce opportunism produces terror, for here is yet another 'leader' using the basest Nazi techniques to turn his people into a giant machine thereby multiplying the sufferings of

12

humanity in the grand manner of all dictators. The fear is that Kongi will be successful and thus add a fresh dimension to universal human disaster.

There is also another side to this within the context of Africa, namely, that Kongi's actions, however apparently extreme, are merely a continuation of the relentless historic process which was responsible for the establishment of successive regimes of which Oba Danlola's royalism is here the last. This historic system is supreme and it tyrannises over all, although its influence is probably felt sharpest in contemporary Africa. Modernism, as represented by Kongi, cannot vary this process nor even really ameliorate the asperities of tradition: it can only give the suffering a new appearance.

Meanwhile Daodu, as the priest of plenitude of Kongi's festival, complains of the excesses of the Messiah of Pain and offers prayers for peace in the community. But this prayer will not be answered. How many of such prayers have ever been answered in the human experience? Instead, the Spirit of Harvest will soon smite the enemies of Kongi and make the latter supreme for the moment.

This aspect of *Kongi's Harvest* is also an extension of traditional practice. For if Daodu is the modern priest of plenitude, the diligent land cultivator, he will still have, like his counterpart in tradition, to succumb to the modern political opportunist as his overlord. In the tradition of many African peoples, the priest, the original owner of the land, has usually been displaced and subordinated by the political chief.[3] The Spirit of Harvest annually smites the priest while upholding the dignity and power of the politician. The point of the failure of Daodu's clever revolt in *Kongi's Harvest,* therefore, is to demonstrate that the idea of this victory of the political schemer over the priest is not just ancient and moribund: it is on the contrary an active principle still very much operative in contemporary Africa.

In other words, for this author contemporary Africa does not really have a clear choice between tradition and modernism: the two operate on more or less the same wave band even though the circumstance may be different. Even in tradition suffering seems to have been accepted as a necessary item of human survival and progress. Thus the sadism and brutality Kongi displays are as true to the tradition that produces kings as that which is now

13

producing 'immortal' African state-builders.

It is little wonder then that the New Yam presented to Kongi is a 'monster yam' which 'grew from Kongi's soil'. The picture that comes to mind is that of some of the Abakaliki or Ekiti prodigious yams six feet tall with hands and legs and head like the statue of a man. The symbolism of the 'monster yam' is, I think, capable of two complementary interpretations. First, it may represent the present, an offspring of the crime and bloodiness of the past which have made corpses of 'living' citizens and driven nature mad. Secondly, it could forecast the future, that Mother Earth is beginning to react to the crime and monstrosity of the Kongi régime and, with a sardonic sense of humour, will give back to the leader as food something to mirror the régime's bloodthirstiness which will eventually poison the body politic.

In whatever way it is interpreted, Kongi's New Yam has made an unusual growth and, although Daodu spent 'a fortune in fertilisers' to help it on, it is Kongi's soil, more than any other thing, that produces the abnormality. In the same way, although the foibles of all the other characters, especially those of Danlola and Daodu, contribute to the progress towards a new régime, it is Kongi's criminal imagination that produces the totalitarian excess. And just as the traditional king, in receiving and eating the first of the new yams thereby tastes the best and bitterest of the community's life and assumes control of all the forces of the land, in the same way Kongi, in accepting the abnormal yam and eating it with the rest of the community, puts himself at the head of this strange régime and, through unrestricted power, rapidly becomes a monster.

There is a convincing atmosphere of a festival in *Kongi's Harvest* with the drumming and revelry and the general impression of plenitude. Rosy and well-fed faces proclaim the mood of merriment. But in the midst of all this Daodu tears the drum and the feast proves to be a mere Bacchanalian orgy. In the midst of it, too, Kongi's bloodthirsty ravings reach a climax. The poison on which both Kongi and the community have been unwittingly feeding has started to do a great damage to the people's health. In this anti-climax the author has only made use of a commonplace occurrence in traditional festivity when in the midst of the most elaborate rejoicings, Esu, the unpredictable one, jumps in to give a sad turn to the merry-making. (See Joan Westroth, 'The Sculpture

14

and Myths of Eshu-Elegta, the Yoruba Trickster', *Africa*, No. 32, pp 336-54.) But here Soyinka has given it a new dimension so that it is the whole community that manifests this anti-climax rather than just a few people made wild by excessive drinking.

The overall design of a festival in *The Strong Breed* is rather different from the one in *Kongi's Harvest*. In *The Strong Breed* the traditional model is that of a purification festival. The end of the year has come again in this unnamed community and the rite of expelling all the evil of the old year is to be performed. The community should enter the new year with a feeling of sanctification and so a Carrier, the scape-goat who will help despatch all the evils of the old year, is to be found. The obvious choice is the idiot Ifada who is god-sent for the purpose.

In tradition the Carrier is a spiritual force and, though a scapegoat, a fortunate one. (See Robin Horton, 'New Year in the Delta', *Nigeria Magazine*, No. 49 (1960), pp. 256-96.) He suffers a bone-racking torment to alleviate others' sufferings and he is best a stranger so as to be completely external to the community's evil he is called upon to shoulder. But in the process he attains a level of spiritual power far superior to that of any other member of the community and so becomes its strongest man. An idiot, then, would be ideal for such a task, for his eventual power will not matter. As he is probably blessed with a higher divine sensitiveness than others in the community he should find the task relatively easy to accomplish.

But Ifada is unwilling and so the strange and ascetic Eman, who has also been acting as Ifada's mentor, is compelled to perform the task since he is the only other stranger in the community. Eman discharges the function with a mysterious ability and we get an insight into his peculiar past. As he gets more and more involved in this rite, the part he is acting ceases to be a role. It becomes clear that this, far from being an accident is, in fact, what his whole life has been moving towards. The Old Man, his father, has also been a Carrier in his time, but this apart, Eman is himself temperamentally suited to the mortifying experience which is the role of the Carrier.

The purpose of the flashback to Eman's earlier life is to show that the role of the sufferer is not new to him. In this formative time he suffers the victimisation of the tutor because of Omae and

15

this casts a shadow on the rest of his life. Even at this early age Eman shows an almost superhuman consistency in pursuing his appointed course. It is this grim determination that dominates the scene between him and Sunma and which the latter completely misinterprets as merely brooding over a lost love. It is this also which makes Sunma's escapism so repugnant to the inherently tragic sensibility of Eman.

In this extremely dark play, Wole Soyinka explores the role of the spiritually elect in a human community. He seems to be anxious to make the point that there is apparently always a choice for the elect between escaping responsibility and taking it up squarely in spite of the prospect of doom. But the truly elect feels an inner compulsion, a tumultuous excitement to act his part. For him escape is impossible, an alternative course of action is unthinkable. He rushes headlong to his task and to inevitable tragedy.

This is the meaning of the statement of the Old Man to Eman:

Ours is a strong breed, my son. It is only a strong breed that can take this boat to the river year after year and wax stronger on it. I have taken each year's evils for over twenty years. I hoped you would follow me.

and later:

Son, it is not the mouth of the boaster that says he belongs to the strong breed. It is the tongue that is red with pain and black with sorrow.

The strong breed stride across human history, not just a straight descent from Old Man to Eman. They are a chain of pivotal persons who ride on the crest of the wave, make the human problems theirs and from age to age sacrifice themselves voluntarily for the common good.

Eman is in this great tradition and it is only those who are within it that know the intensity and pain of the devotion to the human cause. The rest of humanity is either too sensible, like Sunma, to think that the sacrifice is worth it or too naïve like Ifada to appreciate its significance. It is only the elect that have both the will and the temerity to make the plunge and consent to be the sacrificial victim.

The contrast the Old Man draws between the strong-breed and the rest of humanity is also significant:

> Other men would rot and die doing this task year after year. It is strong medicine which only we can take. Our blood is strong like no other.

The image of the Carrier in *The Strong Breed* is, I think, meant to be analogous to the sensibility of the artist, especially the verbal artist, in society. Both the carrier and the artist carry the burden of the human sin and crime of their communities and both are 'strangers' to their immediate communities. Both also seek a periodic purgation of these communities either through the enactment of tragedies and comedies or the cleansing effect of satire. In particular the literary artist, because of the unique articulateness of his medium, can be a very efficient carrier and convey the fullness of his mind. He can help disgorge the rottenness of the human mind for all to see and loath.

To achieve this strength and distinction each member of the strong breed has to make a great sacrifice at birth, namely, the loss of the mother. This means that the child lacks the mother's milk and affection and therefore has the opportunity to grow the hard, the unnatural way and, in some cases, become a genius, for society tends to overdiscipline the individual and so limit his scope for genius. In the same way, the gifted artist sometimes has to stifle the mother's affection in his sensibility, give himself a strange, eccentric nurture and thus be able to evaluate his community against a blind, unflattering standard free of disabling affection.

But how much of the making of the carrier or the artist does the community know? Our experience in this play is that it is very little judging from Sunma's complete misapprehension of Eman's thought and the off-hand manner of Jaguna and his men. For most of the community the ritual of purgation is mere formality and the Carrier's preoccupation a mere, unpleasant diversion. Thus the artist, like the Carrier, is alone in his supreme task and can only commune with past and ancient artists. They alone, because of their own experiences, can fully understand the meaning and significance of events in the living artist's consciousness.

In this little play Wole Soyinka has, characteristically, taken a rather commonplace traditional African event—the purification of

17

a community through a Carrier—to explore the career of the serious artist. The design of a purification festival helps to set in perspective a community conscious of the weight of evil but in which each person is too much of a citizen to dare the evil. For, what person brought up 'naturally' would make the effort to clean up a community? It is in this situation that the true artist comes in and, unhindered by 'good sense' and 'natural loyalty', strikes a discordant note.   *(To be concluded in Number 5)*

NOTES

1. *Oshugbo* is the name for the cult of elders and chiefs who form the executive council in traditional Ijebu government. Ijebu is a sub-tribe of the Yoruba (Western Nigeria). In other parts of Yorubaland this council is called Ogboni. It has both political and ritual functions.
2. *Bere festival:* this festival is now virtually defunct. In its heyday it used to be the occasion for the gathering of all the kings of the Oyo empire. It was also an annual ceremony for paying homage to the Alafin of Oyo, the Emperor.
3. A few examples in Yorubaland are: Oloja Idoko/The Osemawe; The Olukere/The Ogaga; The Balufe/The Ajalorun. In each case, the first mentioned is the displaced priest, the second the contemporary political lord. See also Ulli Beier 'Oloku festival', *Nigeria Magazine*, No. 49 (1956), pp. 168-83.

18

Edwin Thumboo

Most of Kwesi Brew's principal interests are retailed in 'Our Palm-Tree Strength'[1]

> And still I sit here in the dust
> Struggling to understand
> The world and its words
> And so I have sometimes cast
> A hopeful glance over the shoulders of those
> Whose hoes have helped
> A friend to till a thorny ground
> And wondered whether to look
> In fear upon the past or to rejoice;
> To rejoice that we have achieved so much
> That so much has escaped
> The eyes of the gods who hold
> The rod of punishment;
> That the red-clay kitchens
> Of our ancestral homes still
> Teem with the feasts of the year. (p. 62)

While the writing is not notable we are nevertheless struck by a certain old-fashioned dignity much in keeping with the virtues adumbrated: a strong desire to understand, to follow the example of those who are charitable, and an abiding 'faith in humanity'. Brew is conservative, and though this reduces the excitement of his poetry, it saves him from excesses. As we shall see, even when his language sins, the sins are of a predictable kind, falling close to the diction of the Hymnal.

'The Shadow of Laughter' which not only provides the title for his collection, but stands as the introductory poem to the volume, is less declamatory. The start is dramatic:

> No—do not frown at me,
> while these sweet words tumble . . . (p. 1)

Brew seeks ancestral dispensation for his new freedom and individuality.[2] It is out of freedom that joy shall emerge, shall have the strength to break through 'the stupid restraints of a decent world'. He believes the world has taken after 'saddened men' and is therefore hostile to the true impulses of life. As a consequence of the restraints

> We fear the looks in the eyes of our old men,
> Where they sit in the corners
> Of their crumbling huts
> Casting tremulous looks
> At the loud crashing waves.
> For in their hearts
> Rages a storm of tossing surfs,
> And the battered canoes

These attitudes define Brew's position. While they don't wholly explain the main business of his poetry, they tell us what not to expect. Modern life is non-heroic. The old battles with the elements, the unflinching sacrifices are absent, perhaps because the same opportunities do not exist, or if they do, no longer offer the same uncomplicated challenge. Perhaps, again, some acceptable malaise has crept in. Brew is unusually honest and doesn't pretend the twentieth century didn't happen, or that the past can be recovered intact, or that it was glorious. (You never catch him wearing his African heart upon his modern sleeve.)

20

The essential elements of traditional belief remain. The characteristics of the African personality have not been disturbed. The continuum between life and death persists. 'Ancestral Faces' (p. 52) is a specific instance.[3] It is 'the god of my fathers' who calls the poet in 'Through the Forest', where the physical presence is unmistakable.

> Through the forest
> Whitened by the moon
> Come the distant rattles;
> Come the beat of a pulse
> The pulse of the night,
> The pulse of the day.
>
> I hear them
> The rattles;
> Masculine vibrations
> Centuries old. (p. 53)

Brew however, does not surrender to the past, an awkwardness difficult to avoid were the past resurrected too vigorously. The case of Awoonor-Williams amply demonstrates what can happen when a poet is denied responsibility by having themes thrust upon him.

The respect for ancestors has other rarifications. Their role is not purely spiritual. 'The wisdom of our fathers' is a familiar phrase. It represents a whole set of values which exercise an unusual tyranny. Wisdom is a subtle kind of precedence, a most persuasive form of moral or religious injuction. It is the application of principles proceeding from accumulated experiences. When you come to think of it, wisdom is really impersonal. Brew warns us:

> So look not for wisdom
> And guidance
> In their speech, my beloved.
> Let the same fire
> Which chastened their tongue,
> Into silence,
> Teach us—teach us. ('The Search', p. 26)

While the last line is over-insistent, even shrill, the message is clear. Wisdom has to be personally acquired, without outside help. Incidentally, it is interesting, though not surprising, that wisdom is associated with chastening, a shaping of powers through punishment, the imposition of disipline. It would be a pretty simple business to suffer for a period and then reap the benefits. But the grip on reality constantly threatens to slip.

> When we dream of what has gone before
> And what is to come after;
> When the sun comes up over the hills in the mornings
> And sets the way it rose with the moon and stars;
> When at last we hang up our weapons upon our mud walls
> And weep with joy because the battle is over and won . . .
> Do we know indeed what has gone before
> And what is to come after?
>
> ('Questions of Our Time', p. 64)

This stress on the individual's need to renew his conviction, to re-establish his certitude, is responsible for the concreteness of Brew's poetry. It leads to the almost relentless disclosure of his subject. His poems do not have the transparency of Okigbo's or the mercurial escape of thought into image we occasionally notice in Okara's. Brew's poems are, with few exceptions, related to specific situations.

Moreover, his mind is essentially sympathetic and gentle, and civilised, animated by a near-Christian charity. His vigour is of an unusual kind, powerful but non-violent. Few of his images startle or flash. Their effectiveness derives from an apt illumination.

This fits the view of poetry implicit in his work. Brew's is the poetry of situation. He is confident that if disclosed properly, the elements of a situation have their own convincing power. A poet chips away and so lays bare the situation, as a first requirement, and then proceeds to generate out of the other sinews of language, important, but supplementary, meaning.

> When your call came
> I was not at home:
> I had gone abroad
> To look for herbs,

22

Not for today's happiness
But for the troubles of tomorrow.
Back home I am now blamed
That I was not here
When your call came.

('When Your Call Came', p. 10)

Here the poetry is in the anticipation gradually built up by the unfolding event. We feel that things are heading for a climax of sorts, though there is little in the phrasing itself to contribute tension. The language is pared down, left in essential simplicity.

The strategy of allowing the situation to come through forcefully, is based on a special attitude to language. Each word remains firmly denotative. 'When Your Call Came', reads like a translation into English, as if demonstrating the truth of Okara's claim that the cultural impedimenta of language are not easily translatable, that one gets only a basic as against a restlessly suggestive meaning. We feel that we can trust the words to stand firmly in line, without the slightest danger of mischief. The syntax is simple, though the simplicity is, paradoxically, a kind of sophistication.[4] It is there to supply a particular version of things, solid and faithful. There are no procedures to discuss or explicate, no unusual features, no metaphor or simile. If we need to probe, it is into the situation, the emotional content, and not the language. Once the poet's general approach is known, the kind of criticism suitable for concentrated poetry has little to offer. Post-Empsionan readers have come to expect ambiguity, levels of meaning, parallel responses to denotative and connotative meanings, a poetry in which the whole exceeds the parts, because a whole range of elements belonging to words are brought into significant relationship. Brew's poems generally neglect these elements. With few exceptions, his interests are served without them. He sacrifices a number of powerful agencies, the use of sophisticated syntax and the intensities provided by images, just to name two. I am not suggesting that Brew invariably ignores the connotative possibilities, or that he is a *simple* poet; merely that at times he successfully does away with them. And when he does so, the 'normal' expectations of what a poem should be, how it should work, will not help us understand the life of the poem. The power in 'When Your Call Came' depends firmly on the non-aggressiveness of language. Poetry ceases to be a raid into the inarticulate, ceases to throw up metaphors to clutch new areas of experience.

Brew returns to this method in a number of poems, and to suggest what was added to this basic procedure is to provide a description of his mature style. I propose to examine 'The Two Finds' (p. 21) and 'The Heart's Anchor' (p. 56). The first of these poems depicts a situation of pure, uncomplicated feeling.

> I pursued her through the forest
> And along the lonely paths of my heart,
> At last I found the aggrey beads
> I gave her, thrown carelessly
> On the banks of the River Volta.
> I wept for the memories that had
> Been cast away.
>
> I came back home, and found her,
> Lying fast asleep
> On my bed!
> Did she know I had pursued her?
> Was my effort worthwhile, I asked,
> And bent to kiss her on the lips.

This is not even confessional. Freed from restless associations and reduced to their fundamentals, the words function directly. This influences the way we treat the lines. We do not impute any untoward sexuality, nor find cause for discomfort. Brew discloses feeling—'I wept' he says—without shame or shudder. That usual, and at times hypocritical, division between public and private, between feelings displayable and those considered *infra dig*, fails to erect itself. We get a direct conversion of feeling into words and gestures.

But neither 'When Your Call Came' nor 'The Two Finds' are outstanding poems of their kind. Only in 'The Heart's Anchor' does the mode achieve a remarkable success. The language aids the drift of the poem by gathering a dignity, an austerity reminiscent of the Psalms.

24

> I have arrived at last, O my Lord
> At your shrine;
> The songs you asked me to sing
> I have sung them all
> On the desolate sands of my journey.

The tone indicates prayer, incantation even, a direct and nobly simple address of deity. The eventual drama is contained in 'I have arrived *at last* . . .'. He has performed the tasks, sung the songs 'On the desolate sands of my journey' and received signs of coming fulfilment, but soon realises that the peace so fervently sought is still beyond his reach. There are no hints of hysteria—Brew never shakes his fist—though the disappointment is all the more heavily felt by not being made much of. The difficulty of securing an abiding faith recurs in 'Lest We Should Be the Last' (p. 51) and 'Unfaithful Faith' (p. 58). The procedure, substantially that of direct statement, describes a quest in the first poem while the second is a lament for enlightenment withheld.

But Brew, in 'The Heart's Anchor' at any rate, does not deny himself the contributions of connotative meaning, or the metamorphoses of key words. It is 'shrine' that dominates the movement in stanza one. We recognise and without hesitation accept its exclusively religious meaning. And this conditions our understanding of 'arrived', 'journey', 'songs' and 'desolate sands', leading us to the religiousity in stanza two.

> The morning dew filled
> The chambers of my hair
> And I felt the crown of your hand on my head.

The dew, a conventional image of spiritual agency, brings blessing; this '*crown* of your hand' in the last line is, universally, a blessing. We have, then, a clearly established religious context to provide for the doubling of significances.

> I have arrived O my Lord at your shrine.
> I have done the penance you ordered;
> But the peace you promised me stays
> In your heart—beyond my reach.

He has 'arrived' by completing the journey, but also, what is important for our appreciation of the final disappointment, attained to a higher spiritual state. The whole tone and structure of the first two lines require them to be read as statements of fact. He has fulfilled what was prescribed. We are at the dramatic heart of the poem. The dissappointment, as noticed earlier, is all the more acute for its quiet implicitness.

The comprehensiveness of such poetry is limited. While he draws our attention to things we may otherwise miss, the emotional range is narrow. This poses certain dangers and problems. It is not always possible to decide whether the failure of a poem is on account of its language or feebleness of material, or Brew's failure to distinguish the ordinary from the profound.

> I am now too old to look back.
> The urgent future faces me
> And cuts from my sight the end
> That should inevitably come.
> The task that has been assigned to me
> Remains unfinished and almost insurmountable.
> Is it fear of the wasteland at my back
> That keeps me looking ahead,
> Or the lame struggling will to do the work?
> Am I past the middle of the river
> And therefore must go on?
>
> ('The Middle of the River', p. 42)

There is little of interest here. The whole situation is a cliché and Brew does nothing to dispel its triteness. The language fails to shape itself and, consequently, remains pretty ordinary, innocent of any feeling of tragedy, of large undertakings unresolved. The second and concluding stanzas with its 'fitful yearning', lacks the crisp force of Tennyson's 'Ulysses'–though in that poem the means utilised are clearly of a different order. In Brew's piece the tension, the heroism is limp. The lines read like notes and speculations for a poem. Another case of the simple-obvious is 'Nickname': it need not have been written at all.

One other limitation is the degree to which the approach loses its virtues when dealing with a complex relationship. When the drama ceases to be located primarily in the situation, or where it is no longer possible to identify it with a situation, Brew is less successful. This is the case with 'The Harvest of Our Life' (p. 43) in which the action is focussed on the changing, developing consciousness of man.

26

This, Brew's biggest poem, is meant to carry his central reflections. But it is nowhere near an incisive statement. The start of the poem does suggest the basic movement.

> If this is the time
> To master my heart
> Do so!
> Do so now!
> As the clouds float
> Home to their rain-drenched
> Caverns behind the hills.

The clouds retreat, an imagistic confirmation that the movement is propitious. We feel in the presence of an important beginning, of what proves to be the heart's initiation into disciplines and adult intimacies.

The second stanza contains a similar emphasis. What matter, from the point of thematic development, are the first four lines.

> If this is the time
> To master my heart,
> Let me fall an easy victim
> To the pleasures that you hold to my lips
> When the duiker
> Lingers along the pool to drink
> And the ailing leopard
> Turns its dry unbelieving snout away;
> When the dew-drops dry
> Unnoticed on the sinews of the leaf
> And the soft paddling duck
> Webs its way
> Through the subtle
> Entanglement of weeds
> Along the river Prah.

The surrender is expanded and invested with a mixture of tender, severe and explosive images to reflect the duality of the moment, its gentleness as well as the surprise it has in store. The 'ailing leopard' is evocative, one of those images which somehow continues to fascinate and expand both within context and when contemplated alone. But thematic continuity is affected by images which prove too successful and superior. They draw our responses

without inducing a renewal of contact with the main business of the poem. The greater the fascination the surer the dislocation. The contrast they offer to Brew's low-pressure poems is vivid. Brew hasn't the technique to mix the two 'styles'.
The second movement commences with stanza three.

> O, I remember the songs
> You sang that night,
> And the whirl of raffia skirts;
> The speechless pulsations of living bones.
> O, I remember the songs you sang
> Recounting what has gone before
> And what is ours beyond
> The tracks of our thoughts and feet.

Obviously the song and dance recount tribal lore. But clarity is not forthcoming. Either Brew's language has changed its mode of operation or he fails to achieve control. We do not have quick accesses to the poem. The voice of the poem, the 'I', is unable to arrange a fluent accommodation of theme and language. We want but are not able to enter into the world of the poem. Apart from this, the fourth line proves puzzling. Why 'living bones'? The picture evoked of skeletons dancing, is hardly rhythmic or edifying. Why, again, *speechless* pulsations'? Brew requires one narrow quality of the word and gets it, but leaves a number of other painful associations unsuppressed.

The fourth stanza offers in miniature the knowledge provided with initiation.

> You sang of beautiful women
> (The kangaroo-jumps of their youthful breasts)
> Flirting with sportive spirits
> Red-eyed, with red-lips, hoary-red
> With quaffing of frequent libations;
> You sang of feasts and festivals . . .
> And the loading of the dice;
> Why the barndog barked
> At the moon as she sang
> And why the mouse dropped the pearl-corn
> From its teeth and stood forced-humble
> With the soft light of fear in its eyes.

28

It seems hardly possible for a poet as sensitive as Brew to allow that link between kangaroo and breasts. But even discounting that, we still have a curious mixture of sloppy phrasing—'sportive spirits', 'hoary-red'—with some pretty interesting stuff.

In the stanza that follows the initiate reaches a higher state of 'consciousness'. He sees 'a sheen of light' and becomes aware of her with 'hair like the dark eyes of an eagle/over the affairs of men'. From this point the reader finds it hard to keep in touch with the poem. We suspect some symbolic impact but are unable to identify it. The poetry, to a large extent, defeats itself by excluding our understanding.

And yet the river rolled on
And passed over rocks;
While sand in the bed
Bearing the burden of rotten wood
Twigs, grass—a flower—the breath
Of the soul and the bones of thousands
Who should have lived
To fight a war for this or that,
And this or that a ruse
To deceive the mover of the move,
And the mover of the move
Always moved by an uncertainty.

And yet to fight
And yet to conquer;
This was the badge we bore
On the pale texture of our hearts.
And yet to fight
And yet to conquer.

The sea-gulls blow
Like paper-pieces over the hard blue sea
And yet we live to conquer.
So we talked of wars
With their women
And they wept at the foot of the hills.

And the waters rolled on.
And what was old was new

                    And what was new never came to stay.
                    But to skim the gates of change;
                    Forever new; forever old and new;
                    Once-upon-a-time,
                    Never the same,
                    Always at last the same.

Unless we provide a specific value for 'river', we are hard put to
get any meaning going. And it is difficult not to be arbitrary.
Moreover, what does the 'war' relate to? Who is the 'mover'?
These are crude questions, crude but necessary. The compression
is too severe, links are suppressed, and ideas remain embryonic.
Despite the Keatsian echo, the last six lines do suggest, however
unsatisfactorily, the reservoir of power and renewal available to
the initiate. The apparent paradox of an ancient yet potent
cultural force which each generation has to rediscover is something
we understand. But this does not mean that the foreground of
ideas leading to it can be sketchily developed or taken for granted.
Without them the poetry remains inaccessible.

   This section is the metaphysical core of the poem. It comes
between the appearance of the dark lady and the battle for her
possession. Had the poetry not locked its meaning so severely, we
might have risen to the climactic, almost sexual resolution.
Perhaps the 'lady of situations', represents a life-force, a comple-
tion to experience, a final encounter to round off the initiation.
The structural arrangement of the poem points to this.

                    But those who slept with her in those mud huts
                    (Arrows in their grips
                    And bows on their shoulders)
                    Have crawled away soft-bellied,
                    Into hollow chambers
                    Along the road;
                    Lined their walls
                    With smooth white stones;
                    Abandoned the shade
                    That sheltered their peace
                    And call that peace of mind
                    Now floating away with the clouds
                    As peace—
                    That passes understanding.

30

The initiation, understandably, brings change. Sheltered peace is abandoned in favour of positive action.

Brew knows the importance of linking the various movements, especially in a poem of some length. The evidence is there. Lines and phrases recall earlier parts. But this is not really helpful as these parts themselves are imperfectly enunciated. What we miss is inner organisation of the kind in Okigbo's poems, where aspects of the themes develop usefully within a framework. We are able to correlate our responses. 'The Harvest of Our Lives' lacks this firm structure. There is little hope for a reader unless he is willing to devote an excessive amount of time to expand a phrase here and there and generally get the lines going. But many would say this exceeds what can properly be expected of readers, or that it would be altogether an impertinent undertaking.

Brew is capable of shaping his intentions imagistically, a technique essential to the long poem. Images can be developed, patterned, syncopated, used judiciously, to reinforce statement. Not merely by telling us more about what is happening, but by bringing in cogent implications. An example from Brew is 'Waiting':

> When I came to you;
> The door was shut
> I knocked;
> And you opened the door.
> For a shimmering moment
> That stars shone
> Over our heads
> The grass swayed in the wind;
> For they knew
> You and I
> Have touched the rims of the sun together
> In the waters of the Black Nile.
>
> You uttered the word
> And the sun told me
> It was too late in the day,
> So you must leave. (p. 24)

The full emotional explosion accompanying his lover's opening the door, that 'shimmering moment', is imaged in the marked upheaval of star and wind. Nature bestows her approval, providing a cosmic grandeur, the immensity of some unutterably profound communion of synoptic powers. The performance indicates an imaginative capacity of a high order. We feel compelled to understand, to receive the quickly multiplying life.

'The Sea Eats Our Land' (p. 41) contains a further example. Erosion gradually destroys Keta, a town 'built on a narrow strip of land between a lagoon and the sea'. (See *The Shadow of Laughter* p. 41.) The destruction, also seen as punishment for some spiritual ommission, is conveyed simply.

> Here stood our ancestral home:
> The crumbling wall marks the spot.
> Here a sheep was led to slaughter
> To appease the gods and stone
> For faults which our destiny
> Has blossomed into crimes.
> There my cursed father once stood
> And shouted to us, his children,
> To come back from our play
> To our evening meal and sleep.
>
> The clouds were thickening in the red sky
> At night had charmed
> A black power into the pounding waves.
>
> Here once lay Keta.
> Now her golden girls
> Erode into the arms
> Of strange towns.

The foreboding is carried by the middle stanza. It is the waves which destroyed Keta. They have been strengthened by the gathering power of darkness. The image itself is carefully placed to prepare us for the destruction.

Brew's images can be very fetching

> Gamilli's arm has broken into buds ...

or have a certain telling precision:

> ... these tribal marks of the world.

or manage a terrific capture of feeling in

> O there are flowers in Tamele
> That smell like fire.

But there are also disastrous lapses:

> But a vision of your lyrical bosom
> Floats like a ship on the storm
> Of my delirious mind.

Even the suspicion of Freudian undertones fails to retrieve the picture. Heroic proportions do not always secure plain sailing. Brew is guilty of exaggeration, as when in the lines preceding those quoted, he calls the eyes 'Oasis of ecstasy'.

The flow of his poetry is at times disturbed by a 'softness' of phrasing. We find, in 'The Lonely Traveller', (p. 33) for instance. 'sweet energy', 'priceless peace', 'ethereal bliss', 'shores of eternity' and 'genial mists of courage', all within seven lines. The two final lines are, 'Meandering his weary way/On the green and golden hills of Africa!' These vestiges of weaker impulses of English poetry, include:

> With his faith as his spear
> And his past as his shield
> He battled the bondage of bludgeons.

It is not easy to decide whether the defect is one of sensibility or sentiment. Ghanaian poets frequently suffer a lapse in vital creative usage by trusting the surface of a phrase, taking its power for granted. Is it because their longer familiarity with the language bred the kind of contempt which results in an inability to suspect the obvious? It is too prevalent to be explained away as loss of creative pressure.

Brew's style does of course include other contrivances. The most interesting ones are based on syntactical structures and a diction close to proverbial expression. A simple instance is furnished by the following lines from 'Through the Forest':

> Through the forest
> Whitened by the moon
> Come the distant rattles;
> Come the beat of a pulse
> The pulse of the night,
> The pulse of the day. (p. 53)

The pairs of common structures help to concentrate the elements they gather. The first evokes a feeling of the earth alive, rolling in 'her diurnal round', with 'distant rattles' which are akin to Wordsworth's 'ghostly language of the earth'. The pairs are linked by 'pulse' to suggest, in combination, the primal life of the earth.

A more calculated use of structure is the balance of alternatives:

> You sang of beautiful women . . .
> The red blood-line across the necks
> Of sacrificial sheep;
> Of acceptance and refusal of gifts;
> Of sacrifice offered and withheld.
> Of good men and their lot;
> Of good name and its loss; of the die cast
> And the loading of the dice.

The repetition concentrates our attention on the gifts which come with initiation. But 'The Harvest of our Life' is a long poem. Extensive use of the device can prove boring, and give the impression of the same point made repeatedly.

Brew sought suppleness in order to achieve a comprehensive poetic statement. It was, moreover, essential to the life of his staple line.

> And soon, soon the fires,
> The fires will begin to burn,
> The hawk will flutter and turn
> On its wings and swoop for the mouse,
> The dog will run for the hare,
> The hare for its little life.

('The Dry Season', p. 38)

The common syntactical structures and the reptition of words across the lineation, condense phrase and line to produce one dominant suggestion to conclude the poem: this is the dry season and nature is at her most cruel. The repetition of 'soon' and 'fires' carries a suppressed sympathy. And the rhymes 'burn' and 'turn' connect their subjects: 'fire' and 'hawk', both mercilessly destructive. The developing tragedy is epitomised in the hawk's flutter, turn and swoop. The fittest survive, the strong consume the weak.

34

It was suggested earlier that 'The Vulture' read very much like an expanded proverb. Brew frequently pitches his diction is such a way that we feel he is either translating out of traditional sources or modifying them.

> The broken bone cannot be made whole!
> The strong had sheltered in their strength
> The swift had sought life in their speed
> The crippled and the tired heaped out of the way.
> Onto the ant hills . . .

These lines give, in quick firm strokes, the recent state of things in Ghana. The first tells of despair, the second selfishness, the third a loss of courage, the fourth, death of charity. That proverbial ring supplies a solid basis to the dissatisfaction.

Kwesi Brew's work has not received the attention it deserves. His poetry is neither flamboyant, nor does it provoke spectacular analysis. Nor is it readily enlisted to support large and urgent purposes. The poetry is seldom hurried, preferring to move with a confident patience. Few of his poems are memorable in the way that some poems are, staying in the mind as an incantatory whole, independent of the printed text. Their virtues are on the quiet side. These are perhaps reasons for the absence of any really serious discussion of his work, which is a pity, as it is close in spirit to much traditional poetry and could provide insights for a possible rapprochement between English and what the vernaculars have to offer.

NOTES

1. Quotations from Brew's poems are taken from *The Shadow of Laughter* (London 1968). The number in brackets after the title gives the page reference.

2. Lewis Nkosi has a useful comment on the growth of 'individual vision':

   In many areas of Africa the destruction of traditional African values by European imperialism and the concomitant Christianisation of Africans has drastically reversed the role of the poet or artist in the community.

   First there has been a change in the social organisation which has resulted in more emphasis being placed on the individual rather than the communal. Hence the art of communal celebration is being replaced by lonely artistic creation—by an individual vision, so to speak. For the first time the African artist is confronting the community as an individual (even an alienate individual) whose vision may not conform to that of the statesman, the political or the religious leader. (*'Home and Exile,'* London 1965, p. 104.)

'The Search' (p. 26) is a poetic statement of a similar conclusion.

3. Both George Awoonor-Williams (in the interview by Robert Serumaga reported in *Cultural Events*, No. 29, April 1967, p. IV) and Ezekiel Mphahlele ('The Language of African Literature, English Poetry in Africa', *Africa: A Handbook*, p. 400) maintain that Brew 'helps us visualise the various elements that are in ancestral worship and which symbolise a whole way of life.'

4. Gerald Moore in reviewing *Okyeame*, No. 1 (1961) in *Black Orpheus*, No. 10, p. 66, says 'Kwesi Brew's language has weight and a kind of held-back rhythm which keeps the readers attention'. Moore adds that Brew has a 'vivid descriptive gift' and quotes the opening lines of 'A Plea for Mercy' (p. 55) in support:

> We have come to your shrine to worship—
> We the sons of the land.
> The naked cowherd has brought
> The cows safely home,
> And stands silent with his bamboo flute
> Wiping the rain from his brow

We need to qualify the vividness by saying that it results from carefully picked and accurately described details.

Three Crowns Books ♛ ♛ ♛

forthcoming titles are:

Through a Film Darkly   J. C. de Graft

In this new play, the author explores the racial tensions underlying the lives of two married couples. The cause of the hero's hatred of Europeans gradually becomes apparent as the action of this most intelligent play moves to its startling and terrifying conclusion.

People are Living There   Athol Fugard

The action in this play takes place on Milly's fiftieth birthday. Jilted by the flashy lodger with whom she has lived for the past ten years, Milly persuades two of her other lodgers to join her in a gesture of defiance—a wild birthday party. In the kitchen of her Johannesburg boarding-house she, Don and Shorty move through comedy and pathos into the fierce light of self-knowledge.

OXFORD UNIVERSITY PRESS

36

An African
Sentimentalist
Camara
Laye
The African
Child

Paul Edwards
&Kenneth
Ramchand

The note of disapproval for *The African Child* which occurs from
time to time in African journals usually concerns its lack of
commitment to the anti-colonial struggle. For instance, in *The
Literature and Thought of Modern Africa* (London 1966), Claude

Wauthier quotes the following from *Presence Africaine* (p. 144):

Laye resolutely shuts his eyes to the most crucial realities, those which we have always been very careful to reveal to the public here. Has this Guinean, of my own race, who it seems was a very lively boy, really seen nothing but a beautiful, peaceful and maternal Africa? Is it possible that not once has Laye witnessed a single minor extortion by the colonial authorities?

On the other hand the work has been received enthusiastically by its readers in Europe and the West Indies. Its English translator, William Plomer writes in an introduction[1]:

This in some ways deceptively simple story is the work of a 'dark child' uncorrupted by the complexity and dislocation of the world we know. The anxiety aroused in the reader lest so candid a nature should be perhaps smeared or injured by the strain of being 'displaced' in an alien Europe is a measure of the sympathetic interest created by what he has to say and the way he has said it. (p. 8)

Gerald Moore in *Seven African Writers* (London 1962) is led to lament 'a vanishing world so rich in dignity and human values'; and in a way, even a beady-eyed observer like the West Indian novelist V. S. Naipaul yields to its fascination. Commenting in *The Middle Passage* (London 1962) on his difficulties in responding to West Indian novels, Naipaul reflects that 'it is easier to enter the tribal world of an African writer like Camara Laye'. Common to all these comments is the residual feeling that 'we' (the Europeans and the mimic men) have lost sight of a better, simpler, more coherent existence, which 'they' still cling to.

In this article we want to show that *The African Child* is committed to an anti-colonial line on the level of cultural polemics; and to examine its organisation and texture in some detail in order to account for our doubts about its literary quality. These two purposes are not unrelated.

When we discussed this book in the first of a series of Senior Honours seminars at Edinburgh University, students were quick to draw attention to the coherence of *The African Child* in contrast with what they described as the formlessness of the novel paired with it, *The Year in San Fernando* (1965) by the West Indian,

Michael Anthony. As the discussion developed, however, it began to appear that coherence was not strictly speaking a feature of the book, but rather of the society which the book describes. *The African Child* divided easily into two parts: in the first eight chapters, a sense of community is suggested by the use of 'we' and a continuous tense in the verb; in the last four chapters, a narrating 'I' and the past definite tense correspond to the youth's detachment from his sustaining context of African village life. It was at this point that a curious editorial process in most readers' responses was revealed: we found that when our students spoke of 'coherence', they were thinking of the first eight chapters but not the last four. The final chapters had either made no impression, or were simply regarded as a pardonable falling off. The reasons for this are not too difficult to see.

Each of the first eight chapters is built round a recurrent activity or some significant feature in the life of the community: the ancestral snake and guiding spirit; the goldsmith's shop and the making of a trinket; a visit to the country; the rice harvest; the gift of magic; the village school; the night of Konden Diara; and the rite of circumcision. These constitutive elements, successively described, add up to an orderly picture of coherent traditional life and community. Although the 'I' and the past definite tense do occur (significantly, during the circumcision and manhood episode) the predominant 'we' and the continuous tense heighten the sense of unity, immersing the boy's individual consciousness in the character of the community. The three chapters which convey this coherent all-inclusiveness most forcibly are those relating to the creative ritual of the goldsmith's shop, the harvesting climax, and the initiating night of Konden Diara: with such archetypal centres of interest to embellish, Laye can hardly be said to have lacked sources of inspiration. Nevertheless, although the engrossing raw material draws the attention of the reader away from possible deficiencies of expression, we submit that these striking episodes contain weaknesses which, on re-reading, become more and more obtrusive, and are not unrelated to the flatness of the final chapters. To look at each of these three chapters from the early part of the book is to see Laye at his best, but at the same time to trace the first fine cracks in the artefact.

The making of a trinket in the goldsmith's shop is the centre-piece of the most impressive chapter of *The African Child*. A precise description of a technical process in clearly defined phases is the shaping force in the account. Beginning with the formless element of mud out of which the crouching woman has extracted laborious grains of gold for melting in the goldsmith's crucible, the concrete description allows us to see through the hammering and stretching and spinning out of the fragile wire, to the mythic proportions of original creation, beauty and order out of chaos, in the goldsmith's art. It is this mythic pattern implicit in the technical process, not Laye's insistence on an exclusive and local magic, which gives to the goldsmith's incantations the vesture of creative invocation:

> Were they not the spirits of fire and gold, of fire and air, air breathed through the earthen pipes, of fire born of air, of gold married with fire—were not these the spirits he was invoking? Was it not their help and their friendship he was calling upon in this marriage of elemental things? (p. 26)

Between controlled descriptions of aspects of the technical process, however, Laye interjects an inflated commentary which at its worst amounts to a crude insistence upon black mystery—'We could not hear those words, those secret words, those incantations which he addressed to powers that we should not, that we could not hear or see . . .' (p. 27)

Far more important, in fact, than the self-consciously 'impressive' commentary is the way in which the humanity and vulnerability of the people who are sharing in this 'magical' enterprise are kept before our eyes: the typical urgency of the woman to have the work completed, and the father's all too human response to her flattery precede the making of the ornament; the chapter closes with the tough-minded mother complaining that the father is 'ruining his health', as well as that of the little boy who should have been 'playing here in the yard instead of going and breathing the dust and smoke in the workshop'. The finest human touch comes in the final stages of the process, when the woman is watching the marvellous sight of the transformation:

> She was here now, devouring with her eyes the fragile golden wire, following its tranquil and inevitable spirals round the little metal cone which gave the trinket its shape. My father would be watching her out of the corner of his eye, and sometimes I

would see the corners of his mouth twitch into a smile . . . (p. 29)

While Laye makes us aware of this vulnerable humanity in the participants, he also creates a sense of their community in this technical activity. The goldsmith may be the protagonist, but upon him all eyes and hopes are focused: his success will gratify the craving of the woman, excite the mimetic imaginations of the apprentices and inspire the poetic skill of the praise-singer; it will vindicate the mastery of the goldsmith and be a token of the goodwill of the powers that be. At the end, the whole group is conscious of a task shared as well as a wonder achieved, and offer gifts and applause as the goldsmith celebrates with the great dance, the Douga, another universal expression of creative harmony.

In this episode, Laye is not entirely free from an impulse to deny the universal aspects of his culture, but we have tried to show how in this part of *The African Child*, local 'magic' expands into larger myth. It is in the episodes of the rice harvest and of Konden Diara that Laye's doctrinaire intentions seriously begin to threaten his raw material.

The rice harvest episode posits a sense of community, but not in the same way as the goldsmith's shop sequence, and without comprehending as many different individuals. A long perspective on the reapers ('Wasn't it enough to see the ears of rice bowing before the long, gentle wave of those black bodies?') corresponds with an idealising doctrine of peasant soul-harmony:

> Our husbandmen were singing, and as they sang, they reaped; they were singing in chorus, and reaping in unison: their voices and their gestures were all harmonious and in harmony; they were one!—united by the same task, united by the same song. They were bound to one another, united by the same soul: each and every one was tasting the delight, savouring the common pleasure of accomplishing a common task. (p. 51)

It is not Laye's intention in *The African Child* to sustain an illusion that we are experiencing events through the child's consciousness: indeed, the work's pervasive nostalgic effect is deliberately created by the imposition of the older man's mood upon the child's experiences. But here a disguised polemic intention works to the extent that our students felt drawn by this episode to contrast the mechanised and sterile civilisation in which

41

they said they lived with the integrated Being of Laye's people. In this, as we have seen, the students were not unique. If the passage quoted strikes us as being too deeply rooted in stereotypes of innocence and happy peasantry, in the tradition of the European noble savage, it is because Laye wishes to insinuate the same criticism of European civilisation that Rousseau and his followers made. But the trouble is not so much that Camara Laye should use these stereotypes, as that he fails to go very far beyond them. The cause of this failure lies, at least partly, in the author's concern to record the doctrine and no more, rather than to evoke a life in excess of the doctrine but in which that doctrine might be implicit.

The passage may be criticised from another point of view. The picture of an ideally happy, courteous and well-adjusted society is hardly sustained in the description a little later of the goings on at the village school, with the bullying of the smaller boys by the bigger, and the irresponsible violence of the schoolmaster (see pp. 65-78). Nor is it supported by the ironic description of the hospitality afforded Laye at Mamou: 'A former apprentice of my father's . . . had offered me hospitality for the night. This apprentice had written in the most affectionate terms; actually—but perhaps he had forgotten the difference in climate—he lodged me in a dark hut on top of a hill, where I had ample leisure—more than I wanted—to experience the chill nights and the keen air of the Fouta-Djalon'. (p. 121) And when, at Conakry, the uncle suggests that Laye learn a good trade at the technical school, the thoughts of the presumably still uncorrupted youth are as follows: 'Now I *was* ambitious. But I would never realise my ambitions by becoming a manual worker; I had no more respect than most people for such workers.' (p. 129) The suspicion that there is something not entirely pleasant only a little way below the surface of the author's eloquent pastoral becomes irresistible when we add to these examples the comments of the hero's father on his own childhood:

You see, I had no father to look after me, as you had. At least, not for very long: when I was twelve years old I became an orphan; and I had to make my own way in life. It was not easy. The uncles in whose care I was left treated me more like a slave than a nephew . . . (p. 117)

42

If passages like these had been designed to modify or expand Camara Laye's vision of African life, the reader might have looked upon it with more confidence. But it is clear that they have no place either in his polemic intention or in the doctrine which the author feels it necessary to expound in the rice harvest episode and elsewhere.

Further doubts about Laye's purposes are raised by the Konden Diara chapter, with its final cadence—'The secret . . . Do we still have secrets?' (p. 92) This chapter contrasts unfavourably with the one which deals with the trinket-making of the goldsmith. Laye insists throughout the book on the literal fact of magic, and constantly laments a lost world of miracles:

> These miracles—they were miracles indeed—nowadays I think about them as if they were the fabulous event of a far-off past. That past is, however, still quite near: it was only yesterday. But the world rolls on, the world changes, my own world perhaps more rapidly than anyone's; so that it appears as if we are ceasing to be what we were, and that truly we were not exactly ourselves even at the time when these miracles took place before our eyes. Yes the world rolls on, and changes . . .
> (pp. 62-3)

In this quotation, the loss of miracles is ponderously associated in some way with the changing world but above all the author's changing world, and so, presumably with the incursions of Western materialism and technology. In this, the paragraph conforms to the polemic intention of the book. At other points Laye gives specific examples of the magical—in his father's communion with the snake, his mother's with the horses and crocodiles, the 'mute mystery of things' (p. 43), which it is in the countryman's power to perceive, but not in the city-dweller's. There is no suggestion in these instances that the author differentiates between different degrees and kinds of magic. Nor does he seem to think that some of it may be delusory or fraudulent. Yet, this is what the mystery of Konden Diara turns out to be. For as it happens, the roaring of Konden Diara and his thirty lions is explained as a *necessary* fraud, the test which helps bind the age group together. This explanation is perfectly satisfactory, and there is nothing wrong with the author's desire to preserve the sense of wonder and mystery in life.

43

All the same, the Konden Diara episode reflects oddly upon the other explicitly magical incidents in the book, with which it becomes confusingly associated when the author asks his final question—'The secret . . . Do we still have secrets?' To what extent are we to trust his faith in miracles and countrymen's visions? Is it entirely honest of him to imply that the wicked West has emptied the haunted African air? For he would have learned the truth about the 'mystery' of Konden Diara had he stayed in Guinea, and would presumably have practised the same necessary deception on other youngsters in turn. The loss of the 'secret', in consequence, far from having anything to do with the opposition of country and city, Africa and Europe, is simply part of the process of growing up, in which the magic of innocence may very well vanish, perhaps to be replaced by the other magic of experience. Laye's opposition of childhood vision to a sterile maturity appears far too simple, and indeed far too conventional. In fact, two ideas are being confused here in *The African Child,* both going back to the romanticism of Rousseau or Wordsworth (and reappearing in *nègritude* in somewhat disguised forms)—the child's loss of vision, and the corruption of the traditional by the modern. The author's commitment to the doctrine of African innocence and magic corrupted by European technology and rationalism compels him to explain matters in these terms even when, as is the case with Konden Diara, the event does not fit the pattern.

If these flaws of *The African Child* are to some extent compensated for by the engaging nature of the raw material, they appear in an embarrassing way in the last four chapters where once the stiffening of the set pieces has been removed the looseness of the material and the language of the book can no longer be concealed. The last four chapters of *The African Child* in which the 'I' character describes the move from the village to Conakry and his life there, resemble *The Year in San Fernando* closely both in narrative technique and in the similarity of certain crucial experiences. In each book, the narrating character is confronted by a breathtaking seascape; the death of Mrs Chandles is an experience of an ending for Francis in the way that Check's death is for Camara Laye; and in both books, the narrating characters describe adolescent first love. The existence of these virtually parallel passages provides an opportunity to demonstrate positively by comparison some of the weaknesses in Camara Laye's work.

44

Laye's seascape comes after a description of his arrival at Conakry. An attempt is made to capture attention with the stagey sentence 'And then I saw the sea . . .' (the dots are the author's), coming at the end of a paragraph. But the actual description hardly seems to justify this dramatic introduction, for the seascape we are offered is flat:

> I stood a long time looking at its vastness, watching the waves that kept rolling in after one another and finally were broken against the red rocks of the shore. Far off there appeared, in spite of the mist that hung around them, some very green-looking islands. It seemed to me the most astonishing spectacle I had ever seen; from the train, at night, I had only glimpsed what it was like; I had formed no real idea of the vastness of the ocean, and even less of its movement, of the kind of irresistible fascination which comes from its inexhaustibly endless movement. Now the whole spectacle lay before me, it was only with difficulty that I dragged myself away from it. (p. 124)

There is little attempt at imaginative presentation and the author offers only a series of very generalised gestures—'its vastness', 'waves that kept rolling in after one another', 'the vastness of the ocean' again, 'the most astonishing spectacle', 'the kind of irresistible fascination' and so on, concluding with the feeblest and most predictable of assertions. The sea remains uninterruptedly 'out there', without emotional context (apart from the author's laboured insistence that he *did* feel strongly), and lacking any associations in the boy's mind.

Francis' view of the sea in *The Year in San Fernando* comes as a forbidden pleasure: he has strayed into this part of the town while on an errand, with the recurrent picture of an angry Mrs Chandles in his thoughts. The great sprawl of the sea is only one of several lines of radiation at the centre of which is the boy's observing eye:

> The sea lay like a blue blanket. To the right, I could not see much of it as the railway buildings blocked the view, but I watched it sprawling away to the horizon, and to the left I could see at some point down how the coast jutted out and my eyes followed the coast as far as was possible to see. I looked again in front of me and at the horizon and I noticed how the sky just above the water seemed splashed with blood. And I

remembered that Easter evening again. Although it shone, the sun was not plainly seen, for the gathering clouds half-obscured it. It was now midway between the tall sky and sea, and where the sky was clear around it the place was very red, and some of the clouds looked black-red, but the light that fell on the water was as red as blood. I turned away a little from the light and I looked at the towering buildings around and about me. The sunset light was falling upon the wharf too. To the left and by the sea part of the railings was the Fish Market. People had always talked about going down to the wharf for fish. On mornings when the fish had been too expensive at the big market they had said it was murder, and they'd go down to the wharf. So here was where the Fish Market was. Now I knew. Now I knew, also, where the well-known lumber people were. So when the big lumber lorries passed down Romaine Street, I would know about them and where they came from.

> (*The Year in San Fernando*, pp. 129-30)

The lorries that were, earlier in the work, roaring lights from the darkness are now becoming familiar, known. Another piece of knowledge is slotted into place as chance remark in the market about the price of fish is suddenly understood in terms of place 'so here was where the Fish Market was. Now I knew.' But the experience contains more than practical information. The red darkening sky is a persistent image of the shades which seem to the boy to close in upon him as he grows. There is not in this novel, however, any easy opposition between innocent happy childhood and depressed maturity. The sunset raises an echo in memory of a similar one that Francis had watched at Easter:

> The evening was dying now. The sun must have been low over the gulf. I could see the western sky blood-red over the houses, as if the evening had been slain, and was bleeding out. It was sombre thought, but there was also the feeling of splendour in the evening light, and the feeling of happiness and of things being good.
>
> (*The Year in San Fernando*, p. 79)

The acceptance by the boy of growth and decay, and of his consequent joy in a life that remains in many ways painful is a recurrent feature in the novel. Here the Wordsworthian capacity

46

for simultaneous recall and experience, and the ability to draw upon the 'types and symbols' of the natural world, are the means through which acceptance is involuntarily arrived at. Further, indeed, the scene by the sea suggests to the boy, without his consciously realising it, the multitude of paths, radiating lines, his own life may move outwards along. But all this is conveyed through the boy's consciousness, in terms of sights and sounds and memories of these, imaginatively and figuratively, not in the explicit 'philosophising' tone of the contemplative adult we find in *The African Child*.

As another illustration of the deficiencies of these later chapters, there is the description of the death of Check, which reveals impulses towards the stereotype similar to those we have already seen: 'We watched him sleeping and a great hope began to spring in our hearts', 'his features were no longer drawn and his lips appeared to be smiling', even 'Then as the dispensary clock finished the twelve strokes, he died...' (again the dots are Laye's). This last sentence marks with particular clarity the sentimental stylisation of the passage. Check must only be allowed to die in a dramatically 'significant' way as the clock chimes the last stroke of midnight, unfortunately reminding us of the popular Victorian song about 'My grandfather's clock'. The death, in consequence, strikes us as staged, in a way not unlike the feebler death scenes of Dickens.

At this point it is instructive to set beside Camara Laye's words, a similar scene from Michael Anthony, the death of Mrs Chandles:

> By the mid-December, with school having closed for Christmas, I spent the holidays being busy in the house. Mrs Chandles was—as the elderly lady said—just awaiting sentence, though I couldn't think what greater sentence could come to her now. But she was waiting all right. It was strange how hard and untiring the elderly lady worked. For, as she said herself, all she was doing was in vain. I watched her rush in and out of the room, always with hot water on the fire, always with foul smelling bed clothes to wash, and yet she did everything with zest. It was as if she was just getting the feel of the wrestle with death and was enjoying it. I thought she had always been at the side of the dying. I thought maybe it made no difference to her if death won all the time. Mostly, I wondered how was she

47

really feeling inside, and sometimes I thought to myself how much money could Mr Chandles be paying her.

(The Year in San Fernando, p 168)

The realism is not callous. Death is seen through the unblinking eye of the young boy as a messy and degrading business; not a remote and separate state, but something all are involved in, and requiring neighbourly care which is far from sentimental, including as it does the payment of wages, the washing of dirty linen, bad smells, skin and bones and a terror of the dark:

Sometimes she called on me to help her with Mrs Chandles and there was never anything like dismay in her voice. Whenever we were slow and Mrs Chandles soiled the sheets, all she would say was 'Look out!' after it had already happened. This amused me. Immediately she would clean the helpless sick, and getting me to help, she would hold Mrs Chandles to one side of the bed, then to the other, and like that she would put new, clean sheets on the bed. Holding Mrs Chandles was no strain for my arms and she felt just skin and bones. Anyway after putting on the clean sheets the dirty linen would be bundled into a cardboard box to be taken downstairs to wash. But before this was done, Mrs Chandles would be put to lie nice and comfortable on the bed.

At such times I had always tried to do what I had to do without thinking of the sick before me. For her eyes would be like death itself and her body would be as stiff as a board though it did not seem this was on her account. Usually she never seemed to know what was going on. And sometimes while I held her there amidst all the mess I felt as though the stench of the bed clothes was going to suffocate me.

And so looking on these things I knew the end could not be far off now. I had only seen one dead person before, and thinking of that face now, and of this, it was striking how alike were the faces of death. I had gone to the house and had watched that dead man's face and was terrified. I had come out and had run home crying in the dark.

(The Year in San Fernando, pp. 119 and 170)

Sentences like 'I thought she had always been at the side of the dying', and 'it was striking how alike were the faces of death' reverberate beyond their literal significance for the boy and take

48

on a gnomic and more comprehensive meaning. The quality of human endurance illuminates the whole passage, though not in any romantic way through formal heroic or sentimental poses. The woman helper 'did everything with zest' yet the boy wonders 'how was she really feeling inside', and we are given an insight into this possible ambivalence through the boy's own responses—'I had always tried to do what I had to do without thinking of the sick before me . . .' but 'sometimes while I held her there amidst all the mess I felt as though the stench of the bedclothes was going to suffocate me'. The boy is learning about his own strengths and frailties within the processes of growth and decay to which he is discovering himself to be bound. In an adult observer, the tone of what Francis says might often have appeared insensitive. But as the boy speaks, the reader knows what Francis is learning, and what lies ahead. Characteristically of the novel, the reader lives imaginatively the experiences of the boy, but is compelled to measure these experiences against his own maturity, the reverberations of the boy's words and the stark perceptions of the innocent eye.

Again, when Laye describes his love affair with Marie there is a nagging quality of sentimentality and cliché—and added to this is a regular note of owlish priggery:

Would we have danced together if it had been customary to dance in one another's arms? I hardly know what we would have done. I think we would have abstained, although, like all Africans, we have dancing in our blood. (p. 135)

It is the moment I shall never recapture, and which now has only the bitter-sweet charm of something vanished for ever. (p. 137)

'You can breathe!' I would say. 'Here you can breathe!' 'Yes,' Marie would say. (p. 137)

As I grew older I became more passionate; I no longer had merely half-hearted friendships—or even love affairs. I did not have only Marie and Fanta—although at first it was Marie and Fanta I had as friends. But Marie was on holiday at Bela, at her father's; and Fanta was my 'regular' girl. I respected her; and even if I had wanted to go further (and I did not want to), custom would have forbidden it. The rest . . . the rest were unimportant, but they existed nevertheless. Could my mother fail to understand the growing ardour of my blood? (p. 144)

However, the affair with Marie remains unsoiled by such wickedness and appears as scrubbed and disinfected as any Hollywood musical, even to those rainy skies turned blue up above:

And the dreadful sheets of Conakry rain, so wearisome, so interminable when they hung outside the schoolroom windows, became blue skies when I was with Marie . . . (p. 140)

At this stage the author is no longer criticising the breakdown of a way of life and traditional values, or the seduction of country youth by urban vice—he is simply lamenting, as we saw in the Konden Diara episode, having to grow up:

Marie loved me, and I loved her, but we never gave the sweet, the awful name 'love' to what we felt. And may be it was not exactly love, though there was something of that in it. What was it? What could it be? It was certainly something big, something noble: a marvellous tenderness, and an immense happiness. I mean unalloyed happiness, a pure happiness, a happiness still untroubled by desire. But may be that is what love really is. Certainly it was a child-like passion; and we were still children! Officially I had become a man: I had been initiated. But was that enough? Is it enough just to act like a man? It is years alone that makes a man, and I was still not old enough. (pp. 135-136)

Innocence here is little more than an emotive thought, fixed as elsewhere in the work in rigid and unconvincing stances. There is the repetitive, adjectival quality we recognised in the seascape—the author simply falls back on saying over and over again that his love was a 'big', 'noble', 'unalloyed', 'pure' form of 'happiness' (four times) or 'tenderness'. There is the rigged, rhetorical ambiguity— 'What was it? What could it be?'—which the author answers with commonplaces. There is the stereotype that there is something 'pure' about being 'untroubled by desire', and a rather devious attempt to imply that this is what 'love really is', a kind of romantic infantilism. There is the inconsistency about whether innocence is desirable, or whether one should 'become a man', whatever that means, for the author is unable to go beyond the trivial. With threadbare solemnity he arrives at, and rewards his readers with no more than this:

> Is it enough to act like a man? It is years alone that makes a man . . .

When Michael Anthony's boy suffers the first agonies of adolescent love, there is no suggestion that his innocence has, in itself, any moral quality, or that it is 'bad' for him to feel the first stirrings of passion. There is none of the philosophical, knowing tone of Camara Laye, only a dramatic groping towards an understanding of the passions which have suddenly begun to grip him. The reader is only told what Francis feels, not what Francis *should* feel or what the reader should feel. Again the reader is placed in a dual situation, experiencing the events through the innocent senses of the boy, measuring them against his own maturity and understanding. There is no easy opposition, as in Camara Laye, of innocence and experience, but a dramatic representation, even in the awkwardness of the language, of the struggle of the innocent mind with experiences which are barely comprehensible, yet the vehicle by which the boy's mind is to move away from innocence. Here is Francis thinking about the girl Julia:

> I could see her as being very pretty and if I were grown I would certainly ask her for us to get married. I felt strange thinking this way. She would probably laugh if any man asked her for them to get married. She might say she'd only just left school. I wished she did not want to get married to anybody. I liked her.

> (*The Year in San Fernando*, p. 46)

But when Francis discovers Julia and Mr Chandles among the pillars below the house, Anthony is neither tempted into reflections on the loss of innocence nor the sordidness of sex. Instead, the novelist's art intensifies the boy's confusion by combining shock and a pre-existing terror of Mr Chandles with what we recognise as the frustration of adolescent love. The ironic introduction of music, the food of love, to disturb the boy with its short, stabbing blasts is brilliantly conceived:

> I wiped the perspiration round my head with my sleeves. I was feeling desperate. I thought, Why couldn't he take Julia

51

elsewhere so I wouldn't keep coming upon them? I was still trembling with fear. I kept on feeling desperate and then I began trying to calm myself and I said, 'The hell with Julia!' And then I began wondering if Mr Chandles would come in any minute now. I wondered if he would come straight to me and ask me something. I would say I had forgotten the watering-can at the front. I wondered if he would come and be in a temper right away.

I was still trying to be calm and to forget if Mr Chandles would come up to have a word with me. In a strange way Julia kept weighing on my mind. I passed my sleeves all round my head again and now they were wet. Blasts of music started coming from the school. I could hardly think of them but I could hear them coming short and sharp seeming to stab the air. I could hear the low hum of voices in that outer darkness. The blasts stopped. The hum of voices seemed raised now. The first set struck up.

Stardust, they were playing. I liked it but now I did not think of it much. I lay with my heart racing, waiting for Mr Chandles' footsteps, and at the same time I could not help thinking what a dog Julia was. I turned from one side to the other and I felt as if there was a hair on my face. I said to myself, 'She only pretty but she's a tramp!' I turned and removed the wet bed clothes from under my cheek. And I lay in pain for some time.

(*The Year in San Fernando*, pp. 84-5)

It is part of the vision that Anthony's novel promotes not only that the Laye-type reflections should be passed over but that the boy is soon on friendly terms with Julia again.

We have tried to raise doubts about the integrity of *The African Child* both as a recollection of childhood and as a picture of society: the impression of a coherent traditional life conveyed by the carefully chosen set-pieces, not unintentionally, leads the European or European-orientated reader into a denigration of his own culture; the use of stereotypes drawn from the romantic tradition, but without the artistic control of the great romantics, has led many non-Africans to join Camara Laye in a self-indulgent lament for lost innocence; and the comparisons with Michael

52

Anthony's novel help show, we believe, how Laye's polemic intention and self-conscious philosophising get in the way of an imaginative rendering of childhood experience. We would not argue that this philosophising tone necessarily fails in a nostalgic work such as Laye's book sets out to be. What we do claim is that in *The African Child* the tone increasingly lapses into the maudlin and trivial, and that the doctrines propounded are hardly reinforced or sustained (with certain exceptions in the early chapters) by the imaginings of memory. The richer texture of language in the episodes from Michael Anthony invariably led discussion towards the processes of the novel as a whole. In contrast with this, the European or European-orientated reader's self-indulgence or self-flagellation before the simplicities of *The African Child* appears to be carried out with wanton indifference to organic form or expressive language, two ingredients essential before we can speak seriously of imaginative writing.

NOTE
1. All page references to *The African Child* refer to Fontana Books paperback edition (London 1955). This seems to us to convey the qualities of the French original.

PRESENCE AFRICAINE
NEW BILINGUAL REVIEW   No. 71—3rd Quarterly 1969

BOOK REVIEWS — PAN-AFRICAN CULTURAL MANIFESTO

For details concerning free catalogues, subscription rates, availability of back-numbers etc., please write to:
'PRESENCE AFRICAINE'
25 bis, Rue des Ecoles, 75 PARIS 5e

YAMBO OUOLOGUEM

Yambo Ouologuem, *Le Devoir de violence*, Hena Maes-Jelinek, University of Liége, Editions di Seuil, 1968 (An English translation will be published in 1970 by Secker & Warburg followed by publication in African Writers Series, Heinemann 1971) 'But these colonising powers were already too late, seeing that, with the notables, the colonialist long since in power was no other than the Saif, whose game the European conqueror was playing without knowing it.' Like Orwell, who in *Burmese Days* exposed the essential weakness of colonial rule, the young Malian Yambo Ouologuem in his fascinating first novel, *Le Devoir de violence,* presents the white colonialist as a mere pawn of the native potentate. But for him, colonialism was only an episode in the long and cruel history of Africa, one which had little influence on the African people while it lasted, though it eventually helped to give birth to a new type of African elite. The author explodes one by one all the taboos that hide from the world the true image of Africa: Religion—Fetishist, Muslim, Christian—Negro Art, African Civilisation, Ethnology. Similarly, the Blacks themselves, the Whites, the Arabs, the Jews, all are unmasked, their true role exposed. Ouologuem does not accuse; he de-mystifies by painting his own poignant vision of Africa. But however grim and terrible that vision is, yet it is also tender and deeply human.

The novel starts as an epic relating the feats of a dynasty of 'Saifs'. Actually, this epic is a symbolical fresco of African history, a search into the past which brings to light the horror and the shame of orgies of sensuality and violence. The long tribulation of the African people is re-enacted up to our days as a succession of razzias, civil wars, repressions. Throughout the centuries they are and remain a nation of slaves, sold and tortured at will by the Saif and his men. The story of the people runs parallel with the legend of the Saifs; the potentate and his serfs are the main protagonists of the novel. At once mythical and real, a descendant of King Solomon and the Queen of Sheba, the Saif combines the assets of Black, White and Jewish power; he is the very embodiment of oppression. Ironically, the founder of the modern lineage of Saifs was, like Christ, rescued by his mother from the murderous fear of a feudal Herod. Saif ben Isaac El Heit, the contemporary king, is worthy of his bloodthirsty ancestors: he asserts his power through cruelty and brings crime to perfection by devising a devilish game which consists in tormenting, then killing, his victims with asps. If he is sometimes generous, it is always out of self-interest. He is clever and sly, a master at playing fast and loose with the slaves, who see in him their defenders against invaders and colonialists, with the notables, who are forced to support him in exchange for privileges, with the whites, whose interests he appears to serve while secretely undermining their work. He frustrates the latter's efforts to abolish slavery as well as their endeavour to educate the notables and only sends the sons of slaves to their schools. But he is a magnificent figure, a great and terrible emperor, impressive and slightly mysterious. When his son is received officially in France with the words addressed by Louis the Fourteenth to an African prince: 'There is no longer any difference between you and me except from black to white', he and his subjects are in ecstasy at this recognition of equality, though it also heralds the agony of the Saif's Africa.

As the story shifts from myth to reality, everything is reduced to normal dimensions. The Saif is, after all, no more than a slave-trader, a Negro-Jew who stands himself for what is most despised by the rest of the world. The plight of his people is seen through the life story of two of his slaves, who fall deeply in love and give birth to Raymond-Spartacus, the man in whom African tradition and French civilisation will merge. Raymond and his family meet with all the trials current in African life: his mother is raped and killed by the witch-doctor, his father is sold and drugged to death, his brothers die of illness, and his sister is sold as a prostitute and bled to death by a sadist. A brilliant student, Raymond has been sent to France by the Saif, who was quick to perceive how he could use an educated 'slave'. When he hears of the annihilation of his family, Raymond sinks into despair and is finally rescued by a rich protector, himself alienated and anguished, but with whom he experiences a strange and healing love. He marries a Frenchwoman and comes back to his country, where he is welcomed as a saviour by the people, though the Saif remains the real master.

Yambo Ouologuem has succeeded in blending the legendary and the real without ever lapsing into pomposity or sentimentality. He makes no allowance either in his approach to his subject or in his style, now harrowing and bold, though never vulgar, now beautifully unadorned, particularly when he describes the march of the delirious *Zombie* through the forest. The novel is not flawless: its symbolism is sometimes obscure, and one or two scenes of eroticism and violence do not really enhance it. But from the introductory epic to the last scene, when Saif ben Isaac El Heit is shown at last to be fully human and allows the bishop to put an end to his murderous game, the narrative flows like the stream of life. The characters live and suffer and are like real living people. This is a work in which art takes precedence over commitment, in which the author relies on imagination alone to render the fear, cruelty and violence which he sees as the very texture of African life. Why 'the necessity of violence' then? Because we must do violence to ourselves to do away with all misconceptions and see things as they are. To think of colonialism as merely another form of oppression is to be free from its hold and to see Africa in its naked reality. For Ouologuem, the African is not yet emancipated. 'Perhaps,' one slave says, 'this is what a Negro's life is. To be a slave. Sold. Bought, sold again, educated.' In other words, slavery has been given a different form, Raymond-Spartacus knows well enough that he was called back to his country to be the Saif's instrument. But the history of Africa, of his own family, have made a revolutionary out of him, though his future remains an enigma as does the future of Africa. All this is implicit in the inconclusive ending, for the novel does not deliver a 'message'. It describes an Africa in quest of its true self and raises a tragic question.

Hena Maes-Jelinek

LEGSON
KAYIRA
SARIF &
EASMON

Legson Kayira: *Jingala* (Longmans, 1969)
R. S. Easmon: *The Burnt-Out Marriage*
(Nelson, 1967)

Both these recent novels, from opposite
ends of Africa, are unregretful obituaries
for traditional life and values. Both end
with the death of a protagonist who
embodies these values, lives in accordance
with them and is unable to comprehend
the alien moral systems which invade his
family and destroy his authority. It will be
seen from this description that, within the
admittedly telescoped development of
African fiction, they are somewhat old-
fashioned works, written with an apparent
unawareness that this well-trodden ground
offers little to challenge the expectations
of the reader unless it can be surveyed by
an historical imagination which (like
Achebe's) stands to some extent outside
both systems.

Neither Legson Kayira of Malawi nor Dr
Sarif Easmon of Sierra Leone achieve this
kind of objectivity, though both make
valiant efforts to present their doomed
traditionalists with sympathy and even
compassion. For the sympathy is guarded
by a visible conviction that their protagonists are simply on the wrong side, and that

their personal qualities cannot mitigate this
fact. Thus we see not so much a debate as a
defeat, a defeat presented by the authors as
having a kind of historical inevitability.
The time has long gone, however, when the
contemporary cultural scene in Africa
could be presented as the simple ousting of
one set of values and institutions by
another of largely alien inspiration. Rather,
what we see is a co-existence and dynamic
interaction of values and attitudes which
are often as mingled in the individual as
they are in the social context. It is a
confident man who will predict the out-
come of a situation such as this, for it is
one without valid historical precedent. But
certainly traditional Africa cannot be in-
terred with the corpse of Jingala or in-
cinerated in the purgative holocaust which
destroys Francis Briwa at the end of
Easmon's story.

Jingala concentrates upon the relationship of the ageing hero with his schoolboy
son, Gregory. Jingala is a widower with
only this one child to gather to himself.
Liked and respected by his contemporaries
in the highland village, he is an object of
scornful resentment to his son and to the
young girl whom affectionate in-laws have
offered to him as a second wife so soon as
she 'sees her first moon'. Gregory, after a
long absence at a Catholic boarding school,
has been alienated from his father and the
whole life of the village under the influences of Christianity and Western
individualism. He rejects the traditional
emblems of manhood—early marriage and
the setting-up of an independent household—in favour of training for the priesthood, a vocation which probably owes its
attraction precisely to its polarity with the
virile and assertive qualities formerly
associated with the African male.

Whereas Gregory deserts his father
under the lure of education, Liz, Jingala's
destined bride, is seduced by the simplest

of appeals to her dimly-realised desire for the 'glamour' of city life in South Africa. The book shows us the fatal effects of this double desertion upon Jingala, but what makes it rather less than a novel is its failure to show a comparable interest in the effects upon the rather lightly-sketched young pair. There is a statistical probability that Gregory will abandon the vocation of priesthood anyway, for traditional values are not so lightly shed as the book seems to imply, and Africa is scattered with the polygamous compounds of exuberantly lapsed seminarians. As for Liz, a meagre and terrorised existence in the locations of the Reef or a virtual widowhood in Malawi are the real prospects before her.

The Burnt-Out Marriage displays considerable narrative skill, but it too suffers from a certain diagrammatic inevitability of plot. In a thinly-disguised Sierra Leone, Dr Easmon exposes some of the cultural frictions which surround the encounter of Creoles with local peoples in an up-country district. But although he appears to isolate a certain arrogance in his heroine's assumption of her innate superiority to the 'natives', as a Moslem and a Freetown-reared Susu, it soom becomes clear that he shares these assumptions and has built his plot around them. Thus the supposedly progressive Paramount Chief of the Sowanah, Francis Briwa, is doomed to extinction simply by being what he is, a polygamist and, of course, a secret pagan. Both his death by fire and his impotence with his five wives have long been foretold and there is nothing he can do to remedy either. Similarly, his two younger wives, both Susu and one of them Creole by upbringing, cannot be expected to relish or even to accept the obligations they have undertaken as his wives. Makallay, the dominant partner in this discreetly Lesbian relationship, is at once vaunted as a Moslem and turned into a protagonist of monogamy, displaying a relish of adultery, secret liaisons and illegitimate pregnancies, just so long as these are used to undermine her husband's self-respect and in the service of Western individualist romanticism. This passage, from the final cataclysm which destroys Mbriwa and brings Makallay's predictably 'tall, *fair* and handsome' lover and brother leaping upstairs to her rescue, is typical of many in its basically uncritical sentimentality:

The mosquito net and its red cotton lining around the bed were disappearing in thin, curving tongues of fire, and there, through the flames was a gigantic fetish head, carved in black wood, with a fixed cruel stare in its face. The neck was ringed around with cowries and red cotton cloth. It rested on a soap box. Around the base of the box half a dozen small human skulls were neatly arranged. The diamond-shaped opening in the skulls proved them to be the skulls of infants.

Makallay's legs went like jelly under her. So this was Francis's true religion . . . How could Allah allow such things to be? No wonder no child had ever been born to Francis.

Outside, one of two tall young men braced himself in the middle of the sitting-room, then rushed forwards to crash his shoulder against the door.

With the momentum, the door panel was torn right out of the jambs, and man and door flew into the blazing room.

'Oh, Mamakallay!' he cried brokenly, 'Thank God we arrived in time'.

Without regret, the reader watches the final departure of these tiresome girls for the sophisticated delights of Freetown, whose society is infinitely more derivative and insecure than the one so easily disposed of here.

WOLE
SOYINKA

Wole Soyinka: *Poems From Prison* (Rex Collings Ltd., London)

Totally different in effect though it is, the technique of 'Live Burial' reminds one of that of 'Telephone Conversation'—the bantering surface tone lightly spread over the graver implications beneath. Here, however, the surface is more often broken by the sinister undertones. The graver and more sinister suggestions start from the stark first stanza where the narrow confinement 'Sixteen paces/By twenty three' constitutes a lingering 'siege' against the prisoner's 'sanity'. The economy of statement of that first stanza is as good as anything Soyinka produced outside prison, but its starkness is in the present context symbolically reflective of the prisoner's deprived state.

The second stanza is based on the Antigone story. The prisoner becomes Haemon who has allied himself with his lover Antigone against his own father Creon. The analogy has aptness. The son allying himself with an outsider becomes even more hated than the outsider. His attempt to 'unearth/Corpses of Yester Year', is doubly embarrassing because he is a member of the family. The sentence in stanza three—'Seal him Live/In the same necropolis'—is not a literal echo of *Antigone* where Haemon's entry to Antigone's cave and his later death were voluntary. Here the decree is from above. The prisoner is condemned to the same fate as those whose cause he espouses:

> May his ghost mistress
> Point the classic
> Route to Outsiders' Stygian mysteries.

The prisoner is not killed in our poem, only entombed—'Sixteen paces/By twenty-three' and he is watched by guards who are portrayed with a strong hint of sadism. They 'thrill' at the 'constipated groan' of the under-exercised prisoner whose physical state is thus economically suggested. His suffering is in sharp contrast to the implied sniggers of the 'voyeurs' outside as they listen to the 'Muse' singing in a common key, and gloating at their sudden discovery of some point of equality. Then comes the almost throw-away tone of the last stanza lightly covering the chilling physical undertones of the last line:

> 'Our plastic surgeons tend his public
>   image.'

This simultaneously suggests good public relations men piecing together clichés to keep the public happy and more gravely, the damaged physical state of the prisoner being patched up for a public showing. The poem has far more significance than the plight of any one prisoner. It portrays the plight of the individual who runs against juggernaut authority—a theme which occurs all over Soyinka's work, but particularly in *The Strong Breed* and *Kongi's Harvest*. As an author he has always faced the consequence of such a stance—Eman is sacrificed by the people he tried to save (*The Strong Breed*) while Kongi's opponents are detained, even killed. This poem holds no more optimism.

At the start of the second poem, 'Flowers For My Land', the poet takes up a song of the flower people from a distant shore. They ask where their flowers have gone, but their distant cry has echoes in the 'here' of the poet's own land where instead of flowers death is being sown, so that the garlands which result are heavy 'Garlands of Scavengers'. The weight is the weight of guilt; the guilt which arises from man's own act of sowing death for flowers. The application to Nigeria is so obvious that it may blind us to the universality of the guilt. The echo of the song of the flower people is of course a pointer to the world outside Nigeria.

The analogy between flowers and death is meant to juxtapose the potential for life and beauty, and the opposites for which this is exchanged. This is very starkly brought out in two successive stanzas:

Seeking:
Voices of rain in sunshine
Blue kites on ivory-cloud
Towers
Smell of passing Lands on mountain
    flowers.

These images of life, beauty, and grace soon become transformed into their opposites (while Soyinka wittily uses the same words) in:

I saw
Four steel kites, riders
On shrouded towers
Do you think
Their arms are spread to scatter
    mountain flowers?

The kites have grimly become war planes, the clouds cover, and the mountain flowers bombs.

In this situation—of war—voices of dissent (even when they are also of truth) are not tolerated—and this is no specially 'Nigerian' situation. The tares are all too commonly in a position to withhold possession of the lawns from the flowers. In the exigencies of the present, reason and long-term interests are suppressed and crushed. It is against the senselessness of such a situation that the poet makes his ironic call for unity to the weak—'the mangled kind'. Even the words of the call carry in themselves an anticipatory frustration. The tone of the parody 'Orphans of the world/ignite' is ironic.

These two poems represent a triumph of the universal mind over the limitations and the frustrations of a purely local situation, even prison. Soyinka's mind can still reach back into time and outwards to the rest of the world to view the plight of man, the victim of his own stupidity.

Soyinka's poetry must not be interpreted in too limited a sense. He may be starting from fairly obviously identifiable points—his imprisonment and the Nigerian war in these two poems—but his concern is with the values he has always been preoccupied with: truth as it is painfully discovered by the individual; the struggle to remain faithful to this truth; the need for self-sacrifice to enhance the truth; the consciousness that while the mind may still be resolute, the body sometimes falters when the ultimate price is demanded.

Eldred D. Jones

BIBLIO-GRAPHY

Compiled by • Hans Zell

This is the *fourth* in a series of current bibliographies appearing regularly in this journal.

Its aim is to provide comprehensive and up-to-date information on new and recently published literature by African authors. Though essentially a bibliography of *creative* writing, its scope is also inclusive of critical and reference works as well as anthologies. Political, historical, religious literature, etc., are excluded as are children's readers and similar material. The bibliography covers both books and articles; it contains neither reviews nor newspaper articles.

The present listing provides details of new material that has appeared from Spring through Summer 1969. It also cites some items published during the latter part of 1968, details of which were received too late for listing in the previous bibliographies.

The bibliography is arranged in four major sections:

    I. BIBLIOGRAPHIES AND REFERENCE WORKS
    II. CRITICISM
    III. ANTHOLOGIES
    IV. WORKS

In section four, all poetry and plays are identified as such by a brief annotation; all other entries are fiction. Individual poems appearing in periodicals are entered only if they exceed a minimum of two pages. Nationalities of *African* authors are given where known.

In the United States there has been a marked increase in paperback reprints of major works originally published in Britain. These are included here as well.

A cumulative list of periodicals cited in bibliographies nos. 1-4, as well as a directory of major publishers, will be featured in *African Literature Today*, no. 5.

I. BIBLIOGRAPHIES, REFERENCE WORKS

DUDLEY, D. R., and LANG, D. M.; eds.
The Penguin companion to Literature
Vol. 4: Classical and Byzantine, Oriental and African
(Penguin reference books, R 37)
Harmondsworth & Baltimore, Penguin Books, 1969.
360 p. 10s. 6d./$2.25
EAST, N. B.
African Theatre: A checklist of critical materials
New York, Africana Publ. Corp., 1969. (in preparation)
ca. 48 p. ca. $3.00
(An updated and expanded bibliography that originally appeared in the Spring 1969 issue of the *Afro-Asian Theatre Bulletin*)
PARICSY, PAL
A new bibliography of African literature
Part I: An additional bibliography to J. Jahn's 'A bibliography of neo-african literature from Africa, America and the Caribbean'
Part 2: A preliminary bibliography of African writing (from 1965 to the present)
(Studies on Developing Countries, 24)
Budapest, Kultura, 1969.
108 p. ca. $4.00
RAVENSCROFT, ARTHUR et al.
Annual bibliography of Commonwealth Literature 1967
Africa (General); East and Central Africa; Southern Africa; West Africa
in: *Jnl. of Commonwealth Literature*, no. 6, January 1969, p. 3-27
ZELL, HANS M.
Bibliography [of African Literature]
in: *African Literature Today*, no. 2, 1969, p. 57-62
ZELL, HANS M. ed., with SILVER, HELENE,

ABRASH, BARBARA, and MUTISO, GIDEON
The literature of Africa. An annotated bibliographical guide to creative writing by black African authors
New York, Africana Publ. Corp., 1970. ca. 350 p. illus.
ca. $7.50 (ca. $2.95 pap.)

II. CRITICISM

ACHEBE, CHINUA (Nigeria)
'The African writer and the Biafran cause'
in: *The Conch*, v. 1, no. 1, March 1969, p. 8-14
AKSELRAD, MADELEINE
'Albert Memmi et "L'homme dominé"' in:
L'Afrique Littéraire et Artistique, no. 4, April 1969, p. 18-21
ANOZIE, SUNDAY O. (Nigeria)
'A structural approach to Okigbo's "Distances"'
in: *The Conch*, v. 1, no. 1, March 1969, p. 19-29
BADDAH, MONCEF S.
'Contradictions et avenir du théâtre afro-arabe'
in: *L'Afrique Littéraire et Artistique*, no. 5, June 1969, p. 65-71
BISCHOFBERGER, OTTO
Tradition und Wandel aus der Sicht der Romanschriftsteller Kameruns und Nigerias
Schoeneck-Beckenried, Switzerland, Neue Zeitschrift fuer Missionswissenschaft, 1969. 235 p.
BRENCH, A. C.
'Idealist and mystic. Camara Laye'
in: *African Literature Today*, no. 2, 1969, p. 11-31
CHOUPAUT, YVES-MARIE
'L'oracle, une farce répresentative du théâtre africain contemporain'
in: *L'Afrique Littéraire et Artistique*, no. 3, February 1969, p. 73-7

CLARK, JOHN PEPPER (Nigeria)
'The legacy of Caliban'
in: *Black Orpheus*, v. II, no. 1, February 1968, p. 16-39
COUPEZ, A., and KAMANZI, THOMAS; ed.
Littérature courtoise du Rwanda
London & New York, Oxford Univ. Press, 1969. 180 p. 0s. 0d./$9.95
DATHORNE, O. R.
African literature IV: 'Ritual and ceremony in Okigbo's poetry'
in: *Jnl. of Commonwealth Literature*, no. 5, July 1968, p. 79-91
DEBRE, FRANCOIS
'Douce et triste: la poésie malgache'
in: *L'Afrique Littéraire et Artistique*, no. 3, February 1969, p. 3-9
DONAT, CLAUDE
'Avec la jeune troupe de l'institut national des arts le théâtre est bien parti en cote d'ivoire'
in: *L'Afrique Littéraire et Artistique*, no. 3, February 1969, p. 78-82
DONAT, CLAUDE
'Bernard Binlin Dadié'
in: *L'Afrique Littéraire et Artistique*, no. 5, June 1969, p. 16-21
EKOGAMVE, ELIE (Gabon)
'La littérature orale des Fang/The oral literature of the Fang'
in: *African Arts/Arts d'Afrique*, v. 2, no. 4, Summer 1969, p. 14-9 & 77-8
FEUILLET, CLAUDE, and HANRION, REGIS
'Alger, 21 juillet—1er août. Festival culturel panafricain'
in: *Jeune Afrique*, no. 444, 7-13 July, 1969, p. 58-61
FEUSER, WILLFRIED
'Beyond British cultural assumptions: The Ife conference on African writing in English, 16th-19th December 1968'

in: *L'Afrique Actuelle*, no. 35/36, February 1969, p. 47-51

FRESCO, E. M.
'A folktale in the Ketu dialect of Yoruba'
in: *African Notes*, v. 5, no. 1, Oct. 1968, p. 38-60

FRIEDBERGER, HEINZ
'Kenyan writer James Ngugi interviewed by Heinz Friedberger in Nairobi'
in: *Cultural Events in Africa*, no. 50, 1969, p. 8-9

FRIEDBERGER, HEINZ
Interview with Uganda writer Robert Serumaga soon after his first novel, 'Return to the shadows', had been published by Heinemann
in: *Cultural Events in Africa*, no. 53, 1969, p. 7-8

GECAU, JAMES (Kenya)
'The various levels of betrayal in "A wreath for Udomo"'
in: *Busara*, v. II, no 1, 1969, p. 4-10

GOULLI, S. EL (Algeria?)
'Mouloud féraoun'
in: *L'Afrique Littéraire et Artistique*, no. 5, June 1969, p. 6-7

HENNEBELLE, MONIQUE
'Agadir de mohamed kheir-eddine'
in: *L'Afrique Littéraire et Artistique*, no. 5, June 1969, p. 8-16

HINGOT, GEORGES-LOUIS
'Le blanc en proces'
in: *African Arts/Arts d'Afrique*, v. 2, no. 4, Summer 1969, p. 52-6 (Examines African novelists' writing in French)

IKIDDEH, IME (Nigeria)
'James Ngugi as novelist'
in: *African Literature Today*, no. 2, 1969, p. 3-10

IRELE, ABIOLA (Ghana)
'Post-colonial négritude: The political plays of Aime Césaire'
in: *West Africa*, v. 27, January 1968, p. 100-1

JONES, ELDRED (Sierra Leone)
Wole Soyinka's 'The Interpreters'—Reading notes
in: *African Literature Today*, no. 2, 1969, p. 42-50

KILLAM, GORDON D.
The novels of Chinua Achebe
London, Heinemann Educ. Books, 1969. 112 p. 25s. (10s. pap.)
New York, Africana Publ. Corp., 1969. 112 p. $3.95 ($1.75 pap.)

KIMBUGWE, HENRY
'Grace Ogot: the African lady'
in: *East Africa Journal*, v. VI, no. 4, April 1969, p. 23-4

LABURTHE-TOLRA, PHILLIPPE
'Soyinka, ou la Tigritude'
in: *Abbia*, no. 19, March 1968, p. 55-67

LAUTRE, MAXINE
'Wale Ogunyemi interviewed by Maxine Lautre recorded May 1968 in Ibadan'
in: *Cultural Events in Africa*, no. 51, 1969, p. 7-8

MELONE, THOMAS
'Mongo Beti, l'home et le destin'
in: *Présence Africaine*, no. 70, 1969, p. 120-36

MEZU, S. OKECHUKWU (Nigeria)
'Le tragique héros de Chinua Achebe'
in: *L'Afrique Littéraire et Artistique*, no. 4, April 1969, p. 22-5

MPONDO, SIMON (Nigeria)
'L'univers existential de l'intellectuel africain chez Chinua Achebe'
in: *Présence Africaine*, 70, 1969, p. 172-80

NKOSI, LEWIS (South Africa)
'A question of literary stewardship'
in: *Africa Report*, v. 14, nos. 5/6, May/June 1969, p. 69-71 (Book review article)

OKPAKU, JOSEPH (Nigeria)
' Tradition, culture and criticism'
in: *Présence Africaine*, no. 70, 1969, p. 137-46

OLAYEMI, V. (Nigeria)
'Forms of the song in Yoruba folktales'
in: *African Notes*, v. 5, no. 1, Oct. 1968, p. 25-32

P'BITEK, OKOT (Uganda)
'Theatre education in Uganda'
in: *Educational Theatre Journal*, v. 20, August 1968, p. 308

POVEY, JOHN
'African literature's widening range'
in: *Africa Report*, v. 14, nos. 5/6, May/June 1969, p. 67-9 (Book review article)

RAVENSCROFT, ARTHUR
African literature V: 'Novels of disillusion'
in: *Jnl. of Commonwealth Literature*, no. 6, January 1969, p. 120-37

RAVENSCROFT, ARTHUR
Chinua Achebe
(Writers and their work series, 209)
London, Longmans, 1969. 40 p. 3s. 6d.

ROSCOE, A. A.
'Okara's unheeded voice: explication and defense'
in: *Busara*, v. II, no. 1, 1969, p. 16-22

SHELTON, AUSTIN J.
'The articulation of traditional and modern in Igbo literature'
in: *The Conch*, v. 1, no. 1, March 1969, p. 30-49

STOCK, A. G.
'Yeats and Achebe'
in: *Jnl. of Commonwealth Literature*, no. 5, July 1968, p. 105-11

TILLION, GERMAINE *et al.*
'Littérature orale arabo-berbère'
in: *Bull. de liaison, C.N.R.S.*, R.C.P. 43, no. 3, August, 1968, p. 2-34

TIMOTHY, BANKOLE
(Sierra Leone)
'The African writer in the
contemporary world'
in: *African Arts/Arts
d'Afrique*, v. 2, no. 4, summer 1969, p. 38-9
VAN NIEKERK, B. V. D.
*The African image (Négritude) in the poetry of
Léopold Sédar Senghor*
Cape Town, Balkema, 1969.
(in preparation)
VESILLIER, COLETTE
'L'experience africaine de
Raymond Hermantier'
in: *L'Afrique Littéraire et
Artistique*, no. 4, April
1969, p. 62-6
WARREN, STANLEY A.
'Theatre in South Africa'
in: *Educational Theatre
Journal*, v. 20, no. 3, October 1968, p. 408-14
WAUTHIER, CLAUDE
'No ebony tower for African
writers'
in: *Optima (Johannesburg)*,
v. 18, no. 4, December 1968,
p. 194-200
WAUTHIER, CLAUDE
'La trilogie nationaliste du
romancier Kenyan James
Ngugi'
in: *L'Afrique Littéraire et
Artistique*, no. 3, February
1969, p. 10-14

III. ANTHOLOGIES

BEIER, ULLI; ed.
*Political spider. An anthology of stories from 'Black
Orpheus'*
(African writers series, 58)
London, Heinemann Educ.
Books, 1969. 118 p. 6s. 0d.
New York, Africana Publ.
Corp., 1969. 118 p. $1.50
O'SULLIVAN, Rev. JOHN;
ed.
*The new generation; prose
and verse from the secondary schools and training
colleges of Ghana*
Accra, State Publ. Corp.,
1969. 31 p. 25np.

ROTHENBERG, JEROME;
ed.
*Technicians of the sacred: A
range of poetries from
Africa, America, Asia and
Oceania*
(Anchor Books, A 689)
New York, Doubleday,
1969. $3.95
SKINNER, NEIL; ed. and
transl.
Hausa tales and traditions, 3
vols.
London, Cass, 1969. 440 p.
(Vol. I) 126s. od.
New York, Africana Publ.
Corp., 1969. 440 p. (Vol. I)
$15.00
TIBBLE, ANNE; ed.
*African-English literature. A
survey and anthology*
New York, October House,
1969. 304 p. $2.95
(Paperback re-issue of ed.
orig. publ., London & New
York, 1965)

IV. WORKS

ABRAHAMS, PETER
(South Africa)
Tell freedom
New York, Macmillan, 1969.
376 p. $1.50
(Paperback re-issue of ed.
orig. publ. New York, 1954)
ACHEBE, CHINUA
(Nigeria)
No longer at ease
(Premier Books, T 449)
New York, Fawcett, 1969.
$0.75
(Paperback re-issue of ed.
orig. publ. New York, 1960)
ACHEBE, CHINUA
(Nigeria)
Arrow of God
(Anchor Book, A 698)
New York, Doubleday,
1969. 266 p. $1.45
(Paperback re-issue of ed.
orig. publ., New York, 1967)
ACHEBE, CHINUA
(Nigeria)
Things fall apart
(Premier Books, T 450)

New York, Fawcett, 1969.
$0.75
(Paperback re-issue of ed.
orig. publ. New York, 1959)
AIDOO, AMA ATA (Ghana)
'Everything counts'
in: *Zuka*, no. 3, April 1969,
p. 9-13
ALUKO, TIMOTHY MOFO-
LORUNSO (Nigeria)
Chief the honourable minister
(African writers series, 70)
London, Heinemann Educ.
Books, 1970. 160 p. 9s. 0d.
ARMAH, AYI KWEI
(Ghana)
Fragments
Boston, Houghton Mifflin,
1970. (January) $5.95
CISSE, M.
'La mort passe sous les
bancs'
in: *L'Afrique Littéraire et
Artistique*, no. 3, February
1960, p. 21-8
DADIE, BERNARD (Ivory
Coast)
*Sidi, maitre Escroc; Situation difficile; Serment
d'amour*
(Coll. CLE-théâtre)
Yaounde, Ed. C.L.E., 1969.
(in preparation)
New York, Africana Publ.
Corp.; distr.
(Three plays)
DE GRAFT, J. C. (Ghana)
Through a film darkly
(Three Crowns Books)
London, Oxford Univ. Press,
1969. 10s. 0d.
(Play)
DUODO, CAMERON
(Ghana)
The Gab boys
(Fontana Books)
London, Collins, 1969. 6s. 0d.
(Paperback re-issue of ed.
orig. publ., London, 1967)
EKWENSI, CYPRIAN
(Nigeria)
People of the city
(Premier Books, T 455)
New York, Fawcett, 1969.
$0.75

63

Paperback re-issue of ed. o orig. publ. Evanston, 1967)
EKWENSI, CYPRIAN (Nigeria)
Jagua Nana
(Premier Books, T 456)
New York, Fawcett, 1969. $0.75
(Paperback re-issue of ed. orig. publ. London, 1961)
FUGARD, ATHOL (South Africa)
People are living there
(Three Crown Books)
London, Oxford Univ. Press, 1969. 10s. 0d.
(Play)
GOULLI, S. EL (Algeria?)
'Tickets! Tickets!'
in: *L'Afrique Littéraire et Artistique*, no. 4, April 1969, p. 26-9
HIGO, AIG (Nigeria)
Five Poems
in: *Black Orpheus*, v. II, no. 1, February 1968, p. 42-3
KAREITHI, P. M. (Kenya)
Kaburi bila Msalaba
Nairobi, East African Publ. House, 1969. 128 p. EAshs 4/95
(Novel in Swahili)
KARIARA, JONATHAN (Kenya)
'A bride for Africa'
in: *Zuka*, no. 3, April 1969, p. 32-5
KIMBUGWE, HENRY S. (Kenya)
'The colourful stranger'
in: *Zuka*, no. 3, April 1969, p. 5-8
LAYE, CAMARA (Guinea)
The dark child
(Noonday Paperbacks, N 365)
New York, Farrar, Straus & Giroux, 1969. $1.95
(Paperback re-issue of ed. orig. publ. New York, 1954)
LO LIYONG, TABAN (Uganda)
Fixions
(African writers series, 69)
London, Heinemann Educ. Books, 1969. 96 p. 7s. 0d.
(Poetry)

LO LIYONG, TABAN (Uganda)
Synthetism
(Modern African Library)
Nairobi, East African Publ. House, 1969. (in preparation)
LO LIYONG, TABAN (Uganda)
'Student's lament'
in: *Busara*, v. II, no. 1, 1969, p. 25-33
(A long poem)
MAHMOUD, MOSTAFA
'Le héros'
in: *Présence Africaine*, no. 69, 1969, p. 204-7
MAMMERI, MAULOUD
Les Isefra, poèmes de Si Mohand
(Coll. Domaine Maghrébin)
Edition bilingue berbère-français
Paris, Maspero, 1969. 480 p. F 24.65
MATSELE, ROBINSON (South Africa)
'A concert suit' (A short story)
in: *Présence Africaine*, 70, 1969, p. 200-5
MAZRUI, ALI A. (Uganda)
'The ninth in queue'
in: *Zuka*, no. 3, April 1969, p. 14-20
MHELEMA, MAJORIE
'A child is born'
in: *Zuka*, no. 3, April 1969, p. 39-41
MODUPE, PRINCE (Guinea)
A royal African
New York, Praeger, 1969. 168 p. $4.95
(Re-issue of 'I was a savage', orig. publ. London, 1958)
MOORE, BAI T. (Liberia)
'La femme au serpent noir'
in: *L'Afrique Littéraire et Artistique*, no. 5, June, 1969, p. 22-31
NABWIRE, CONSTANCE (Uganda)
'Teda'
in: *East Africa Jnl.*, v. VI, no. 1, January 1969, p. 19-22

NGINGA, JOHN (Kenya)
'The wound of joy'
in: *Busara*, v. II, no. 1, 1969, p. 34-43
NGUBIAH, S. N. (Kenya)
'A curse from God'
in: *Busara*, v. II, no. 1, 1969, p. 11-14
NGUGI, JAMES (Kenya)
'The black bird'
in: *Zuka*, no. 3, April 1969, p. 21-7
NGUGI, JAMES (Kenya)
Weep not child
New York, Macmillan, 1969. 154 p. $1.50
(Paperback re-issue of ed. orig. publ. Evanston, 1967)
NUGI, PAUL (Kenya)
'This side of town'
in: *East African Jnl.*, v. VI, no. 1, January 1969, p. 9-13
NWANIKI, NGUREH (Kenya)
'Home'
in: *Zuka*, no. 3, April 1969, p. 30-1
OBIECHINA, EMMANUEL N. (Nigeria)
'An after Christmas dream'
in: *The Conch*, v. 1, March 1969, p. 4-7
ODEKU, E. LATUNDE (Nigeria)
Whispers from the night
Ibadan, Author (c/o Univ. of Ibadan), 1969. 136 p.
OGIERIAIKHI, EMWINMA (Nigeria)
Oba Ovonramwen and Oba Ewuakpe
London, Univ. of London Press, 1969. 3s. 6d.
(Two short historical plays)
OKAI, JOHN (Ghana)
'Fugue for waterfrogs. A poem in three movements'
in: *African Arts/Arts d'Afrique*, v. 2, no. 4, Summer 1969, p. 26-9
OKIGBO, CHRISTOPHER (Nigeria)
'Poems prophesying war: Path of Thunder'
in: *Black Orpheus*, v. II, no. 1, February 1968, p. 5-11
(Six poems)

P'BITEK, OKOT (Uganda)
Song of prisoner
(Modern African Library)
Nairobi, East African Publ.
House, 1969. (in preparation)

P'BITEK, OKOT (Uganda)
Song of Ocol
(Modern African Library)
Nairobi, East African Publ.
House, 1969. (in preparation)

QLUDEHE-MACGOYE, MAJORIE (Kenya)
Ultimatum
in: *East Africa Jnl.*, v. VI, no. 1, January 1969, p. 43-7

SELLASIE, SAHLE (Ethiopia)
'The woman of Azer'
in: *Zuka*, no. 3, April 1969, p. 37-8

SENGHOR, LEOPOLD SEDAR (Senegal)
Nocturnes
(Transl. from the French by Clive Wake and John Reed)
African writers series, 71)
London, Heinemann Educ. Books, 1970. 64 p. 8s. 0d.

SOYINKA, WOLE (Nigeria)
Three short plays
(Three Crowns Book)
London & New York, Oxford Univ. Press, 1969. 128 p. 6s. 0d./$1.25
(Orig. publ. as *Five Plays* London, 1964. Contains: 'The Swamp dwellers', 'The trials of Brother Jero', and 'The strong breed')

SOYINKA, WOLE (Nigeria)
Poems from prison
London, Rex Collings, 1969. 3 p. 1s. 6d.

TCHICAYA U'TAMSI, GERALD FELIX (Congo-Brazzaville)
Poems
(Transl. from the French by Gerald Moore)
(African writers series, 72)
London, Heinemann Educ. Books, 1970. 96 p. 8s. 6d.

TIMOTHY, BANKOLE (Sierra Leone)
'Sama and the barber'
in: *African Arts/Arts d'Afrique*, v. 2, no. 4, Summer 1969, p. 39-41

TSARO-WIWA, KEN (Nigeria)
'Poems prophesying war: A voice in the wind'
in: *Black Orpheus*, v. II, no. 1, February 1968, p. 12-15

UMEASIEGBU, REMS NNA (Nigeria)
The way we lived
(Afican writers series, 61)
London, Heinemann Educ. Books, 1969. 139 p. 6s. 6d. illus.
New York, Humanities Press; distr. $1.00
(Ibo customs and stories)

WACIUMBA, CHARITY (Kenya)
Daughter of Mumbi
Nairobi, East African Publ. House, 1969. EAshs. 7/00 $2.00

WAGACHIA, BERNARD MBUI (Kenya)
'The night of the women'
in: *Busara*, v. II, no. 1, 1969, p. 46-51

Note: *East Africa Journal*, v. VI, no. 1, January 1969, is a special literary issue of East African creative writing. There is poetry—not listed in this bibliography—by Okot p'Bitek, Okoth-Ogendo, Tony Mphahele, Amin Kassam, Kenneth Watene, Khadambi Asalache, and a great many more.

INDEX

African Literature Today
Numbers 1-4